Lecture Notes in Artificial Intelligence   8779

Subseries of Lecture Notes in Computer Science

LNAI Series Editors

Randy Goebel
   University of Alberta, Edmonton, Canada
Yuzuru Tanaka
   Hokkaido University, Sapporo, Japan
Wolfgang Wahlster
   DFKI and Saarland University, Saarbrücken, Germany

LNAI Founding Series Editor

Joerg Siekmann
   DFKI and Saarland University, Saarbrücken, Germany

T0213837

Abdelhamid Bouchachia (Ed.)

Adaptive and Intelligent Systems

Third International Conference, ICAIS 2014
Bournemouth, UK, September 8-10, 2014
Proceedings

Springer

Volume Editor

Abdelhamid Bouchachia
Bournemouth University
Faculty of Science and Technology
Fern Barrow
Poole, Dorset, BH12 5BB, UK
E-mail: abouchachia@bournemouth.ac.uk

ISSN 0302-9743   e-ISSN 1611-3349
ISBN 978-3-319-11297-8   e-ISBN 978-3-319-11298-5
DOI 10.1007/978-3-319-11298-5
Springer Cham Heidelberg New York Dordrecht London

Library of Congress Control Number: 2014947557

LNCS Sublibrary: SL 7 – Artificial Intelligence

Typesetting: Camera-ready by author, data conversion by Scientific Publishing Services, Chennai, India

Printed on acid-free paper

Springer is part of Springer Science+Business Media (www.springer.com)

Preface

Adaptation plays a central role in dynamically changing systems. It is about the ability of the system to "responsively" self-adjust upon change in the surrounding environment. Like living creatures that have evolved over millions of years developing ecological systems due to their self-adaptation and fitness capacity to the dynamic environment, systems undergo similar cycles to improve or at least not weaken their performance when internal or external changes take place. Internal or endogenous change bears on the physical structure of the system (hardware and/or software components) due mainly to faults, knowledge inconsistency, etc. it requires a certain number of adaptivity features such as flexible deployment, self-testing, self-healing and self-correction. Extraneous change touches on the environment implication such as the operational mode or regime, non-stationarity of input, new knowledge facts, the need to cooperate with other systems, etc. these two classes of change shed light on the research avenues in smart and autonomous systems.

To meet the challenges of these systems, a sustainable effort needs to be developed: (1) adequate operational structures involving notions like self-healing, self-testing, reconfiguration, etc.; (2) appropriate design concepts encompassing self-x properties (self-organization, self-monitoring, etc.) to allow for autonomy and optimal behaviour in the (dynamically changing) environment; (3) efficient computational algorithms targeting dynamic setting, life-long learning, evolving and adaptive behaviour and structure. For this three-fold development direction, various design and computational models stemming from machine learning, statistics, metaphors of nature inspired from biological and cognitive plausibility, etc. can be of central relevance. Due to its versatility, online adaptation is involved in various research areas which are covered by the International Conference on Adaptive and Intelligent Systems (ICAIS): neutral networks, data mining, pattern recognition, computational intelligence, smart and agent-based systems, distributed systems, ubiquitous environments, Internet, system engineering, hardware, etc. the ICAIS conference strives to sharpen its focus on issues related to online adaptation and learning in dynamically evolving environments and to expand the understanding of all these inter-related concepts.

ICAIS is a biennial event. After the very successful ICAIS 2009 and ICAIS 2011, the conference witnessed another success this year. ICAIS 2014 received 32 submissions from 11 countries around the world (Argentina, Austria, Brazil, Canada, China, Czeck Republic, Germany, Poland, Portugal, Tunisia, UK) which underwent a rigorous and tough peer-review by three reviewers. Based on the referees' reports, the Program Committee selected 19 full papers.

ICAIS 2014 was enhanced by 3 keynote speeches and 1 invited talk given by internationally renowned researchers, presenting insights and ideas in the research areas covered by the conference. The rest of the program featured interesting sessions. Overall we had 4 sessions: 1- Advances in feature selection consisting of 4 papers 2- Clustering and classification techniques consisting of 6 papers 3- Adaptive optimization consisting of 5 papers 4- Time series analysis 4 papers

Although this set of sessions does not cover the topics of the conference, it is a very good mix proving fresh insight in some of the techniques related to adaptive and intelligent systems.

This volume and the whole conference are of course the result of team effort. My thanks go to the local organizers, particularly to Tobias Baker, the Steering Committee, the publicity chair and especially the Program Committee members and the reviewers for their cooperation in the shaping of the conference and running the refereeing process. I highly appreciate the hard work and timely feedback of the referees who did an excellent job. I would like to thank all the authors and participants for their interest in ICAIS 2014. Thank you for your time and effort in preparing and submitting your papers and your patience throughout the long process. Your work is the backbone of this conference.

The support of the University of Bournemouth and the Faculty of Science and Technology was crucial in making this event happen. I also thank the technical sponsors, IEEE Computational Society and International Neural Networks Society for their trust in ICAIS, and Springer for enabling the publication of this volume.

We worked hard to make ICAIS 2014 an enticing and informative event.

July 2014   Abdelhamid Bouchachia

Organization

ICAIS 2014 is organized by the department of Computing, Faculty of Science & Technology, Bournemouth University.

Executive Committee

Conference Chair

Abdelhamid Bouchachia   Bournemouth University, UK

Advisory Committee

Nikola Kasabov   Auckland University, New Zealand
Xin Yao   University of Birmingham, UK
Djamel Ziou   University of Sherbrooke, Canada
Plamen Angelov   University of Lancaster, UK
Witold Pedrycz   University of Edmonton, Canada
Janusz Kacprzyk   Polish Academy of Sciences, Poland

Program Committee

Plamen Angelov, UK
Emili Balaguer-Ballester, UK
Albert Bifet, New Zealand
Nizar Bouguila, Canada
Ahmed Bouridane, UK
Martin Butz, Germany
Heloisa Camargo, Brazil
André de Carvalho, Brazil
Damien Fay, UK
Joao Gama, Portugal
Haibo He, USA
Eyke Huellermeier, Germany
Ata Kaban, UK
Frank Klawonn, Germany
Mario Koeppen, Japan
Lukasz Kurgan, USA

Stéphane Lecoeuche, France
Ahmad Lotfi, UK
Edwin Lughofer, Austria
Trevor Martin, UK
Jose Antonio Iglesias Martínez, Spain
Christophe Marsala, France
Hammadi Nait-Charif, UK
Marcin Paprzycki, Poland
Jose de Jesus Rubio, Mexico
Ali Salah, Turkey
Daniel Sanchez, Spain
Moamar Sayed-Mouchweh, France
Igor Škrjanc, Slovenia
Vaclav Snasel, Czech Republic
Alexey Tsymbal, Germany

Additional Reviewers

Heysem Kaya, Turkey   Hande Alemdar, Turkey
Aljaz Osojnik, Slovenia   Vânia G. Almeida, Portugal

Local Organizing Committee

Tobias Baker   Bournemouth University, UK
Hammadi Nait-Charif   Bournemouth University, UK
Emili Balaguer-Ballester   Bournemouth University, UK
Damien Fay   Bournemouth University, UK

Sponsoring Institutions

Bournemouth University, UK
Faculty of Science and Technology, Bournemouth University, UK
The International Neural Networks Society

Invited Talks

Feature Extraction for Change Detection

Ludmila Kuncheva

School of Computer Science, Bangor University
Dean Street, Bangor, Gwynedd, LL57 1UT, United Kingdom
l.i.kuncheva@bangor.ac.uk

An online classifier is only accurate if the distribution of the incoming data is the same as the distribution of the data the classifier was trained upon. Therefore, detecting a change and retraining the classifier accordingly is an important task. This talk will challenge the concept of change and change detectability from unsupervised streaming data. What constitutes a change? The answer is uniquely determined by the context. But in order to have change detection methods that work across problems, the relevant features must be exposed. The talk will be focused on feature extraction for the purposes of change detection.

Distributed Data Stream Mining

João Gama

LIAAD - INESC Porto, Laboratory of Artificial Intelligence and Decision Support
University of Porto, Portugal
joao.jgama@gmail.com

The phenomenal growth of mobile and embedded devices coupled with their ever-increasing computational and communications capacity presents an exciting new opportunity for real-time, distributed intelligent data analysis in ubiquitous environments. In these contexts centralized approaches have limitations due to communication constraints, power consumption (e.g. in sensor networks), and privacy concerns. Distributed online algorithms are highly needed to address the above concerns. The focus of this talk is on distributed stream mining algorithms that are highly scalable, computationally efficient and resource-aware. These features enable the continued operation of data stream mining algorithms in highly dynamic mobile and ubiquitous environments.

Music Lessons and Other Exercises

Kurt Geihs

University of Kassel, EECS Department|Distributed Systems
Wilhelmshöher Allee 73, D-34121 Kassel, Germany
geihs@uni-kassel.de

For more than a decade researchers have explored software systems that dynamically adapt their behavior at run-time in response to changes in their operational environments, user preferences, and underlying computing infrastructure. Our particular focus has been on context-aware, self-adaptive applications in ubiquitous computing scenarios. In my presentation I will discuss lessons learned from three projects in the realm of self-adaptive systems. Some of these insights relate to purely technical concerns. Others touch on socio-technical concerns that substantially influence the users' acceptance of self-adaptive applications. Our experiments have shown that both kinds of concerns are important. We claim that an interdisciplinary software development methodology is needed in order to produce socially aware applications that are both acceptable and accepted.

Adaptive Ambient Intelligence and Smart Environments

Ahmad Lotfi

School of Science and Technology, Nottingham Trent University
Clifton Campus, Clifton Lane, Nottingham, NG11 8NS, United Kingdom
ahmad.lotfi@ntu.ac.uk

Ambient Intelligence refers to a digital environment that proactively supports people in their daily lives. It is an emerging discipline that brings intelligence to our living environments, makes those environments sensitive to us, and adapt according to the user's needs. By enriching an environment with appropriate sensors and interconnected devices, the environment would be able to sense changes and support decisions that benefit the users of that environment. Such smart environments could help to reduce the energy consumption, increase user's comfort, improve security and productivity, etc. One specific area of interest is the application of ambient intelligence in Ambient Assisted Living, where the home environment provides assistance with daily living activities for people with disabilities. In my presentation, I will provide a review of the technologies and environments that comprises ambient intelligence, as well as how changes in the environment are reflected in the overall design of an adaptive ambient intelligence environment.

Table of Contents

Advances in Feature Selection

Clustering and Classification

Adaptive Optimization

Advances in Time Series Analysis

A Hierarchical Infinite Generalized Dirichlet Mixture Model with Feature Selection

Wentao Fan[1], Hassen Sallay[2], Nizar Bouguila[3], and Sami Bourouis[4]

[1] Department of Computer Science and Technology, Huaqiao University, China
fwt@hqu.edu.cn
[2] Al Imam Mohammad Ibn Saud Islamic University (IMSIU), Riyadh, Saudi Arabia
hmsallay@imamu.edu.sa
[3] Concordia University, Montreal, QC, Canada
nizar.bouguila@concordia.ca
[4] Taif University, Taif, Saudi Arabia
s.bourouis@tu.edu.sa

Abstract. We propose a nonparametric Bayesian approach, based on hierarchical Dirichlet processes and generalized Dirichlet distributions, for simultaneous clustering and feature selection. The resulting statistical model is learned within a variational framework that we have developed. The merits of the developed model are shown via extensive simulations and experiments when applied to the challenging problem of images categorization.

Keywords: Clustering, mixture model, feature selection, generalized Dirichlet, variational inference, image databases.

1 Introduction

Dirichlet process (DP) has became as one of the most popular nonparametric Bayesian techniques [12,10]. It can be viewed as a stochastic process and can be considered as distribution over distributions, also. Recently, hierarchical DP [20,19] has been developed as a hierarchical nonparametric Bayesian model and has shown promising results to the problem of model-based clustering of grouped data with sharing clusters. It is built on the DP and involves Bayesian hierarchy where the base measure for a DP is itself distributed according to a DP. The hierarchical DP framework is particularly useful in problems involving the modeling of grouped data where observations are organized into groups, and allow these groups to remain statistically linked by sharing mixture components [20,19]. As several other statistical approaches, existing hierarchical DP-based models considers the Gaussian assumption. Unlike, these existing works, in this paper, we focus on a specific form of hierarchical DP mixture model where each observation within a group is drawn from a mixture of generalized Dirichlet (GD) distributions. We are mainly motivated by the fact that the generalized Dirichlet distribution has been shown to be efficient in modeling high-dimensional proportional data (i.e. normalized histograms) in a variety of applications from different disciplines (e.g. computer vision, data mining, pattern recognition) [5,6,8,9].

A. Bouchachia (Ed.): ICAIS 2014, LNAI 8779, pp. 1–10, 2014.
© Springer International Publishing Switzerland 2014

Having the hierarchical infinite generalized Dirichlet mixture model in hand, a principled variational approach is developed to learn its parameters. To validate the overall statistical framework a challenging application, which has attracted the attention of the computer vision community recently [2,16], namely the classification of images containing categories of animals is considered. The rest of this paper is organized as follows. In the next section, we propose our model. Section 3 develops our variational learning procedure. Section 4 is devoted to the experimental results. Finally, we conclude the paper in Section 5.

2 The Model

2.1 The Hierarchical Dirichlet Process Mixture Model

Let H be a distribution over some probability space Θ and γ be a positive real number, then a random distribution G follows a DP with a base distribution H and concentration parameter γ, denoted as $G \sim \mathrm{DP}(\gamma, H)$, if

$$(G(A_1), \ldots, G(A_t)) \sim \mathrm{Dir}(\gamma H(A_1), \ldots, \gamma H(A_t)) \tag{1}$$

where $(A_1, \ldots, A_t)$ is the set of finite partitions of Θ, and Dir is a finite-dimensional Dirichlet. Now, let us introduce the general setting of a two-level hierarchical Dirichlet process: Assume that we have a grouped data set, in which each group is associated with an infinite mixture model (a DP G_j). This indexed set of DPs $\{G_j\}$ shares a base distribution G_0, which is itself distributed as a DP:

$$G_0 \sim \mathrm{DP}(\gamma, H) \quad G_j \sim \mathrm{DP}(\lambda, G_0) \quad \text{for each } j, j \in \{1, \ldots, M\} \tag{2}$$

where j is an index for each group of data. In this work, we represent a hierarchical DP in a more intuitive and straightforward form through two stick-breaking constructions which involves a global-level and a group-level construction [18,11]. In the global-level construction, the global measure G_0 is distributed according to a $\mathrm{DP}(\gamma, H)$ and can be described using a stick-breaking representation

$$\psi'_k \sim \mathrm{Beta}(1, \gamma) \quad \Omega_k \sim H \quad \psi_k = \psi'_k \prod_{s=1}^{k-1}(1 - \psi'_s) \quad G_0 = \sum_{k=1}^{\infty} \psi_k \delta_{\Omega_k} \tag{3}$$

where $\{\Omega_k\}$ is a set of independent random variables distributed according to H, δ_{Ω_k} is an atom at Ω_k. The random variables ψ_k are the stick-breaking weights that satisfy $\sum_{k=1}^{\infty} \psi_k = 1$, and are obtained by recursively breaking a unit length stick into an infinite number of pieces. In this work, we apply the conventional stick-breaking representation [21] to construct each group-level DP G_j

$$\pi'_{jt} \sim \mathrm{Beta}(1, \lambda) \quad \varpi_{jt} \sim G_0 \quad \pi_{jt} = \pi'_{jt} \prod_{s=1}^{t-1}(1 - \pi'_{js}) \quad G_j = \sum_{t=1}^{\infty} \pi_{jt} \delta_{\varpi_{jt}}$$

where $\delta_{\varpi_{jt}}$ are group-level atoms at ϖ_{jt}, $\{\pi_{jt}\}$ is a set of stick-breaking weights which satisfies $\sum_{t=1}^{\infty} \pi_{jt} = 1$. Since ϖ_{jt} is distributed according to the base distribution G_0, it takes on the value Ω_k with probability ψ_k. This can also represented using a binary latent variable W_{jtk} as an indicator variable, such that $W_{jtk} \in \{0, 1\}$, $W_{jtk} = 1$ if ϖ_{jt} maps to the base-level atom Ω_k which is indexed by k; otherwise, $W_{jtk} = 0$. Then, we can have $\varpi_{jt} = \Omega_k^{W_{jtk}}$. As a result, group-level atoms ϖ_{jt} do not need to be explicitly represented which further simplifies the inference process as it shall be clearer later. The indicator variable $\boldsymbol{W} = (W_{jt1}, W_{jt2}, \ldots)$ is distributed according to $\boldsymbol{\psi}$ in the form

$$p(\boldsymbol{W}|\boldsymbol{\psi}) = \prod_{j=1}^{M} \prod_{t=1}^{\infty} \prod_{k=1}^{\infty} \psi_k^{W_{jtk}} \tag{4}$$

Since $\boldsymbol{\psi}$ is a function of $\boldsymbol{\psi}'$ according to a stick-breaking construction, then

$$p(\boldsymbol{W}|\boldsymbol{\psi}') = \prod_{j=1}^{M} \prod_{t=1}^{\infty} \prod_{k=1}^{\infty} \left[\psi_k' \prod_{s=1}^{k-1} (1 - \psi_s') \right]^{W_{jtk}} \tag{5}$$

The prior distribution of $\boldsymbol{\psi}'$ is a specific Beta distribution

$$p(\boldsymbol{\psi}') = \prod_{k=1}^{\infty} \text{Beta}(1, \gamma_k) = \prod_{k=1}^{\infty} \gamma_k (1 - \psi_k')^{\gamma_k - 1} \tag{6}$$

Let i index the observations within each group j, we assume that each θ_{ji} is a factor corresponding to an observation X_{ji}, and the factors $\boldsymbol{\theta}_j = (\theta_{j1}, \theta_{j2}, \ldots)$ are distributed according to DP G_j, one for each j: $\theta_{ji}|G_j \sim G_j, X_{ji}|\theta_{ji} \sim F(\theta_{ji})$, where $F(\theta_{ji})$ represents the distribution of the observation X_{ji} given θ_{ji}. According to Eq.(2), the base distribution H of G_0 provides the prior for θ_{ji}. This setting forms the definition of a *hierarchical DP mixture model*, where each group is associated with a mixture model, and the components are shared among these mixtures due to the sharing of atoms Ω_k among all G_j. Furthermore, since each θ_{ji} is distributed according to G_j, it takes the value ϖ_{jt} with probability π_{jt}. Next, we introduce a binary latent variable $Z_{jit} \in \{0, 1\}$ as an indicator variable. That is, $Z_{jit} = 1$ if θ_{ji} is associated with component t and maps to the group-level atom ϖ_{jt}; otherwise, $Z_{jit} = 0$. Therefore, we have $\theta_{ji} = \varpi_{jt}^{Z_{jit}}$. Since ϖ_{jt} also maps to the global-level atom Ω_k, we then have $\theta_{ji} = \varpi_{jt}^{Z_{jit}} = \Omega_k^{W_{jtk}Z_{jit}}$. The indicator variable $\boldsymbol{Z} = (Z_{ji1}, Z_{ji2}, \ldots)$ is distributed according to $\boldsymbol{\pi}$ as

$$p(\boldsymbol{Z}|\boldsymbol{\pi}) = \prod_{j=1}^{M} \prod_{i=1}^{N} \prod_{t=1}^{\infty} \pi_{jt}^{Z_{jit}} \tag{7}$$

According to the stick-breaking construction, $\boldsymbol{\pi}$ is a function of $\boldsymbol{\pi}'$. We then have

$$p(\boldsymbol{Z}|\boldsymbol{\pi}') = \prod_{j=1}^{M} \prod_{i=1}^{N} \prod_{t=1}^{\infty} [\pi_{jt}' \prod_{s=1}^{t-1} (1 - \pi_{js}')]^{Z_{jit}} \tag{8}$$

$$p(\boldsymbol{\pi'}) = \prod_{j=1}^{M} \prod_{t=1}^{\infty} \text{Beta}(1, \lambda_{jt}) = \prod_{j=1}^{M} \prod_{t=1}^{\infty} \lambda_{jt}(1 - \pi'_{jt})^{\lambda_{jt}-1} \qquad (9)$$

2.2 Hierarchical DP Mixture Model of GD Distributions with Feature Selection

Assume that we have a D-dimensional vector $\boldsymbol{Y} = (Y_1, \ldots, Y_D)$ drawn from a GD distribution with parameters $\boldsymbol{\alpha} = (\alpha_1, \ldots, \alpha_D)$ and $\boldsymbol{\beta}_j = (\beta_1, \ldots, \beta_D)$

$$\text{GD}(\boldsymbol{Y}|\boldsymbol{\alpha}, \boldsymbol{\beta}) = \prod_{l=1}^{D} \frac{\Gamma(\alpha_l + \beta_l)}{\Gamma(\alpha_l)\Gamma(\beta_l)} Y_l^{\alpha_l - 1} \Big(1 - \sum_{f=1}^{l} Y_f\Big)^{\gamma_l} \qquad (10)$$

where $\sum_{l=1}^{D} Y_l < 1$ and $0 < Y_l < 1$ for $l = 1, \ldots, D$, $\alpha_l > 0$, $\beta_l > 0$, $\gamma_l = \beta_l - \alpha_{l+1} - \beta_{l+1}$ for $l = 1, \ldots, D-1$, $\gamma_D = \beta_D - 1$, and $\Gamma(\cdot)$ is the gamma function. Based on an interesting mathematical property of the GD distribution which is thoroughly discussed in [7], we can transform the original data point $\boldsymbol{Y}$ using a geometric transformation into another D-dimensional data point $\boldsymbol{X}$ with independent features in the form of $\text{GD}(\boldsymbol{X}|\boldsymbol{\alpha}, \boldsymbol{\beta}) = \prod_{l=1}^{D} \text{Beta}(X_l|\alpha_l, \beta_l)$, where $\boldsymbol{X} = (X_1, \ldots, X_D)$, $X_1 = Y_1$ and $X_l = Y_l/(1 - \sum_{f=1}^{l-1} Y_f)$ for $l > 1$, and $\text{Beta}(X_l|\alpha_l, \beta_l)$ is a Beta distribution defined with parameters $\{\alpha_l, \beta_l\}$. Now let us consider a data set $\mathcal{X}$ that contains N random vectors separated into M groups, then each vector $\boldsymbol{X}_{ji} = (X_{ji1}, \ldots, X_{jiD})$ is represented in a D-dimensional space and is drawn from a hierarchical infinite GD mixture model.

In practice, not all the features are important, some of them may be irrelevant and may even degrade the clustering performance. Therefore, feature selection technique is important and is adopted here as a tool to chooses the "best" feature subset. The most common feature selection technique, in the context of unsupervised learning, defines an irrelevant feature as the one having a distribution independent from class labels [13]. Therefore, in our work the distribution of each feature X_l can be defined by

$$p(X_{jil}) = \text{Beta}(X_{jil}|\alpha_{kl}, \beta_{kl})^{\phi_{jil}} \text{Beta}(X_{jil}|\alpha'_l, \beta'_l)^{1-\phi_{jil}} \qquad (11)$$

where ϕ_{jil} is a binary latent variable represents the feature relevance indicator, such that $\phi_{jil} = 0$ denotes the feature l of group j is irrelevant (i.e. noise) and follows a Beta distribution: $\text{Beta}(X_{jil}|\alpha'_l, \beta'_l)$; otherwise, the feature X_{jil} is relevant. The prior distribution of $\boldsymbol{\phi}$ is defined as

$$p(\boldsymbol{\phi}|\boldsymbol{\epsilon}) = \prod_{j=1}^{M} \prod_{i=1}^{N} \prod_{l=1}^{D} \epsilon_{l_1}^{\phi_{jil}} \epsilon_{l_2}^{1-\phi_{jil}} \qquad (12)$$

where each ϕ_{jil} is a Bernoulli variable such that $p(\phi_{jil} = 1) = \epsilon_{l_1}$ and $p(\phi_{jil} = 0) = \epsilon_{l_2}$. The vector $\boldsymbol{\epsilon} = (\epsilon_1, \ldots, \epsilon_D)$ represents the features saliencies such that

$\epsilon_l = (\epsilon_{l_1}, \epsilon_{l_2})$ and $\epsilon_{l_1} + \epsilon_{l_2} = 1$. Furthermore, a Dirichlet distribution is chosen over ϵ as

$$p(\epsilon) = \prod_{l=1}^{D} \mathrm{Dir}(\epsilon_l | \boldsymbol{\xi}) = \prod_{l=1}^{D} \frac{\Gamma(\xi_1 + \xi_2)}{\Gamma(\xi_1)\Gamma(\xi_2)} \epsilon_{l_1}^{\xi_1 - 1} \epsilon_{l_2}^{\xi_2 - 1} \qquad (13)$$

In the next step, we need to introduce Gamma prior distributions for parameters α, β, α' and β'.

3 Variational Model Learning

In order to simplify notations, we define $\Theta = (\Xi, \Lambda)$ as the set of latent and unknown random variables, where $\Xi = \{\boldsymbol{Z}, \boldsymbol{\phi}\}$ and $\Lambda = \{\boldsymbol{W}, \boldsymbol{\epsilon}, \boldsymbol{\psi}, \boldsymbol{\pi}', \boldsymbol{\alpha}, \boldsymbol{\beta}, \boldsymbol{\alpha}', \boldsymbol{\beta}'\}$. Variational inference [1,3] is a deterministic approximation technique that is used to find tractable approximations for posteriors of a variety of statistical models. The goal is to find an approximation $Q(\Theta)$ to the true posterior distribution $p(\Theta | \mathcal{X})$ by maximizing the lower bound of $\ln p(\mathcal{X})$:

$$\mathcal{L}(Q) = \int Q(\Theta) \ln[p(\mathcal{X}, \Theta) / Q(\Theta)] d\Theta \qquad (14)$$

In this work, we adopt factorial approximation which is commonly used in variational inference [3] to factorize $Q(\Theta)$ into disjoint tractable distributions. Moreover, we apply a truncation technique as in [4] to truncate the variational approximations of global- and group-level Dirichlet process at K and T. It is noteworthy that the truncation levels K and T are variational parameters which can be freely initialized and will be optimized automatically during the learning process. By using truncated stick-breaking and factorization, the approximated posterior distribution $q(\Theta)$ can be fully factorized into disjoint distributions as

$$q(\Theta) = q(\boldsymbol{Z})q(\boldsymbol{W})q(\boldsymbol{\phi})q(\boldsymbol{\pi}')q(\boldsymbol{\psi}')q(\boldsymbol{\alpha})q(\boldsymbol{\beta})q(\boldsymbol{\alpha}')q(\boldsymbol{\beta}')q(\boldsymbol{\epsilon}) \qquad (15)$$

In our work, variational inference is performed based on a natural gradient method as introduced in [17]. The main idea is that, since our model has conjugate priors, the functional form of each factor in the variational posterior distribution is known. Therefore, the lower bound $\mathcal{L}(q)$ can be considered as a function of the parameters of these distributions by taking general parametric forms of these distributions. The optimization of variational factors is then obtained by maximizing the lower bound with respect to these parameters. In our case, the functional form of each variational factor is the same as its conjugate prior distribution, namely Discrete for $\boldsymbol{Z}$ and $\boldsymbol{W}$, Bernoulli for $\boldsymbol{\phi}$, Dirichlet for $\boldsymbol{\epsilon}$, Beta for $\boldsymbol{\psi}'$ and $\boldsymbol{\pi}'$, and Gamma for α, β, α' and β'. Therefore, the parametric forms for these variational posterior distributions can be defined as the following

$$q(\boldsymbol{Z}) = \prod_{j=1}^{M} \prod_{i=1}^{N} \prod_{t=1}^{T} \rho_{jit}^{Z_{jit}} \qquad q(\boldsymbol{W}) = \prod_{j=1}^{M} \prod_{t=1}^{T} \prod_{k=1}^{K} \vartheta_{jtk}^{W_{jtk}} \qquad (16)$$

$$q(\boldsymbol{\phi}) = \prod_{j=1}^{M} \prod_{i=1}^{N} \prod_{l=1}^{D} \varphi_{jil}^{\phi_{jil}} (1 - \varphi_{jil})^{1-\phi_{jil}} \quad q(\boldsymbol{\epsilon}) = \prod_{l=1}^{D} \text{Dir}(\epsilon_l | \boldsymbol{\xi}^*) \tag{17}$$

$$q(\boldsymbol{\pi}') = \prod_{j=1}^{M} \prod_{t=1}^{T} \text{Beta}(\pi'_{jt} | a_{jt}, b_{jt}) \quad q(\boldsymbol{\psi}') = \prod_{k=1}^{K} \text{Beta}(\psi'_k | c_k, d_k) \tag{18}$$

$$q(\boldsymbol{\alpha}) = \prod_{k=1}^{K} \prod_{l=1}^{D} \mathcal{G}(\alpha_{kl} | \tilde{u}_{kl}, \tilde{v}_{kl}) \quad q(\boldsymbol{\beta}) = \prod_{k=1}^{K} \prod_{l=1}^{D} \mathcal{G}(\beta_{kl} | \tilde{g}_{kl}, \tilde{h}_{kl}) \tag{19}$$

$$q(\boldsymbol{\alpha}') = \prod_{l=1}^{D} \mathcal{G}(\alpha'_l | \tilde{u}'_l, \tilde{v}'_l) \quad q(\boldsymbol{\beta}') = \prod_{l=1}^{D} \mathcal{G}(\beta'_l | \tilde{g}'_l, \tilde{h}'_l) \tag{20}$$

Consequently, the parameterized lower bound $\mathcal{L}(q)$ can be obtained by substituting Eqs.(16)~(20) into Eq.(14). Maximizing this bound with respect to these parameters then gives the required re-estimation equations. The variational inference for our model can be performed then as an EM-like algorithm.

4 Experimental Results

In this part, we validate the proposed hierarchical infinite GD mixture model with feature selection (referred to as *HInGDFs*) through a real-world application concerning images categorization. In our case, we concentrate on the problem of discriminating different images of breeds of cats and dogs, which is a specific type of object categorization. This problem is extremely challenging since cats and dogs are highly deformable and different breeds may differ only by a few subtle phenotypic details [15]. In our experiments, we initialize the global truncation level K to 800, and the group truncation level T to 100. The hyperparameters λ_{jt} and γ_k are initialized to 0.05. The initial values of hyperparameters u_{kl}, g_{kl}, u'_l, v'_l for the conjugate Beta priors are set to 0.1, and v_{kl}, h_{kl}, v'_l, h'_l are set to 0.01. The hyperparameters ξ_1 and ξ_2 of the feature saliency are both initialized to 0.5. These specific choices were found convenient according to our experiments.

4.1 Experimental Setting

We perform the categorization of cats and dogs using the proposed *HInGDFs* model and the bag-of-visual words representation. Our methodology are summarized as follows: First, we extract the 128-dimensional scale-invariant feature transform (SIFT) [14] descriptors from each image using the Difference-of-Gaussians (DoG) interest point detectors and then normalized. Then, these extracted SIFT features are modeled using our *HInGDFs*. Specifically, each image $\mathcal{I}_j$ is considered as a "group" and is therefore associated with a Dirichlet process mixture (infinite mixture) model G_j. Thus, each extracted SIFT feature vector X_{ji} of the image $\mathcal{I}_j$ is supposed to be drawn from the infinite mixture model G_j, where the mixture components of G_j can be considered as "visual words". A global vocabulary is constructed and is shared among all groups (images) through the common global infinite mixture model G_0 of our hierarchical model. This setting matches the desired design of a hierarchical Dirichlet process mixture model. It is noteworthy that an important step in image categorization approaches with bag-of-visual words representation is the construction of visual vocabulary. Nevertheless, most of the previously invented approaches have to apply a separate vector quantization algorithm (such as K-means) to build a visual vocabulary, where the vocabulary size is normally manually selected. In our approach, the construction of the visual vocabulary is part of our mixture framework, and therefore the size of the vocabulary (i.e., the number of mixture components in the global-level mixture model) can be automatically inferred from the data thanks to the property of nonparametric Bayesian model. Since the goal of our experiment is to determine which image category (breeds of cats and dogs) that a testing image $\mathcal{I}_j$ belongs to, we also need to introduce an indicator variable B_{jm} associated with each image (or group) in our hierarchical Dirichlet process mixture framework. B_{jm} means image $\mathcal{I}_j$ is from category m and is drawn from another infinite mixture model which is truncated at level J. This means that we need to add a new level of hierarchy to our hierarchical infinite mixture model with a sharing vocabulary among all image categories. In this experiment, we truncate J to 50 and initialize the hyperparameter of the mixing probability of B_{jm} to 0.05. Finally, we assign a testing image to a given category according to Bayes' decision rule.

4.2   Data Set

In this work, we evaluate the effectiveness of the proposed approach for categorizing cats and dogs using a publicly available database namely the Oxford-IIIT Pet database [15][1]. It contains 7,349 images of cats and dogs, and is composed of 12 different breeds of cats and 25 different breeds of dogs. Each of these breeds contains about 200 images. Some sample images of this database are displayed in Fig. 1 (cats) and Fig. 2 (dogs). This database is randomly divided into two partitions: one for training (to learn the model and build the visual vocabulary), the other one for testing.

Results. In our experiments, we demonstrate the advantages of the proposed *HInGDFs* approach by comparing its performance with two other mixture models including the hierarchical infinite GD mixture model without feature selection (*HInGD*) and the hierarchical infinite Gaussian mixture model with feature selection (*HInGFs*). To make a fair comparison, all of these models are learned using variational inference and we evaluated the categorization performance by running the approach 30 times. In the first part of our experiments, we measure the performance of our approach for categorizing cats (12 breeds) and dogs (25 breeds), respectively. The average categorization performances of our approach

---

[1] Database available at: http://www.robots.ox.ac.uk/~vgg/data/pets/

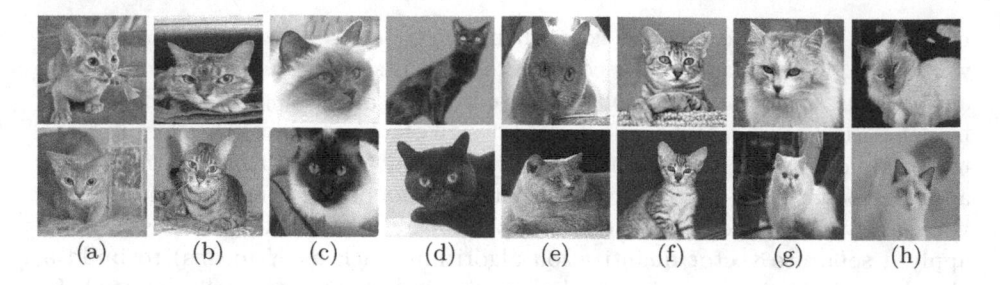

Fig. 1. Sample cat images from the Oxford-IIIT Pet database. (a) Abyssinian, (b) Bengal, (c) Birman, (d) Bombay, (e) British Shorthair, (f) Egyptian Mau, (g) Persian, (h) Ragdoll.

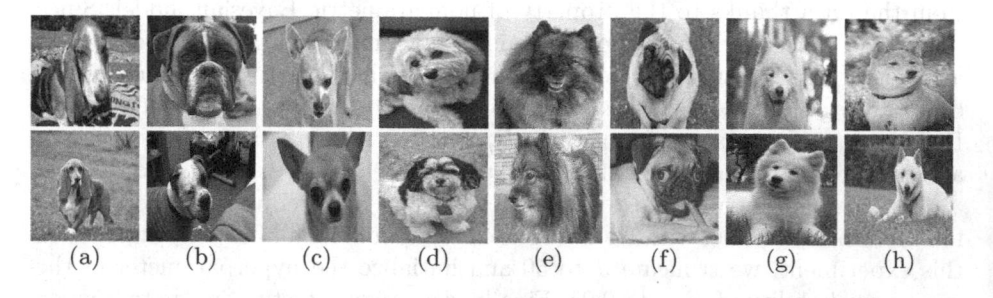

Fig. 2. Sample dog images from the Oxford-IIIT Pet database. (a) Basset hound, (b) Boxer, (c) Chihuahua, (d) Havanese, (e) Keeshond, (f) Pug, (g) Samyod, (h) Shiba inu.

and the two other tested approaches are shown in Table 1. As we can see from this table, our approach (*HInGDFs*) provided the highest categorization accuracy among all tested approaches. Moreover, *HInGDFs* outperformed *HInGD* and *HInGFs* which demonstrates the advantage of incorporating a feature selection scheme into our framework and verifies that the GD mixture model has better modeling capability for proportional data than Gaussian. Next, we have evaluated all approaches for the whole Oxford-IIIT Pet database (i.e., we do not separate cat and dog images). The corresponding results are shown in Table 1. Based on the obtained results, the proposed approach provides again the best categorization accuracy rate (42.73%) as compared toHInGD (39.58%) and

Table 1. The average categorization performance (%) and the standard deviation obtained over 30 runs using different approaches. The values in parenthesis are the standard deviations of the corresponding quantities.

Method	Cats	Dogs	Both
HInGDFs	56.38 (0.95)	44.23 (1.21)	42.94 (1.05)
HInGD	52.92 (1.46)	40.86 (1.07)	39.58 (1.19)
HInGFs	48.65 (1.39)	37.52 (1.13)	35.27 (0.93)

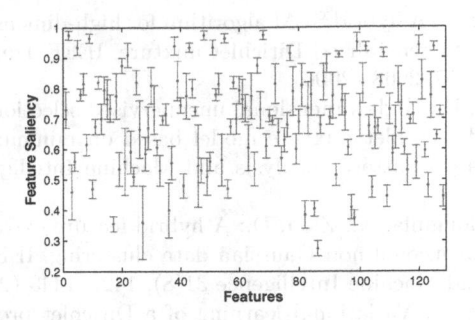

Fig. 3. Feature saliencies of different features calculated by *HInGDFs*

HInGFs (35.27%) approaches. Furthermore, the corresponding feature saliencies of the 128-dimensional SIFT vectors obtained by the proposed are illustrated in Fig. 3. According to this figure, it is clear that the different features do not contribute equally in the categorization, since they have different relevance degrees.

5 Conclusion

In this paper, we have developed a nonparametric Bayesian approach for data modeling, classification, and feature selection, using both hierarchical DP and generalized Dirichlet distributions which allows to model data without the need to define, a priori, the complexity of the entire model. In order to learn the parameters of the proposed model we have derived an inference procedure that relies on variational Bayes. The validation of the model has been based on a challenging application namely images categorization. We are currently working on the extension of our learning framework to online settings to handle the problem of dynamic data modeling.

Acknowledgments. The second author would like to thank King Abdulaziz City for Science and Technology (KACST), Kingdom of Saudi Arabia, for their funding support under grant number 11-INF1787-08.

References

1. Attias, H.: A variational Bayes framework for graphical models. In: Proc. of Advances in Neural Information Processing Systems (NIPS), pp. 209–215 (1999)
2. Berg, T., Forsyth, D.: Animals on the web. In: 2006 IEEE Computer Society Conference on Computer Vision and Pattern Recognition, vol. 2, pp. 1463–1470 (2006)
3. Bishop, C.M.: Pattern Recognition and Machine Learning. Springer (2006)
4. Blei, D.M., Jordan, M.I.: Variational inference for Dirichlet process mixtures. Bayesian Analysis 1, 121–144 (2005)

5. Bouguila, N., Ziou, D.: A hybrid SEM algorithm for high-dimensional unsupervised learning using a finite generalized Dirichlet mixture. IEEE Transactions on Image Processing 15(9), 2657–2668 (2006)
6. Bouguila, N., Ziou, D.: High-dimensional unsupervised selection and estimation of a finite generalized Dirichlet mixture model based on minimum message length. IEEE Transactions on Pattern Analysis and Machine Intelligence 29(10), 1716–1731 (2007)
7. Boutemedjet, S., Bouguila, N., Ziou, D.: A hybrid feature extraction selection approach for high-dimensional non-Gaussian data clustering. IEEE Transactions on Pattern Analysis and Machine Intelligence 31(8), 1429–1443 (2009)
8. Fan, W., Bouguila, N.: Variational learning of a Dirichlet process of generalized Dirichlet distributions for simultaneous clustering and feature selection. Pattern Recognition 46(10), 2754–2769 (2013)
9. Fan, W., Bouguila, N., Ziou, D.: Unsupervised hybrid feature extraction selection for high-dimensional non-gaussian data clustering with variational inference. IEEE Transactions on Knowlege and Data Engineering 25(7), 1670–1685 (2013)
10. Ferguson, T.S.: Bayesian Density Estimation by Mixtures of Normal Distributions. Recent Advances in Statistics 24, 287–302 (1983)
11. Ishwaran, H., James, L.F.: Gibbs sampling methods for stick-breaking priors. Journal of the American Statistical Association 96, 161–173 (2001)
12. Korwar, R.M., Hollander, M.: Contributions to the theory of Dirichlet processes. The Annals of Probability 1, 705–711 (1973)
13. Law, M.H.C., Figueiredo, M.A.T., Jain, A.K.: Simultaneous feature selection and clustering using mixture models. IEEE Transactions on Pattern Analysis and Machine Intelligence 26(9), 1154–1166 (2004)
14. Lowe, D.G.: Distinctive image features from scale-invariant keypoints. International Journal of Computer Vision 60(2), 91–110 (2004)
15. Parkhi, O.M., Vedaldi, A., Zisserman, A., Jawahar, C.V.: Cats and dogs. In: IEEE Conference on Computer Vision and Pattern Recognition (CVPR), pp. 3498–3505 (2012)
16. Ramanan, D., Forsyth, D.A.: Using temporal coherence to build models of animals. In: Proc. of the 9th IEEE International Conference on Computer Vision (ICCV), pp. 338–345. IEEE Computer Society (2003)
17. Sato, M.: Online model selection based on the variational Bayes. Neural Computation 13, 1649–1681 (2001)
18. Sethuraman, J.: A constructive definition of Dirichlet priors. Statistica Sinica 4, 639–650 (1994)
19. Teh, Y.W., Jordan, M.I.: Hierarchical Bayesian Nonparametric Models with Applications. In: Hjort, N., Holmes, C., Müller, P., Walker, S. (eds.) Bayesian Nonparametrics: Principles and Practice. Cambridge University Press (2010)
20. Teh, Y.W., Jordan, M.I., Beal, M.J., Blei, D.M.: Hierarchical Dirichlet processes. Journal of the American Statistical Association 101(476), 1566–1581 (2006)
21. Wang, C., Paisley, J.W., Blei, D.M.: Online variational inference for the hierarchical Dirichlet process. Journal of Machine Learning Research - Proceedings Track 15, 752–760 (2011)

Importance of Feature Selection for Recurrent Neural Network Based Forecasting of Building Thermal Comfort

Martin Macas[1], Fabio Moretti[2], Fiorella Lauro[2], Stefano Pizzuti[2],
Mauro Annunziato[2], Alessandro Fonti[3], Gabriele Comodi[3],
and Andrea Giantomassi[4]

[1] Department of Cybernetics, Czech Technical University in Prague,
Prague, Czech Republic
mmacas@seznam.cz
[2] Unità Tecnica Tecnologie Avanzate per l'Energia e l'Industria,
ENEA (Italian National Agency for New Technologies, Energy and Sustainable
Economic Development), Cassacia Research Center, Roma, Italy
[3] Dipartimento di Ingegneria Industriale e Scienze Matematiche,
Università Politecnica delle Marche, Ancona, Italy
[4] Dipartimento di Ingegneria dell'Informazione,
Università Politecnica delle Marche, Ancona, Italy

Abstract. The paper demonstrates the importance of feature selection for recurrent neural network applied to problem of one hour ahead forecasting of thermal comfort for office building heated by gas. Although the accuracy of the forecasting is similar for both the feed-forward and the recurrent network, the removal of features leads to accuracy reduction much earlier for the feed-forward network. The recurrent network can perform well even with less than 50% of features. This brings significant benefits in scenarios, where the neural network is used as a blackbox model of thermal comfort, which is called by an optimizer that minimizes the deviance from a target value. The reduction of input dimensionality can lead to reduction of costs related to measurement equipment, data transfer and also computational demands of optimization.

Keywords: Forecasting, thermal comfort, gas, heating, neural networks, feature selection.

1 Introduction

Although artificial neural networks are very popular soft-computing techniques used in industrial applications, recurrent neural networks are not used so often like the feed-forward models. One possible cause is the fact that their training is usually much more difficult and more complex recurrent models are more sensitive to over-fitting. It can be therefore crucial to perform a proper selection of network inputs, which can simplify the training and can lead to a better generalization abilities [4], [2]. A proper input selection was observed to be very important particularly in real-world applications [8].

A. Bouchachia (Ed.): ICAIS 2014, LNAI 8779, pp. 11–19, 2014.

In this paper, a simple recurrent neural network model is adopted. The resulting network can be further used as a data-based black box model for optimization of the building heating. At each hour, a building management system finds the indoor air temperature set points that lead to a minimum output of the consumption model and a proper level of thermal comfort. For this purpose, it is crucial to reach a good prediction accuracy of both consumption and thermal comfort. Since the cost function is highly nonlinear and multi-modal, population based metaheuristical optimization can be used with advantage. Because the neural network is used in optimization loop many times, it is also crucial to have the network as smallest as possible. Moreover, if the optimization is performed remotely, one must minimize the amount of data that are measured and transferred from the building to the optimization agent. All these requirements imply a critical need for a proper selection of features, which leads to reasonable data acquisition requirements and proper prediction accuracy.

We focus on one hour ahead forecasting of thermal discomfort in particular gas-heated office building. The comfort is assessed in terms of Predicted Mean Vote model. First we demonstrate that accuracy of the recurrent model is higher than the accuracy of feed-forward network. The main conclusion however is that sensitivity based feature selection can help the recurrent network to reach much higher reduction of the input dimensionality by simultaneously keeping a good accuracy level. This phenomenon has been observed also in study [3] focused on the prediction of heating gas consumption.

In Section 2, we briefly describe all the methods used in the experimental part, which is described in section 3. Some final discussion and conclusions can be found in Section 4.

Fig. 1. Outside of F40 building

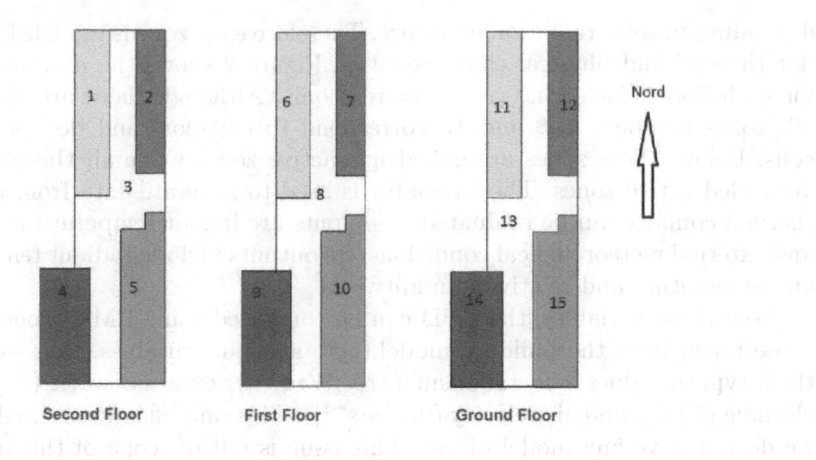

Fig. 2. Partitioning of F40 building zones

2 Data and Methods

2.1 Thermal Comfort Model

To asses a thermal comfort inside particular zones, we used Predicted Mean Vote model (PMV). The model was developed by P. O. Fanger using heat balance equations and empirical studies about skin temperature to define comfort. The model has two outputs. One is PMV value, which is a continuous variable between -3 and $+3$. Its ideal value is zero. Positive PMV means too hot environment and the negative PMV corresponds to cold environment. The comfort zone is for PMV between -0.5 and $+0.5$. The second output of PMV model is Predicted Percentage of Dissatisfied (PPD), which is always greater than 5%. In our experiments we used implementation from Technical University of Eindhoven, Netherland [10].

2.2 F40 Building Model

A real office building located at ENEA (Cassacia Research Centre, Rome, Italy) was considered as a case study (see Figure 1). The building is composed of three floors and a thermal subplant in the basement. The building is equipped with an advanced monitoring system aimed at collecting data about the environmental conditions and electrical and thermal energy consumption. In the building there are 41 offices of different size with a floor area ranging from 14 to 36 m^2, 2 EDP rooms each of about 20 m^2, 4 Laboratories,1 Control Room and 2 Meeting Rooms. Each office room has from 1 up to 2 occupants.

In order to simulate the variables of interest, a MATLAB Simulink simulator based on HAMBASE model ([7], [9]) was developed. In particular, the building was divided into 15 different zones according to different thermal behavior depending to solar radiation exposure. Therefore each zone is modeled with similar thermal and physical characteristics. Figure 2 shows the division of zones for each floor. Each zone covers more rooms. Although there are 15 zones at all, zones numbers 3, 8 and 13 correspond to corridors and do not have fan coils. Below, these zones are called non-active zones while all the other zones are called active zones. The simulator is used to generate data from which the thermal comfort can be evaluated. Its inputs are indoor temperature set points and external meteorological conditions. Its outputs include radiant temperature, air temperature and relative humidity.

From those variables, the PPD can be computed using PMV model. Among those taken from the building model,there are four variables, that were set to their typical values - metabolism (70 $[Wm^{-2}]$), external work (0 $[Wm^{-2}]$), clothing (1 $[-]$), and air velocity (0.1 $[ms^{-1}]$). This simplification is used, because we do not have any model of yet. This issue is out of scope of this paper and will be solved in future work.

2.3 Data

A potential remote control agent would be based on a simple data-driven black box model (here it is a surrogate of the simulator). Metaheuristical algorithms can use such model to optimise temperature set point of the zones so as to keep a predefined comfort level or to minimise thermal consumption and maximise user's comfort. Optimized temperature set points would be then applied to the simulator in order to evaluate the resulting energy savings and comfort. The optimization issue is not covered by this paper, which is devoted only to black box modeling. We used the simulator with the following settings.

To obtain valid and reliable results, we simulated four heating seasons - 2005/2006, 2006/2007, 2007/2008 and 2008/2009. Each data set consists of 75 days which corresponds to $75 \times 24 = 1800$ hourly data instances. The data from the first heating season are called the training data and are used for both the training and feature selection. The data from 2006/2007 are used for selection of the best number of inputs. And the data from 2007/2008 and 2008/2009 are used for the final validation of methods.

The behavior of supply water temperature set point was controlled by a simple weather compensation rule. To excite the dynamics of the system in a proper degree, we also added a random component. The value of the set point is Gaussian random number with standard deviation $10°\ C$ and mean equal to $70 - 2T_e$, where T_e is the external temperature. If the generated number is out of feasibility interval $\langle 35; 70 \rangle°\ C$, the value of water temperature set point is replaced by uniformly distributed random number from this feasibility interval. The behavior of inside air temperature set points differs for daytime and nighttime hours. Between 6 a.m. and 8 p.m., they are also Gaussian random numbers with mean $21°\ C$ and standard deviation $1°\ C$. Moreover, there is a saturation under $19°\ C$ and above $23°\ C$. Between 8 p.m. and 6 a.m., there is a nighttime regime and all the set points are $17°\ C$.

The whole set of features used as inputs for our neural networks is described in Table 1. The first 12 features are the set point values for air temperatures (held constant within each hour) at hour t in 12 active zones (zones that have at least one fan coil). The 13rd feature is the supply water temperature set point at hour t. The remaining features describe the external environment climatic conditions in previous hour $t - 1$. All the meteorological data are obtained from real measurements in Roma Ciampino location. The predicted variable is the PPD value averaged over all active zones and all samples within hour t.

Table 1. The description of features in the original set

Number	Feature
1	Air temperature set point in active zone 1 [$^\circ$ C]
⋮	
12	Air temperature set point in active zone 12 [$^\circ$ C]
13	Supply water temperature set point [$^\circ$ C]
14	Diffuse solar radiation [Wm^{-2}]
15	Exterior air temperature [$^\circ$ C]
16	Direct solar radiation (plane normal to the direction)[Wm^{-2}]
17	Cloud cover(1...8)
18	Relative humidity outside [%]
19	Wind velocity [ms^{-1}]
20	Wind direction [degrees from north]

2.4 Neural Networks

In the underlying experiments, the two simple models were used. The first one is the feed-forward neural network with one hidden layer trained by Levenberg-Marquardt algorithm. This is one of the most popular methods used in neural network applications. The second network is the recurrent neural network with one hidden layer whose delayed outputs are connected back to the input [1]. The network was trained also by the Levenberg-Marquardt algorithm. This popular algorithm is used, because of its relatively high speed, and because it is highly recommended as a first-choice supervised algorithm by Matlab Neural Network toolbox, although it does require more memory than other algorithms [5]. Moreover, the use of the same training method highlights the difference between models and feature selection procedures.

Both networks were simulated in Neural Network Toolbox for Matlab [5]. For the reasons described in section 3 justified also by preliminary experiments, only one unit networks are used here. The hidden and output neurons use the sigmoid and linear transfer function, respectively. The mean squared error was minimized by training procedure. The training was stopped after 100 epochs without any improvement or after the number of training epochs exceeded 300 or if the error gradient reached 10^{-7}.

2.5   Feature Selection

Although both studied neural networks are nonlinear, they significantly differ in their dynamics and a feature selection should be adapted for particular network. To select proper features tailored for particular network, we decided to use a well known sensitivity based method developed by Moody [6]. It is called Sensitivity based Pruning (SBP) algorithm. It evaluates a change in training mean squared error (MSE) that would be obtained if ith input's influence was removed from the network. The removal of influence of input is simply modeled by replacing it by its average value. Let $\mathbf{x}_j(t) = (x_{1j}, \ldots, x_{ij}, \ldots, x_{Dj})$, be the jth of N instances of the input vector (N is the size of the training data set). Let $\mathbf{x}_j^i(t) = (x_{1j}, \ldots, \sum_j x_{ij}/N, \ldots, x_{Dj})$ be jth instance modified at ith position. For each data instance j, partial sensitivity is defined by

$$S_{ij} = (f(\mathbf{x}_j^i) - y_i)^2 - (f(\mathbf{x}_j) - y_i))^2, \tag{1}$$

where f is the neural network function and y_i is the target value for ith data instance. Further, the sensitivity of the network to variable i is defined as:

$$S_i = \frac{\sum_j S_{ij}}{N} \tag{2}$$

In our implementation of SBP, the algorithm starts with the full set of features ($D = 20$). At each step, a target neural network is trained. Further, its sensitivity is computed for particular inputs and the feature, for which the sensitivity is smallest is removed from the data. Note, that a new neural network is trained at each backward step.

An obvious question is, how many features to select. To answer this question, we test the neural networks with different number of inputs on an independent testing data set 2006/2007 and select the proper number of inputs according to its testing error. The final errors of the methods are estimated on the 2007/2008 and 2008/2009 data sets, which are not used in any part of the predictor design process.

3   Experiments

In this section, we experimentally compare how much benefit the feature selection brings for feed-forward and recurrent neural network. From preliminary experiment performed on training data set 2005/2006, we choose neural networks with only one hidden unit. For the two or three neurons in the hidden

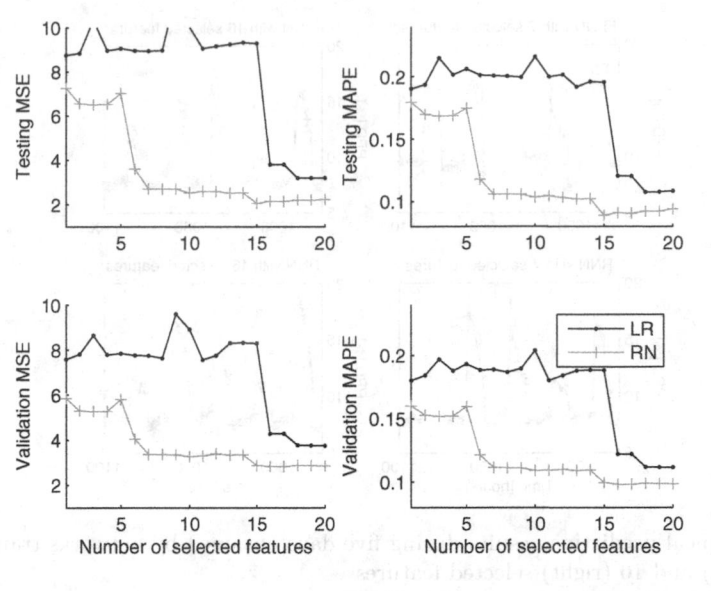

Fig. 3. The dependence of errors on number of selected features. Based on the testing error curve, it was decided to select 7 features for RNN and 16 features for FF.

layer, the average of error estimate (computed over multiple runs) was similar, but the standard deviation value was much higher. Therefore, it seems to be "less risky" to use only one hidden unit topologies for both networks.

First, the training set 2005/2006 was used for feature selection and subsequent training.

Second, the error obtained for different numbers of selected features was estimated on testing set 2006/2007. This error can be found in the upper part of Figure 3. From a brief analysis of the upper subfigures, one can observe, that the feed-forward neural network gives reasonable testing error for 16 and more inputs. On the other hand, the recurrent neural network can perform reasonably well even with 7 features. The term "reasonable" means that the prediction is not disrupted too much. The difference is demonstrated in Figure 4, where the upper-left part shows a bad prediction results obtained by feed-forward network with 7 inputs (MSE approximately equal to 9). On the other hand, the lower part shows a reasonably good prediction obtained by recurrent neural network (MSE approximately equal to 3). Thus, according to the evaluation on the test data, one would chose 16 features and only 7 features as the final number of inputs for feed-forward network or recurrent network, respectively.

Third, the final models were validated on separate validation set 2007/2008 and 2008/2009. This error can be found in the lower-left part of Figure 3. One can see that the comparison results for the two methods are the same for both the testing and validation data. This means that the testing data sufficiently represent the behavior of the system and can be used for the final model selection. The

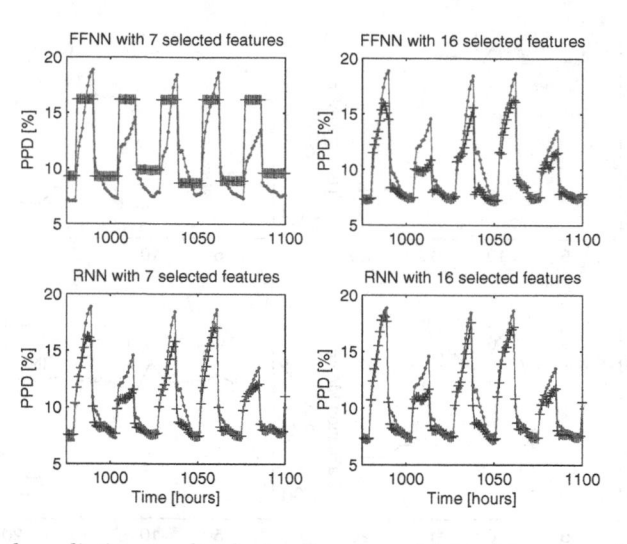

Fig. 4. Typical prediction results during five days obtained by networks trained with only 7 (left) and 16 (right) selected features

Table 2. The feature numbers (see Table 1 for feature names) in the same order as they were removed from the feature set by the backward feature elimination procedure. E.g. for both methods, the feature number 8 (air temperature set point in active zone 8) was removed as the first one.

Feed-forward	8 9 13 14	15 16 10 18 6 12 17 7 20	2 3 4 5 11 19 1
Recurrent	8 9 10 11	12 13 17 18 19 20 16 6 7	14 15 1 2 3 4 5

most important conclusion is that the recurrent model can perform much better for much smaller numbers of input features than the feed-forward networks.

4   Discussion and Conclusions

The main conclusion of the paper is that for our prediction problem, the feature selection, which is based on sensitivity of the network to the removal of features, leads to a significant reduction of input dimensionality without increasing of the MSE. For the recurrent model such a reduction is much higher (13 of 20 inputs were removed). Thus, we are able to reduce the input dimensionality for recurrent network by more than 50%. This also means that a real benefit of recurrent neural network is in possibility of having a much simpler process of data acquisition (remote transfer) and faster computation of network outputs.

The fact that we used such small networks can seem quite strange, but it can be related to small training data consisting of one heating season measurement. For much bigger data, bigger networks could be more suitable, and the results can be different. However, in a real-plant case, one usually does not have enough time to collect multiple heating seasons data and the small networks must be used.

Finally, we describe the feature selection result itself. In Table 2, one can find the order, in which the features were removed from the original set. Although we averaged 20 runs, the feature selection was the same for most runs (19 of 20), thus we show the most typical result. The air temperature set points in active zones number 8 and 9 (zones 10 and 11 in Fig. 2 were the worst features filtered out for both networks.

The findings from this paper will be directly used in our recent experiments with optimization of building heating. However, in such a real case, the training data generated by the procedure described here are not sufficient for a proper optimization. We propose to use the described methodology only to get a first inaccurate surrogate model. Every hour, this model is used to find new set points. The suboptimal set points are applied and their response (thermal comfort) is measured. Those newly measured data would be given to an adaptation mechanism of the neural network, the network is adapted and the process repeats in the next hour.

In future, we also want to focus on some more sophisticated feature selection methods and also more complex neural models of thermal comfort or gas heating consumption.

Acknowledgments. The research was supported by the Czech Science Foundation project no. 13-21696P, "Feature selection for temporal context aware models of multivariate time series".

References

1. Elman, J.L.: Finding structure in time. Cognitive Science 14(2), 179–211 (1990)
2. de Jesús Rubio, J.: Evolving intelligent algorithms for the modelling of brain and eye signals. Applied Soft Computing 14, Part B, 259–268 (2014)
3. Macas, M., Lauro, F., Moretti, F., Pizzuti, S., Annunziato, M., Fonti, A., Comodi, G., Giantomassi, A.: Sensitivity based feature selection for recurrent neural network applied to forecasting of heating gas consumption. In: de la Puerta, J.G., et al. (eds.) International Joint Conference SOCO'14-CISIS'14-ICEUTE'14. AISC, vol. 299, pp. 259–268. Springer, Heidelberg (2014)
4. Macaš, M., Lhotská, L.: Wrapper feature selection significantly improves nonlinear prediction of electricity spot prices. In: 2013 IEEE International Conference on Systems, Man, and Cybernetics (SMC), pp. 1171–1174 (2013)
5. Mathworks: Neural Network Toolbox for Matlab ver. 2012b (2012)
6. Moody, J.E.: The effective number of parameters: An analysis of generalization and regularization in nonlinear learning systems. In: NIPS, pp. 847–854. Morgan Kaufmann (1991)
7. Schijndel, A.W.M.V.: HAMLab: Integrated heat air and moisture modeling and simulation. Ph.D. thesis, Technische Universiteit, Eindhoven (2007), http://archbps1.campus.tue.nl/bpswiki/index.php/Hamlab
8. Villar, J.R., González, S., Sedano, J., Corchado, E., Puigpinós, L., de Ciurana, J.: Meta-heuristic improvements applied for steel sheet incremental cold shaping. Memetic Computing 4(4), 249–261 (2012)
9. de Wit, M.: HAMBASE: Heat, Air and Moisture Model for Building and Systems Evaluation. Technische Universiteit Eindhoven, Faculteit Bouwkunde (2006)
10. de Wit, M.: Calculation of the predicted mean vote (pmv) and the predicted percentage of dissatisfied (ppd) according Fanger. Online Matlab SW (1998)

Classifying Textures with Only 10 Visual-Words Using Hidden Markov Models with Dirichlet Mixtures

Elise Epaillard[1], Nizar Bouguila[2], and Djemel Ziou[3]

[1] Department of Electrical and Computer Engineering
[2] Concordia Institute for Information Systems Engineering,
Concordia University, Montreal, Quebec, Canada
[3] MOIVRE, Département d'informatique,
Université de Sherbrooke, Sherbrooke, Quebec, Canada
e_epail@encs.concordia.ca, nizar.bouguila@concordia.ca,
djemel.ziou@usherbrooke.ca

Abstract. This work presents what we think to be the first application of Dirichlet-based Hidden Markov Models (HMM) to real-world data. Initially developed in [5], this model has only been tested on controlled synthetic data, showing promising results for classification tasks. Its capabilities on proportional data are investigated and leveraged for texture classification. Comparison to HMM with Gaussian mixtures and to nearest-neighbor classifiers is conducted and a generalized Bhattacharyya distance for series of histograms is proposed. We show that HMM with Dirichlet mixtures outperforms other tested classifiers. Using the popular bag-of-words approach, the Dirichlet-based HMM proves its ability to discriminate well between 25 textures from challenging data sets using a global dictionary of 10 words only. This seems to represent the smallest dictionary ever used to this purpose and raises the question of the need of hundreds-word dictionaries most often used in the literature for the data sets we have tested.

Keywords: Hidden Markov models, Dirichlet mixtures, texture classification, Bhattacharyya distance, bag-of-visual-words.

1   Introduction

Most of our natural environment can be interpreted as textures, in the sense it is mainly composed of more or less repetitive patterns involving some spatial dynamics. Their thorough study is of great importance and texture categorization, segmentation, and synthesis have been the topics of unnumbered studies with applications as various as medical imaging [9], special effects [2], remote sensing [21], etc. This paper tackles the classification task by proposing the use of a data-tailored classifier of the HMM family for proportional data.

HMMs for texture applications - HMMs have been seldom used for texture classification purpose though their capabilities to unravel latent structures of textures that direct observations could not provide alone has been brought to light long ago [14]. Their capabilities have then been investigated in the wavelet domain [8,17,20] giving

A. Bouchachia (Ed.): ICAIS 2014, LNAI 8779, pp. 20–28, 2014.

promising results, but no further study seems to have been led with HMMs. As dynamical processes, they seem however particularly appropriate to model textures that naturally embed spatial dynamics.

HMMs in other application fields - HMMs are already extensively used in numerous fields involving latent temporal dynamics such as speech processing [16], object and gesture classification [3,6], or anomaly detection [1,10]. The training process of the HMMs itself is quite standardized, and newly developed approaches mostly focus on their initialization in terms of topology, parameters estimation or algorithmic complexity [1,3,6,10], arguing that the initial tuning has a direct impact on results accuracy. To the opposite, the choice of emission probability distribution functions is seldom discussed and mixtures of Gaussian are most often used for their mathematical and practical convenience, without strong justification. In this paper, we propose to use mixtures of Dirichlet as emission probability distributions, as developed in [5], for proportional data modeling. The rationale behind this is the capability of Dirichlet distribution, because of its compact support $[0,1]$, to better model proportional data [4] which is an usual outcome of stochastic representations (e.g. histograms).

Bag-of-words and affiliated methods for texture representation - One popular texture representation approach is the bag-of-words (BoW) method. First introduced as the image counterpart of document classification works, it has been broadly employed and shown to be efficient for texture classification tasks [12]. Among the numerous studies employing it, [15] proposes two approaches known for their good performance in text classification, namely Probabilistic Latent Semantic Indexing and Non-negative Matrix Factorization. A sparse image representation is used by first detecting local regions of interest with Harris- and Hessian-affine detectors and then extracting SIFT [13] in these regions. A global texton-dictionary is built with an optimal number of textons found to be 500 as a trade-off between computational load and performance. Classification is finally led in an unsupervised manner. In [23], local regions are also detected and then normalized to be mapped into subspaces. Texton-dictionaries of size 100 are built from different feature types (intensity and gradient) with several linear and non-linear embedding methods and a Support Vector Machine (SVM) classifier is used. In [12], a method based on the projection of a set of points from a high-dimensional space to a randomly chosen low-dimensional subspace, referred to as random projections (RP), is developed. Images are seen as an ensemble of patches from which RP features are extracted. Rotation-invariance is obtained by sorting the pixels intensity or the pixels differences projections. Each texture class is represented by a BoW model of 40 to 80 textons, leading to a full dictionary of 1000 to 2000 words. Classification is performed using nearest-neighbor (NN) and SVM classifiers. [22] makes use of fractal analysis to describe textures at different resolutions. The authors provide an interesting comparison of multifractal spectrum (MFS) and histograms. Their analysis shows that MFS overcomes the issue of the loss of spatial distribution information inherent to histograms by providing a multilayer aspect to key points count. In comparison, we propose to use series of histograms over image patches to help maintaining partial information about the spatial distribution of the key points (textons). This makes the comparison of our method with this one of high interest.

Contributions of our work - In all these works, the dictionary size used goes from one hundred up to a few thousands words. Our main contributions are to show that a well-tailored classifier can achieve state-of-the-art results with a dictionary as small as of 10 visual-words leading to the most compact representation ever reported, and that HMMs with Dirichlet Mixtures model (HMMDM) can be efficiently used on real-world data. Furthermore, our original representation uses series of histograms and gives rise, for comparison with NN classification, to the need of a similarity measure for ordered multiple histograms. This led us to generalize the Bhattacharyya distance to this case.

This paper is organized as follows: Section 2 details the method's main steps, Section 3 reports our experimental results and provides elements of comparison as well as results interpretation. We finally conclude in Section 4 and present some ideas to be studied in our future work on the topic.

2   Application to Texture Classification

A common way to obtain proportional data from images is to work with a BoW strategy. In our work, the quality of the extracted features is not crucial to assess the performance of a classifier relatively to other classifiers, and we therefore simply use SIFT [13] and a two-stage k-means clustering to build a texton-dictionary.

HMMDM has in practice a big restriction on input data dimension that we empirically found to be of the order of 10 (higher dimensions lead intermediate matrices to be singular, causing invertibility issues). While this number is very small as a dictionary size, we choose to give it a try and to perform our experiments with a global dictionary of only 10 words. To the best of our knowledge, this constitutes the smallest dictionary ever reported for experiments over large texture data sets, several orders lower than usual ones (500 words in [15] and 1000 in [12] for a 25-class representation). However, it is worthwhile noticing that 10 words theoretically have the capability to represent much more than 25 classes. Supposing that only 2 value levels are allowed for each word (e.g. *present* or *absent*), 2^{10} configurations are possible. Though the intra-class variability probably reduces the effective number of classes that could be discriminated with such a naive representation, we state that there is no need of hundreds of words to represent distinctively a few dozens classes.

2.1   Textons Dictionary Building

The SIFT detector proposed in [13] is used on each image with dense sampling (no local region detector is used). Due to the nature of SIFT features itself, the number of extracted descriptors varies from around 100 up to 7000, depending on the texture class,. In order not to take any advantage of this clue, a k-means clustering is performed for each image lowering down the number of features to 60. As this paper focuses on the classification method, no further study has been conducted to optimize this value which is a trade-off between the image representation precision and the computational load of this step. A set of N images is randomly selected from each of the c classes to form a training set. By the aforementioned process, 60 SIFT features per image are extracted. A second k-means clustering is then applied to the gathering of all the training set features, i.e. $60 \times c \times N$ SIFT vectors, from which 10 centers are obtained, forming the global dictionary.

2.2   Series of Histograms Computation

As mentioned earlier, we consider here textures as being quite repetitive patterns involving some spatial dynamics. We propose to embed these spatial dynamics into each image representation by scanning the image following a predefined path and building a corresponding series of histograms. Each image is divided into P patches of equal size, and the scan path is arbitrarily defined as going from row to row, from the left to the right. For each patch, all originally extracted features (i.e. the ones obtained before any clustering) are assigned to their nearest SIFT-word in the dictionary. This operation results in a series of P 10-bin histograms (which can also be interpreted as a 2D-histogram) representing the image. This process is used in both training and testing phases.

2.3   Model Computation and Classification

Each texture type is modeled by an HMM that is trained using the N available training series of histograms of the corresponding texture class. We compare two types of emission probability distributions; Dirichlet Mixture Models [5] and Gaussian Mixtures Models which are the most commonly used emission functions in HMMs applications. Same numbers of states K, and mixture components M, have been used in both cases, empirically determined by making them vary from 1 to 4, values which keep the model computation tractable. It has been noticed that when the product KM is too large (above 12 here), some class models fail to be estimated (matrices singularities appear at some point, stopping the whole estimation process). The best results have been obtained for KM products equal to 8 or 9.

Changing the probability distributions from mixtures of Gaussian to mixtures of Dirichlet involves modifying the parameters estimation step in the EM-algorithm, keeping the rest of the HMM algorithm unchanged. The details of the distributions substitution are discussed in [5]. The model's parameters initialization has been shown intractable if accurately computed [5]. Following [5], KM single Dirichlet distributions are initialized and then assigned to the HMM states in an ordered manner, while other parameters are randomly initialized.

As a new image arrives, all its SIFT features are computed and allocated to the different histograms bins depending on their location and value. Once the series of histograms is built, its likelihood with respect to each class model is computed using a forward algorithm and the image is classified into the category of highest likelihood.

2.4   Baseline Method

To quantify the performance of the HMMDM classifier, a baseline method using an NN classifier is implemented. The Bhattacharyya distance between two histograms G and H

$$d(G, H) = \sqrt{1 - \sum_i \sqrt{G(i)} \sqrt{H(i)}}, \tag{1}$$

where i denotes the bin number [7], can be straightforwardly generalized to series of N histograms by

$$d(G_N, H_N) = \sqrt{1 - \frac{1}{N} \sum_{n=1}^{N} \sum_{i} \sqrt{G_n(i)} \sqrt{H_n(i)}} \, . \qquad (2)$$

The number of histograms in our case is equal to the number of patches in the image. However, this distance, denoted *BD1* later, is clearly not robust to translation. Working at the patch level, if P patches are used then, P translated patterns exist. Hence, we propose the following patch-translation robust distance, denoted *BD2*:

$$d_{tr}(G_N, H_N) = \min_{p \in [1, P]} d(G_N, H_N^p) \, , \qquad (3)$$

where the superscript p stands for the translation of the first patch of G_N source image onto the pth patch of H_N source image, spatially warping around the other patches.

3 Experimental Results

3.1 Results

We propose to assess the performance of the HMMDM classifier on proportional data comparing it to HMMGM and NN classifiers. To the best of our knowledge, this work represents its first use on real-world data. [5] which first introduced it only presents experiments on synthetic data, generated from a known HMMDM. Therefore, the capabilities of HMMDM have to be investigated and leveraged on real-world data. Our experiments are performed on the two recent challenging natural texture images data sets from UIUC [11] and UMD [22], and compared with other BoW-based methods.

UIUC and UMD data sets contain 1000 images of size 480x640 and 1280x960 pixels, respectively, divided up into 25 different classes (40 instances in each). They are challenging by the variety of 2D and 3D transformations and illumination variations present in it. For fair results comparison, the UMD data set is downsampled to the same resolution as the UIUC one. Sample images are presented in Fig. 1.

The experimental results presented here have been obtained fixing $M = K = 3$ and $P = 12$ with random training sets of $N = 5, 10, 20$ images of each class, running the algorithm 50 times. Results are reported in Figs 2 and 3. The F-score [18] of the proposed approach with $N = 20$ is 94.3% on the UMD data set and 91.7% on the UIUC one (only accuracy is reported on the graphs).

As mentioned earlier, the choice of working with a 10-word dictionary is induced by the HMMDM model itself. Using more words degrades the overall performance mainly because of the divergence of the estimation algorithm for some classes. One way to overcome this issue would be to force the estimation process to stop before it diverges, i.e. as soon as the transition probability and the emission probability matrices are estimated, and to rely on the initial parameters for the emission distributions. This would lead to less accurate models but may allow the use of a slightly larger number of visual-words. More investigation is needed to find an optimum between the number of words and the models' accuracy needed. Even in this case, the number of words used will still be several orders lower usual dictionary sizes for this type of applications.

Fig. 1. Sample images from the UMD (top) and UIUC (bottom) data sets

3.2 Comparison and Interpretation

From our experiments, it is clear that the HMMDM classifier can be used for real texture classification purpose and outperforms NN classifiers independently of the data set. It is worth noticing that the use of a dynamical model is not sufficient to get good classification accuracy. Working with appropriate emission probability distributions that match with features properties is essential and the use of HMMs with non-suited probability emission functions dramatically degrades the results even compared to a simple NN classifier. Careful study of features properties is therefore crucial for choosing these distributions. Experiments with HMMGM even led to the misclassification of entire classes which is critical for recognition applications. HMMDM performs better than the other tested classifiers even with a training set reduced to 5 images. As expected, larger training sets improve the accuracy.

Rank statistics of order 3 and 5 show that most of time, even when not well-classified, the likelihood of the query with respect to its ground truth class is high. Introduction of a prior might help to improve the performance of the HMMDM classifier. For instance, we did not take advantage of the information about SIFT density extracted at the first clustering level while it varies a lot depending on the texture class and could thus provide a valuable clue.

Our proposed patch-translation robust Bhattacharyya distance (*BD2*) systematically improves the results of NN classification with respect to a simpler generalization (*BD1*) and gives acceptable accuracy on the UMD data set despite its simplicity. It however seems less versatile than HMM classifiers as the results on the UIUC data set are significantly more degraded with respect to the ones obtained with HMMDM.

We compare our approach with [12,15,22,23], briefly presented in the introductory part. All these studies use BoW strategies or similar texture representation and therefore constitute good references to assess the performance of our method. On the UIUC data set, [15] achieves 77.2% of accuracy using 500 textons (but unsupervised classification), [12], 95.8% with 1000 textons, and [23], 97.9% with 100 textons. MFS approach [22] leads to 92.7% of accuracy and ours to 91.4% using 10 textons. On the UMD data set, we achieve an accuracy of 93.9%, equal to the one reported in [22], while [12]

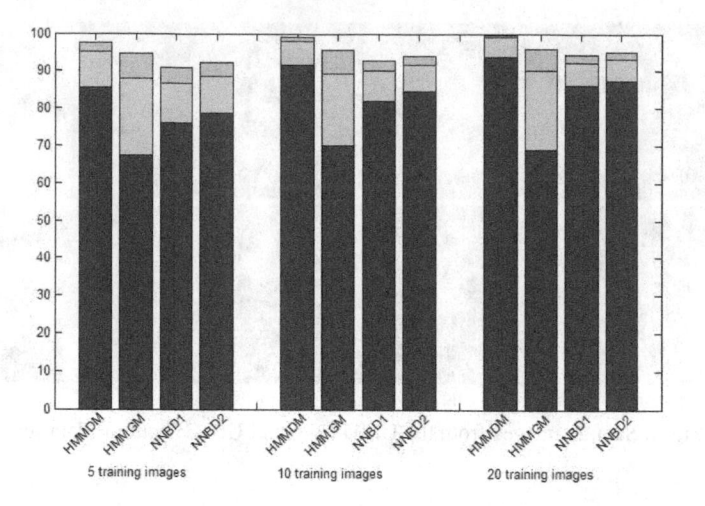

Fig. 2. Accuracy (in blue) and rank statistics of order 3 (in green) and 5 (in orange) for the different classifiers on the UMD data set using 5, 10, and 20 training images per class.

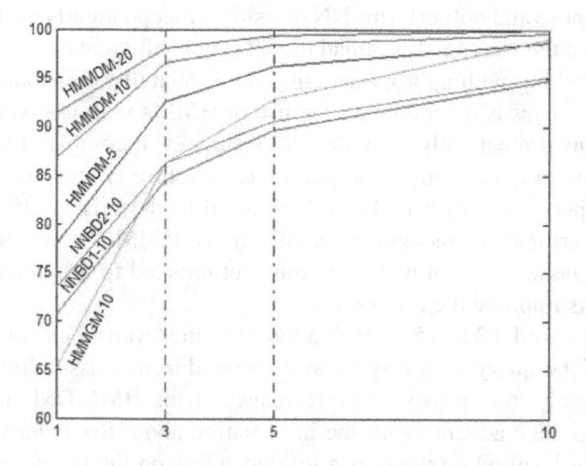

Fig. 3. Rank statistics of order 1 (recall), 3, 5, and 10 for the different classifiers on the UIUC data set. The number after the '-' indicates the number of training images per class.

and [23] reach 98.7% and 98.2%, respectively. In all cases, 20 training images per class have been used. Correct classification rate of our method falls only few percents below current top state-of-the-art methods [12,23], while using a dictionary 10 to 100 times smaller. This shows the potential power of the HMMDM for proportional data. Moreover, these results might be further improved with more appropriate features and optimized parameters.

One weakness of histograms is the loss of spatial information in the image representation. We overcome this issue by considering series of histograms over patches while [22] proposes a multi-resolution representation with MFS features. Both methods achieve same or close results over the two tested data sets, showing that series of histograms can also help to solve this point while being more straightforward.

The good results obtained while using an approximate clustering method for features extraction (double stage k-means clustering, allowing easy convergence towards local extrema), tend to confirm the observation made in [19] regarding the estimation precision needed for the clusters centers to efficiently model data for classification tasks. Indeed, in their study, the authors have shown that good accuracy results could be obtained even if the dictionary textons were selected at random. These conclusions open a window towards lower complexity algorithms in this field, especially for applications involving restricted memory size for image representation storage.

4 Conclusion

We presented a method based on a double stage clustering SIFT features to form a very compact 10-word dictionary. Series of histograms are used to keep partial spatial information and Dirichlet-based HMMs to perform classification, outperforming other tested classifiers. Our initial guess that 10 words had the capability to discriminate well among few dozens of classes proves to be true in these applications. Despite the huge changes of scale, rotation, illumination and even more challenging 3D-transformations present in the data sets used, our roughly determined 10-word dictionary performs classification with a very acceptable accuracy. Though further investigation is needed to get a definite conclusion, this result raises the question of the necessity of the hundreds-word dictionaries most often used in the literature.

In its current setting, our approach cannot appropriately handle dynamic data as the model's parameters cannot evolve over time. Future work will strive to extend the model to online settings, making it more application-versatile and robust to time-varying environments (e.g. video surveillance data).

References

1. Andrade, E.L., Blunsden, S., Fisher, R.B.: Hidden Markov models for optical flow analysis in crowds. In: Proc. ICPR, pp. 460–463 (2006)
2. Bertalmío, M., Vese, L.A., Sapiro, G., Osher, S.: Simultaneous structure and texture image inpainting. IEEE Transactions on Image Processing 12(8), 882–889 (2003)
3. Bicego, M., Castellani, U., Murino, V.: A hidden Markov model approach for appearance-based 3D object recognition. Pattern Recognition Letters 26(16), 2588–2599 (2005)
4. Bouguila, N., Ziou, D., Vaillancourt, J.: Unsupervised learning of a finite mixture model based on the dirichlet distribution and its application. IEEE Transactions on Image Processing 13(11), 1533–1543 (2004)
5. Chen, L., Barber, D., Odobez, J.M.: Dynamical dirichlet mixture model. IDIAP-RR 02, IDIAP (2007)
6. Cholewa, M., Glomb, P.: Estimation of the number of states for gesture recognition with hidden Markov models based on the number of critical points in time sequence. Pattern Recognition Letters 34(5), 574–579 (2013)
7. Dubuisson, S.: The computation of the Bhattacharyya distance between histograms without histograms. In: Proc. IPTA, pp. 373–378 (2010)

8. Fan, G., Xia, X.G.: Wavelet-based texture analysis and synthesis using hidden Markov models. IEEE Transactions on Circuits and Systems 1: Fundamental Theory and Applications 50(1), 106–120 (2003)
9. van Ginneken, B., Katsuragawa, S., ter Haar Romeny, B.M., Doi, K., Viergever, M.A.: Automatic detection of abnormalities in chest radiographs using local texture analysis. IEEE Transactions on Medical Imaging 21(2), 139–149 (2002)
10. Jiang, F., Wu, Y., Katsaggelos, A.K.: Abnormal event detection from surveillance video by dynamic hierarchical clustering. In: Proc. ICIP, pp. 145–148 (2007)
11. Lazebnik, S., Schmid, C., Ponce, J.: A sparse texture representation using local affine regions. IEEE Transactions on Pattern Analysis and Machine Intelligence 27(8), 1265–1278 (2005)
12. Liu, L., Fieguth, P.W., Clausi, D.A., Kuang, G.: Sorted random projections for robust rotation-invariant texture classification. Pattern Recognition 45(6), 2405–2418 (2012)
13. Lowe, D.G.: Object recognition from local scale-invariant features. In: Proc. ICCV (1999)
14. Povlow, B.R., Dunn, S.M.: Texture classification using noncausal hidden Markov models. IEEE Transactions on Pattern Analysis and Machine Intelligence 17(10), 1010–1014 (1995)
15. Qin, L., Zheng, Q., Jiang, S., Huang, Q., Gao, W.: Unsupervised texture classification: Automatically discover and classify texture patterns. Image and Vision Computing 26(5), 647–656 (2008)
16. Rabiner, L.R., Juang, B.H.: An introduction to hidden Markov models. IEEE ASSP Magazine 3(1), 4–16 (1986)
17. Salles, E.O.T., Ling, L.L.: Texture classification by means of hmm modeling of am-fm features. In: Proc. ICIP, pp. 182–185 (2001)
18. Sasaki, Y.: The truth of the f-measure. School of Computer Science. University of Manchester (2007)
19. Varma, M., Zisserman, A.: A statistical approach to material classification using image patch exemplars. IEEE Transactions on Pattern Analysis and Machine Intelligence 31(11), 2032–2047 (2009)
20. Xu, Q., Yang, J., Siyi, D.: Color texture analysis using the wavelet-based hidden Markov model. Pattern Recognition Letters 26(11), 1710–1719 (2005)
21. Xu, S., Fang, T., Li, D., Wang, S.: Object classification of aerial images with bag-of-visual words. IEEE Geoscience and Remote Sensing Letters 7(2), 366–370 (2010)
22. Xu, Y., Ji, H., Fermüller, C.: Viewpoint invariant texture description using fractal analysis. International Journal of Computer Vision 83(1), 85–100 (2009)
23. Yang, X., Tian, Y.: Texture representations using subspace embeddings. Pattern Recognition Letters 34(10), 1130–1137 (2013)

A Novel Method for Scene Categorization Using an Improved Visual Vocabulary Approach*

Tarek Elguebaly[1] and Nizar Bouguila[2]

[1] Department of Electrical and Computer Engineering,
Faculty of Engineering and Computer Science,
Concordia University
t_elgue@encs.concordia.ca
[2] Concordia Institute for Information Systems Engineering,
Faculty of Engineering and Computer Science,
Concordia University
nizar.bouguila@concordia.ca

Abstract. The performance of any scene categorization system depends on the scene representation algorithm used. Lately, the Bag of Visual Words (BoVW) approach has indisputably become the method of choice for this crucial task. Nevertheless, the BoVW approach has various flaws. First, the K-means clustering algorithm for visual dictionary creation is based solely on the Euclidean distance. Second, the size of the visual vocabulary is a user-supplied parameter which is unpractical as the final categorization depends critically on the chosen number of visual words. Finally, classifying each descriptor to only one visual word is unrealistic because it does not consider the uncertainty present in the image descriptor level. Therefore, in this paper, we propose a simple solution for these problems. Our algorithm uses the Asymmetric Generalized Gaussian mixture (AGGM) to model the distribution of the visual words. Our choice is based on the fact that the Asymmetric Generalized Gaussian distribution (AGGD) can fit different shapes of observed non-Gaussian and asymmetric data. To automatically determine the number of visual words, the number of mixture components in our case, we employed the Minimum Message length (MML) criterion. We propose to use a soft assignment by exploiting the probability for each descriptor to belong to each visual word and thus considering the uncertainty present in the image descriptor level. In addition, the efficacy of the proposed algorithm is validated by applying it to scene categorization.

1 Introduction

With the widespread diffusion of portable device, millions of users produce, edit, and share huge amounts of image and videos every day. Flickr, one of the many on-line services that allow sharing digital visual content, has an impressive

---

* The authors would like to thank the Natural Sciences and Engineering Research Council of Canada (NSERC).

A. Bouchachia (Ed.): ICAIS 2014, LNAI 8779, pp. 29–39, 2014.
© Springer International Publishing Switzerland 2014

amount of over half a billion pictures by 2012. Thus, users searching in these multimedia collections are in need of automatic methods to help them explore such multimedia spaces. Therefore, nowadays, computerized categorization and classification of images and their properties is of essential importance for the automatic organization, selection and retrieval of the huge amount of visual content surrounding us. In particular, automatically recognizing various scenes in images has received a lot of attention because of its potential number of applications such as object recognition and detection [1] and content-based image indexing and retrieval [2]. Scene categorization refers to the task of grouping images into semantically meaningful categories. The performance of a scene categorization system depends mainly on two components, namely, image representation and classification.

Image representation is the task of choosing the best features or signatures which can describe and summarize important visual properties of the image. There are mainly two types of features, local and global. Global descriptors consist of features computed on the whole image, therefore, they have the ability to represent the entire image with a single vector. Consequently, they don't need any further representation and can be directly used for classification. They usually use low level features such as color, texture, etc. One of the widely used methods in this category is the GIST representation which uses perceptual dimensions (naturalness, openness, roughness, expansion, ruggedness) in order to represent the dominant spatial structure of a scene [3]. On the other hand, local descriptors are computed at multiple points in the image in order to represent the characteristics of the different regions in the image; thus allowing a better representation of the image content. Furthermore, they are more robust to occlusion and clutter. Scale Invariant Feature Transform (SIFT) descriptors are created by representing the blurred image in multiple orientation planes and scales which make them invariant to image scaling translation, to rotation and partially to illumination changes [4]. Speeded Up Robust Features (SURF) is a robust local feature detector inspired by SIFT [5]. It uses an integer approximation to the determinant of Hessian blob detector. For features, it uses the sum of the Haar wavelet response around the point of interest which can be computed with the aid of the integral image. In this paper we are interested in local descriptors. For local descriptor, an image representation task is needed in order to produce a single vector per image from an unordered set of feature vectors computed for the various interest points found in the image. Recently, the BoVW approach exhibits very good performance in image categorization and scene classification [6]. BoVW approach is used to identify a set of key-points which are in some way prototypes of a certain types of image patch. Generally, the visual words are found using a simple k-means algorithm with Euclidean distance as the clustering metric. After creating the visual dictionary or codebook, The key-points are used to map each image's set of patch descriptors to a histogram over key-points. However, the BoVW approach has several flaws such as its need for a predefined codebook size, dependence on the chosen set of visual words, and the use of hard assignment clustering for histogram creation. In this paper, we are trying to overcome these issues by using an AGGM model. The advantage of the considered model is that it has the required flexibility to fit different shapes of observed non-Gaussian and asymmetric descriptors. Furthermore, we use the Expectation-Maximization (EM) algorithm for mixture parameters estimation. In order to choose the best codebook size M, we start by choosing a large initial value for M and derive the structure of the mixture by letting the estimates of some of the mixing probability to be zero. Therefore, this method aims at finding the best overall model in the entire set of available models rather than selecting one among a set of candidate models. Thus, we end up with M visual words where each keypoint is represented by an AGGD. Finally, we use a soft assignment clustering approach to map each image's set of patch descriptors to a histogram over keypoints. Our approach uses the probability for each descriptor to belong to each visual word, hence, consider the uncertainty present in the image descriptor level. Image classification is the final stage for any scene categorization system. While classification might be easy for human beings it is very hard for machines. Recently, several classification methods were introduced such as naive Bayes [7] and Support Vector Machine (SVM) [8]. Naive bayes classifier is a simple probabilistic classifier based on applying Bayes' theorem with naive independence assumptions. SVM constructs a hyperplane in a high-dimensional space, which allow for a good separation between classes.

This paper is organized as follows. Section 2 describes the AGGM model and gives a complete learning algorithm. In Section 3, we assess the performance of the new model for scene categorization while comparing it to other BOVW models. Our last section is devoted to the conclusion. and some perspectives.

2 AGGM Model

If a D-dimensional random variable $\vec{X} = [X_1, \ldots, X_D]^T$ follows an AGGD with parameters $\vec{\mu}$, $\vec{\beta}$, $\vec{\sigma}_l$, and $\vec{\sigma}_r$, then the density function is given by.

$$p(\vec{X}|\vec{\mu}, \vec{\beta}, \vec{\sigma}_l, \vec{\sigma}_r) = \prod_{d=1}^{D} \frac{\beta_d \left[\frac{\Gamma(3/\beta_d)}{\Gamma(1/\beta_d)}\right]^{1/2}}{(\sigma_{l_d} + \sigma_{r_d})\Gamma(1/\beta_d)} \begin{cases} \exp\left[-A(\beta_d)\left(\frac{\mu_d - X_d}{\sigma_{l_d}}\right)^{\beta_d}\right] \text{if } X_d < \mu_d \\ \exp\left[-A(\beta_d)\left(\frac{X_d - \mu_d}{\sigma_{r_d}}\right)^{\beta_d}\right] \text{if } X_d \geq \mu_d \end{cases} \quad (1)$$

where $A(\beta_d) = \left[\frac{\Gamma(3/\beta_d)}{\Gamma(1/\beta_d)}\right]^{\beta_d/2}$ and $\Gamma(.)$ is the Gamma function given by: $\Gamma(x) = \int_0^\infty t^{x-1}e^{-t}dt$, $x > 0$. $\vec{\mu} = (\mu_1, \ldots, \mu_D)$, $\vec{\sigma}_l = (\sigma_{l_1}, \ldots, \sigma_{l_D})$, $\vec{\sigma}_r = (\sigma_{r_1}, \ldots, \sigma_{r_D})$, and $\vec{\beta} = (\beta_1, \ldots, \beta_D)$ denote the distribution mean, left standard deviation, right standard deviation, and the shape parameter for the D-dimensional AGGD, respectively. The parameter $\vec{\beta}$ controls the shape of the probability density function (pdf). The larger the value, the flatter the pdf; and the smaller the value, the more picked the pdf. This means that $\vec{\beta}$ determines the decay rate of the density function. The AGGD is chosen to be able to fit, in analytically simple and realistic way, symmetric or non-symmetric data by the combination of the left and right variances. Therefore, if $\vec{X}$ follows a mixture of M AGGDs, it can be expressed as follows:

$$p(\vec{X}|\Theta) = \sum_{j=1}^{M} p_j p(\vec{X}|\xi_j) \tag{2}$$

where $\xi_j = (\vec{\mu}_j, \vec{\beta}_j, \vec{\sigma}_{l_j}, \vec{\sigma}_{r_j})$ is the set of parameters of the jth component; p_j $(0 \leq p_j \geq 1$ and $p_j = 1)$ are the mixing proportions. As for the symbol $\Theta = (P, \xi)$, it refers to the entire set of parameters to be estimated, knowing that $P = (p_1, \ldots, p_M)$ and $\xi = (\xi_1, \ldots, \xi_M)$. Let $\mathcal{X} = (\vec{X}_1, \ldots, \vec{X}_N)$ be a set of N independent and identical distributed vectors, assumed to arise from a finite AGGM with M components. Hence, the likelihood corresponding to this case is $p(\mathcal{X}|\Theta) = \prod_{i=1}^{N} \sum_{j=1}^{M} p_j p(\vec{X}_i|\xi_j)$. We introduce an M dimensional vector, $\vec{Z}_i = (Z_{i1}, \ldots, Z_{iM})$, known by the unobserved or missing vector that indicates to which component $\vec{X}_i$ belongs; such that: Z_{ij} will be equal to 1 if $\vec{X}_i$ belongs to class j or 0, otherwise. The complete-data likelihood is then

$$p(\mathcal{X}, Z|\Theta) = \prod_{i=1}^{N} \prod_{j=1}^{M} \left(p_j p(\vec{X}_i|\xi_j) \right)^{Z_{ij}} \tag{3}$$

2.1   Expectation-Maximization

The EM algorithm represents an elegant and powerful method to estimate the parameters of a mixture model by maximizing the likelihood, supposing that the number of mixture components M is known. Therefore the EM algorithm consists of getting the mixture parameters that maximize the log-likelihood function given by

$$L(\Theta, Z, \mathcal{X}) = \sum_{j=1}^{M} \sum_{i=1}^{N} Z_{ij} \log \left(p(\vec{X}_i|\xi_j)p_j \right) \tag{4}$$

However, before applying the EM algorithm, we need to choose some initial values for the mixture parameters. In our case, we use the K-means algorithm to choose the initial values. Then, we employ the EM iterative algorithm which produces a sequence of estimates to the mixture parameters $\Theta^{(t)}$, for $t = 0, \ldots$, until a certain convergence criterion is satisfied through two different steps: the expectation and maximization. In the expectation step, we use the current values for the parameters to evaluate the responsibilities defined as the posterior probability that the ith observation arises from the jth component of the mixture as follows:

$$\hat{Z}_{ij}^{(t)} = \frac{p(\vec{X}_i|\xi_j^{(t-1)})p_j^{(t-1)}}{\sum_{j=1}^{M} p(\vec{X}_i|\xi_j^{(t-1)})p_j^{(t-1)}} \tag{5}$$

where t denotes the current iteration step, and $(\xi^{(t)}, p_j^{(t)})$ are the current evaluations of the parameters. Now, using these expectations, the goal is to maximize the complete data log-likelihood with respect to our model parameters. This can be done by calculating the gradient of the log-likelihood with respect to p_j, $\vec{\mu}_j$, $\vec{\beta}_j$, $\vec{\sigma}_{l_j}$, and $\vec{\sigma}_{r_j}$. When estimating p_j we actually need to introduce Lagrange multiplier to ensure that the constraints $p_j > 0$ and $\sum_{j=1}^{M} p_j = 1$ are satisfied. Thus, the augmented log-likelihood function can be expressed by:

$$\Phi(\Theta, Z, \mathcal{X}, \Lambda) = \sum_{i=1}^{N} \sum_{j=1}^{M} Z_{ij} \log \left(p(\vec{X}_i | \xi_j) p_j \right) + \Lambda(1 - \sum_{j=1}^{M} p_j) \qquad (6)$$

where Λ is the Lagrange multiplier. Differentiating the augmented function with respect to p_j we get:

$$\hat{p}_j = \frac{1}{N} \sum_{i=1}^{N} p(j | \vec{X}_i) \qquad j=1, \ldots, M \qquad (7)$$

Note that the gradients with respect to $\vec{\mu}$, $\vec{\beta}$, $\vec{\sigma}_l$ and $\vec{\sigma}_r$ are non-linear, therefore we have used the Newton-Raphson method to estimate these parameters as done in [9].

2.2   Minimum Message Length

Various model selection methods have been introduced to estimate the number of components of a mixture. Here, we adopt the MML approach [10] where the optimal number of classes of the mixture is obtained by minimizing the following [11]:

$$MessLens \approx -\log p(\Theta) + \frac{N_p}{2} - \frac{1}{2} \log 12 + \frac{1}{2} \log |F(\Theta)| - L(\mathcal{X}, \Theta, Z) \qquad (8)$$

where $p(\Theta)$ is the prior probability, $|F(\Theta)|$ is the determinant of the Fisher information matrix of minus the log-likelihood of the mixture, and N_p is the number of parameters to be estimated and is equal to $M(4d + 1)$ in our case. Note that, $p(\Theta)$ and $|F(\Theta)|$ are given in [9]. Thus, the overall algorithm for AGGM can be summed up in 1. Note that, in order to initialize the parameters, we used the K-Means algorithm. Furthermore, we initialized both the left and right standard deviations with the standard deviation values obtained from the K-Means, as for the values of the shape parameters we initialized them to 2. It is noteworthy that this is equivalent actually to reducing the AGGM to a simple GM at the initialization step.

Algorithm 1. Overall algorithm for AGGM

Input: $\mathcal{X}$
Output: Θ, M^*
   1. For $M = 1 : M_{max}$ do
     (a) Initialization
     (b) Repeat until convergence
        i. The Expectation step using Eq.5.
        ii. The Maximization step using Eq.7 and the Newton-Raphson algorithm
     (c) Calculate the associated message length using Eq.(8)
   2. Select the model M^* with the smallest message length value

---

3   Scene Categorization

This section investigates automatic scene categorization, which focuses on the task of assigning images to predefined categories. For example, an image may be categorized as an office, forest, or street scene. Applications of automatic scene categorization may be found in various applications such as content-based image retrieval, object recognition, and image understanding. Scene recognition, also known as scene classification or scene categorization, is a crucial process of the human vision system that enables us to immediately and accurately examine the surrounding environment. Generally, scene categorization methods include two main tasks: feature extraction and image representation and scene classification.

Careful selection of appropriate features is critical for scene categorization because images possess unique characteristics that must be considered. Feature extraction methods can be classified into local and global. Global feature methods are inspired by the human perception of scenes, therefore, they extract enough visual information to accurately recognize the functional and categorical properties and overlooked most of the perceptual information concerning the objects and their locations in the scene. In other words, global features are low-level attributes that represent semantic information of the scene such as color, texture, and frequency information. The work in [2] consider the hierarchical classification of vacation images by combining binary Bayesian classifiers and low-level features. In [12], color, texture, and frequency information were employed to infer high-level properties for indoor-outdoor classification. Nevertheless, the most significant work was proposed in [3] where the authors suggest the use of a spatial envelope to capture the overall gist of the scene and employed it to classify eight categories of a natural scene image data set. Even though, global features have the ability to represent the entire image with a single vector, thus, don't need any further representation; they are not sufficient for illustrating semantic information of images. On the other hand, image keypoints or local interest points have become very popular and achieved certain success in visual recognition, image retrieval, scene modeling/categorization, etc., due to their robustness to occlusions, geometric deformations and illumination variations. These approaches model the image content by automatically detecting salient image patches on which individual features are computed. Then, the resulting representation is built as a collection of these local descriptors. Therefore, The first step of the local feature extraction framework is to find a set of distinctive keypoints that can be reliably localized under varying imaging conditions, viewpoint and scale changes, and in the presence of noise. Different scale invariant detectors have been developed over the past few years and among the most important we can find Laplacian of Gaussian (LoG), Difference of Gaussian (DoG), Harris-Laplace, Hessian-Laplace, Maximally Stable Extremal Regions (MSER) [13] or Speeded-Up Robust Features (SURF) [5]. Once a set of interest regions has been detected from an image, their content needs to be encoded in a descriptor that is suitable for discriminative matching. Scale-invariant feature transform (SIFT) descriptors, originally introduced in [4], are multi-image representations of an image neighbourhood. This descriptor aims to achieve robustness to lighting variations and small positional shifts by encoding the image information in a localized set of gradient orientation histograms. Speeded Up Robust Features (SURF) is another well-known detector/descriptor partly inspired by the SIFT descriptor. SURF is based on sums of 2-dimensional Haar wavelet responses and makes an efficient use of integral images, thus, is several times faster than SIFT. In this paper, we decide to use dense sampling because it has shown to provide better performance than interest points for scene classification. Thus, we use dense PCA-SIFT descriptors of 16×16 pixel patches computed over a grid with spacing of 8 pixels[1].

Given a set of patch descriptions for each image the next main step is to produce a single vector per image. The well known BoVW approach has been widely applied for image representation by identifying a set of key-points that are in some way prototypes of a certain types of image patch. This approach is derived from text analysis wherein a document is represented by word frequencies. The analogy to representing a text document by its word count frequencies is made possible by labeling each feature vector as a visual word. Then, the K-means clustering approach is used to create a dictionary of visual words. This codebook is then used to quantize the extracted features by simply assigning the label of the closest cluster centroid. Therefore, the final representation of an image is the frequency counts or histogram of visual words. The BoVW approach is an highly effective method for image representation. However there appear to be a number of areas where its categorization performance could be improved by application of more advanced machine learning techniques. Firstly, the image histogram can be viewed as a way for representing the set of input feature vectors by an estimate of their density distribution. However, a histogram is a crude representation of this inherently continuous density profile. Secondly, the size of the visual vocabulary is a user-supplied parameter which is unpractical as the final categorization depends critically on the chosen number of visual words. In this paper, we are trying to overcome these issues by modeling each visual word in the codebook by an asymmetric generalized Gaussian distribution capable of modeling different shapes of observed non-Gaussian and heavy tailed data. By treating each mixture component as a visual word it is clear that the AGGM is a direct generalization of the histogram for approximating a density model. In addition, asymmetrical Gaussian mixture model can emphasize different feature components shapes depending on the structure they are trying to represent, hence, clustering is not based solely on the Euclidean distance. Moreover, the BoVW approach depends strongly on predicting the ideal codebook size which is a difficult and database-dependent task. Some image collections can be well described with small visual vocabulary while others may need a codebook with thousands of visual words. Thus, automatically choosing the most appropriate size of codebook depending on the given dataset itself can be a good improvement of the BoVW approach. This can be done by using the MML approach to choose the right number of components in the mixture and therefore choosing the best size for the visual vocabulary. Finally, allowing each patch vector to be classified to one visual word is unreliable and noise intolerant. We propose a new soft

---

[1] Source code of PCA-SIFT:http://www.cs.cmu.edu/~yke/pcasift

weighting technique by using the posterior probabilities that the given feature vector observation arises from each component of the mixture. This approach permits soft assignment by allowing a feature vector to contribute to more than one visual word if necessary. Note that, we used two scenarios for constructing the visual words dictionary: per-category and all-at-once training. In per category training, we have simply performed the keypoint generation independently on a per-category basis, and then combining the resulting keypoints. This can be done, by constructing a dictionary or an AGGM model for each class, then, we combine the set of AGGDs together and divide the mixture components prior probability by the number of categories to ensure they summed to one. In the case of all-at-once training, we use patch descriptors from the different scene categories to build one dictionary or a super AGGM model. Our codebook generation approach for both scenarios can be summarized in 2 Recently, particular attention has been devoted to Support Vector Machines (SVM) as a classification method. SVMs have often been found to provide superior classification results than other widely used pattern recognition methods, such as the maximum likelihood and neural network classifiers. Thus, SVMs are very attractive for scenes classification. SVM classification is essentially a binary (two-class) classification technique, which has to be modified to handle the multiclass tasks based upon one-vs-all trained SVMs. Therefore, we have used a multi-class classifier based upon one-vs-all trained SVMs.

Algorithm 2. Visual vocabulary construction

Input: Training Set, M_{max}

Output: $\Theta_{super}, M^*_{super}$

1 **Local feature extraction:** we use dense PCA-SIFT descriptors of 16×16 pixel patches computed over a grid with spacing of 8 pixels. Hence, each patch is modeled by a 36-dimensional vector.

2 **if** *per-category training* **then**

    1. Use the AGGM estimation algorithm proposed in 1 to construct a visual dictionary for each scene category. Thus, we will end up with K AGGMs for the K scene categories.

    2. Combine the K AGGMs into one super AGGM by simply combining the set of AGGDs together and dividing the mixture components prior probability by the number of categories to ensure they summed to one. Hence, we end up with an AGGM model for all scene categories.

3 **if** *all-at-once training* **then**

    1. Add patches from all categories together.

    2. Use the AGGM estimation algorithm proposed in 1 to construct one visual dictionary for all the scenes.

3.1   Evaluation

We have tested our approach on the SUN dataset. The SUN dataset captures a full variety of 899 scene categories and is by far the largest scene recognition dataset. We have used 397 well-sampled categories for which there are at least 100 unique photographs. Following [14], we have used 50 images per class for training. Fig. 1 shows some sample images from different scenes in the dataset.

In order to evaluate the performance of our approach for Codebook generation, we have used four well-known metrics, overall accuracy, average precision, average recall, and F-measure [15]. The overall accuracy is the simplest and most intuitive evaluation measure for classifiers. It is defined as

$$Accuracy = \frac{\text{Number of images correctly classified}}{\text{Total number of images}} \tag{9}$$

The overall accuracy can be derived from the confusion matrix by averaging the values on the diagonal. Precision represents the percentage of detected true positives to the total number of items detected by the algorithm. Recall is the percentage of number of detected true positives by the algorithm to the total number of true positives in the dataset: $Precision = \frac{TP}{TP+FP}$, $Recall = \frac{TP}{TP+FN}$, where TP is the total number of true positives correctly classified by the algorithm, FP is the total number of false positives, and FN is the number of true positives that were wrongly classified as negatives.

3.2   Results

In order to validate our method, we compared it with the well known BOVW with both the K-means clustering approach and the Gaussian Mixture models (GMM). Table 1 shows the results for the three methods under consideration when we use per class training as well as when all training images are used. From experimental results, we can conclude that the AGGM outperform the two other methods for scene categorization. Furthermore, we found that using images from all classes at once for training has higher efficiency because it takes account of discriminative information between different classes.

Table 1. Methods' evaluations for the SUN dataset

	K-means-category	k-means-all	GMM-category	GMM-all	AGGM-category	AGGM-all
Accuracy	36.47%	36.96%	37.68%	38.74%	40.01%	**41.33%**
Precision	48.09%	48.29%	49.04%	49.30%	51.56%	**52.12%**
Recall	32.67%	33.39%	36.90%	36.93%	37.33%	**37.86%**
F-measure	38.90%	39.48%	42.11%	42.27%	43.31%	**43.86%**

Fig. 1. Sample images from the SUN dataset; First Row: (a) Abbey, (b) Airplane cabin, (c) Airport terminal, (d) Alley, (e) Amusement arcade, (f) Amusement park, (g) Apartment building, (h) Apse; Second Row: (a) Aquarium, (b) Cabin, (c) Candy store, (d) Office, (e) Oilrig, (f) Parking Garage, (g) Raft, (h) Village

4   Conclusion

In this study, an improved visual vocabulary approach is implemented for extracting important keypoints in scenes. Our method proposes to use a soft assignment and thus considers the uncertainty present in the image descriptor level. Furthermore, our approach uses the Asymmetric Generalized Gaussian mixture (AGGM) to model the distribution of the visual words allowing the model to fit different shapes of observed non-Gaussian and asymmetric data. Last but not least, our method is able to choose the right size of the visual vocabulary, thus, sidestepping the problem of having a prefixed value in advance. From the results obtained it is clear that the use of our algorithm has helped to improve classification accuracy.

References

1. Torralba, A., Murphy, K.P., Freeman, W.T., Rubin, M.: Context-based vision system for place and object recognition. In: IEEE International Conference on Computer Vision (ICCV), pp. 273–280 (2003)
2. Vailaya, A., Figueiredo, M.A.T., Jain, A.K., Zhang, H.-J.: Image classification for content-based indexing. IEEE Transactions on Image Processing 10(1), 117–130 (2001)
3. Oliva, A., Torralba, A.: Modeling the shape of the scene: a holistic representation of the spatial envelope. International Journal of Computer Vision 42(3), 145–175 (2001)
4. Lowe, D.G.: Object recognition from local scale-invariant features. In: IEEE International Conference on Computer Vision (ICCV), pp. 1150–1157 (1999)
5. Bay, H., Tuytelaars, T., Van Gool, L.: SURF: Speeded up robust features. In: Leonardis, A., Bischof, H., Pinz, A. (eds.) ECCV 2006, Part I. LNCS, vol. 3951, pp. 404–417. Springer, Heidelberg (2006)
6. Sivic, J., Zisserman, A.: Video google: A text retrieval approach to object matching in videos. In: IEEE International Conference on Computer Vision (ICCV), pp. 1470–1477 (2003)

7. Rish, I.: An empirical study of the naive bayes classifier. In: International Joint Conference on Artificial Intelligence (IJCAI), pp. 41–46 (2001)
8. Cortes, C., Vapnik, V.: Support-vector networks. Machine Learning 20(3), 273–297 (1995)
9. Elguebaly, T., Bouguila, N.: Finite asymmetric generalized gaussian mixture models learning for infrared object detection. Computer Vision and Image Understanding 117(12), 1659–1671 (2013)
10. Wallace, C.S., Boulton, D.M.: An information measure for classification. The Computer Journal 11(2), 185–194 (1968)
11. Figueiredo, M.A., Jain, A.K.: Unsupervised learning of finite mixture models. IEEE Transactions on Pattern Analysis and Machine Intelligence 24(3), 381–396 (2002)
12. Szummer, M., Picard, R.W.: Indoor-outdoor image classification. In: International Workshop on Content-Based Access of Image and Video Databases (CAIVD), pp. 42–51 (1998)
13. Matas, J., Chum, O., Urban, M., Pajdla, T.: Robust wide baseline stereo from maximally stable extremal regions. In: British Machine Vision Conference (BMVC), pp. 384–393 (2002)
14. Xiao, J., Hays, J., Ehinger, K., Oliva, A., Torralba, A.: Sun database: Large-scale scene recognition from abbey to zoo. In: IEEE Conference on Computer Vision and Pattern Recognition (CVPR), pp. 3485–3492 (2010)
15. Maddalena, L., Petrosino, A.: A self-organizing approach to background subtraction for visual surveillance application. IEEE Transactions on Image Processing 17(7), 1168–1177 (2008)

Learning Sentiment from Students' Feedback for Real-Time Interventions in Classrooms

Nabeela Altrabsheh, Mihaela Cocea, and Sanaz Fallahkhair

School of Computing, University of Portsmouth,
Lion Terrace, Portsmouth, United Kingdom
{nabeela.altrabsheh,mihaela.cocea,sanaz.fallahkhair}@port.ac.uk

Abstract. Knowledge about users sentiments can be used for a variety of adaptation purposes. In the case of teaching, knowledge about students sentiments can be used to address problems like confusion and boredom which affect students engagement. For this purpose, we looked at several methods that could be used for learning sentiment from students feedback. Thus, Naive Bayes, Complement Naive Bayes (CNB), Maximum Entropy and Support Vector Machine (SVM) were trained using real students' feedback. Two classifiers stand out as better at learning sentiment, with SVM resulting in the highest accuracy at 94%, followed by CNB at 84%. We also experimented with the use of the neutral class and the results indicated that, generally, classifiers perform better when the neutral class is excluded.

1 Introduction

Students feedback can help the lecturers understand their students learning behaviour [5] and improve teaching [19]. Taking feedback can highlight different issues that the student may have with the lecture. One example of this is when the student does not understand part of the lecture or a specific example. Another example is when the lecturers' teaching pace is too fast or too slow. Feedback is usually collected at the end of the unit, but it is more beneficial taken in real-time.

Collecting feedback in real-time has numerous benefits for the lecturer and their students, such as improvement in teaching [19] and understanding students' learning behaviour [5]. Moreover, students' feedback improves communication between the lecturer and the students [5], allowing the lecturer to have an overall summary of the students opinion.

One way of collecting feedback in real-time is using Student Response Systems (SRS) which is a term used for devices that collect real-time data from students. Clickers, mobile phones and social media are types of SRS that have been used in the past to collect feedback in real time. Despite their usefulness in collecting real-time feedback, SRS systems can not be used to their full advantage without support for the analysis of the collected data. For example, in a study using Twitter to collect feedback, the lecturer had to read through all the students' tweets sequentially [16]; therefore, the lecturer had to read from the beginning

A. Bouchachia (Ed.): ICAIS 2014, LNAI 8779, pp. 40–49, 2014.

to understand the tweets, causing time loss. Furthermore, other research showed concern that using this tool will put such an additional workload onto the lecturers that they would require additional training to effectively use the tweets as feedback [26].

To address this problem we propose the creation of a system that will automatically analyse students' feedback in real-time and present them to the lecturer. The system will be trained offline, to insure there will be no delay in presenting the results to the lecturer. The system will visualise the students' feedback in a meaningful way giving the lecturer the most important information from the feedback. To analyse the students' feedback we propose the use of sentiment analysis.

Sentiment analysis, an application of natural language processing, computational linguistics and text analytics, identifies and retrieves information from the text. Sentiment analysis can be applied to general data, although it is more effective when applied to specific domains [23] because word meanings and sentiment may differ across domains. An example for this is the word 'early' which may reflect negative subjectivity in education as in the instance "The lecture is too early!". Then again, when describing a parcel service such as "The parcel arrived early", this is most likely a positive sentiment.

One scenario that shows the benefits of the system is described in the following. Rob, a lecturer, has just finished presenting an example, and he wanted to know whether to move on to the next part of the lecture. He looks at the visualisation provided by our system, illustrating different proportions of positive, negative and neutral sentiment. He cans also see frequent words with their polarity. He found words such as 'example', 'confused','complicated' and 'lost' show on the screen with the negative polarity. He then looks at the percentage of negative feedback, which is 60 percent of the class, the neutral is 30 percent and the positive is 10 percent. He then decided to explain the example in a different way.

To insure that the system delivers optimal results, there is need of studying and designing sentiment analysis models that are trained with real students feedback. In this paper we focus on assessing the ability of several machine learning techniques to learn sentiment from students' textual feedback. Consequently we trained four models, i.e. Naive Bayes, Complement Naive Bayes, Maximum Entropy and Support Vector Machine, and compared their performance.

The rest of the paper is organised as follows. Related research is presented in section 2. The data corpus used for this study is presented in Section 3. The sentiment analysis models are presented in Section 4, followed by results and discussion in Section 5. To finish, conclusions and future work are outlined in Section 6.

2   Related Work

Sentiment analysis looks at the polarity of sentiment. In most cases, researchers are interested in the positive and negative sentiments, although some researchers advocate the use of a neutral category as well.

Agarwal et al. [1] investigated the contribution of the neutral class to the performance of classifiers by comparing 2-class (Positive/Negative) models with 3-class (Positive/Negative/Neutral) models. They found that the 2-class models have higher accuracy; however, other researchers obtained a good performance for the 3-class models [3].

We believe that a neutral class is needed in a real life applications for education, while acknowledging that enough training data labelled as neutral is necessary to get good results. For this paper, we used the method proposed by Agarwal et al. [1], comparing the model with and without the neutral class, to investigate the effect of the neutral class on the performance of classifiers in the educational domain.

There have been some studies about sentiment analysis for education, however they have been focused mainly on e-learning [17, 24], with some exceptions looking at classroom learning. For example, in Munezero [15], sentiment analysis was applied in-class to detect students' emotions from students' learning diaries. This work, however, did no look at real-time interventions based on the analysed feedback.

Machine learning sentiment analysis approaches have four main steps: collecting the data, preprocessing it, selecting the features and applying the machine learning techniques. These are reviewed in the following subsections.

2.1 Preprocessing

Preprocessing is the process of cleaning the data from noise such as removing special characters. It increases the accuracy of the results by reducing errors in the data [2]. There are different types of preprocessing used according to where the data is collected from; for example, data collected from Twitter needs extra preprocessing such as removing hashtags, retweets and links. Some of the most common general preprocessing techniques [20] that will be used in our experiments are:

- Remove stop words: Removal of the stop words will help reduce index space, improve response time, and improve effectiveness. There is not one set of stop words that can be removed. Stop words can be words such as 'a', 'the' and 'there'. More examples can be found in [20];
- Remove punctuation: Removal of punctuation, such as question and exclamation marks, has been applied by Prasad [20]. However, exclamation marks can indicate the presence of emotion such as in the sentence 'I passed!!!'; here the exclamation may mean strong positive sentiment or strong joy emotion. Moreover, the question mark may represent confusion. Most of the researchers removed numbers and punctuation, therefore for this paper we decided to eliminate it; however, it will be investigated in the future;
- Remove numbers: Numbers in chat language can represent words; for example, 'to' or 'too' can be written as '2', 'for' can be written as '4' and the word 'great' can be written in chat language as 'gr8'. However, most of the

time numbers do not have meaning by themselves and are irrelevant in sentiment analysis. In most sentiment analysis research numbers are removed; therefore, we also remove them for our experiments;

- Convert text to lower or upper case: converting the letters into upper or lower case is used to match occurrences in the training data. Words in capitals sometimes suggests strong emotion [20]. However, this will not be investigated in the experiments presented in this paper;
- Spelling check/Removing repeated letters: Spelling can be corrected by removing extra letters such as in Prasad [20] and Ortigosa et al. [17]. Go et al. [9] replaced the letters with two letters. However, Agarwal et al. [1] replaced the letters with three letters. In our research, we replaced repeated letters with two letters, as most words in English have a maximum of two repeated letters. However, this affects words which should be single letters, such as 'looooove', which will become 'loove' and, therefore, it will not be matched to other occurrences of 'love'. On the other hand, it covers most common situations, rather than exceptions.

2.2   Features

Feature selection allows a more accurate analysis of the sentiments and detailed summarization of the results. One of the most common feature is n-grams [1, 9]. An n-gram is a sequence of n items from a text. It can be letters, syllables, or words. The most common n-gram is unigram which is selecting single words, as found in many research works [1, 8, 27]. Consequently, for the purpose of this paper, unigrams alone will be experimented with.

2.3   Machine Learning Techniques

In the educational domain, Tan et al. [23] and Troussas et al. [25] found Naive Bayes to be the best technique, while Song et al. [22] used Support Vector Machines. This research indicates that different machine learning techniques give different results even for the same domain, prompting a need for testing several techniques. The techniques used in our experiments are Naive Bayes (NB), Complement Naive Bayes (CNB), Maximum Entropy (ME), and Support Vector Machines (SVM), due to their popularity and high results in previous research.

3   Data Corpus

We used two methods for data collection: real-time collection of feedback in lectures and end of unit feedback. The first method we used is real-time feedback from computing lectures at the University of Portsmouth. The lectures included postgraduate and undergraduate level students.

Due to the difficult circumstances in collecting real-time students' feedback, we collected end of unit student feedback from various institutes. The total amount of data is 1036 instances, as shown in Table 1.

Table 1. Data Sources

Data Source	Number of instances
End of Unit Other Institutes	768
End of Unit University of Portsmouth	117
Real-time feedback University of Portsmouth	190

The data was labelled by three experts, one with background in data mining (including sentiment analysis) and two with background in linguistics. The labels were assigned using a majority rule. When there was no majority, the neutral label was assigned. To verify the reliability of the labels provided by the three experts, we looked at inter-rater reliability. The percent agreement was 80.6%, the Fleiss kappa [7] was 0.625 and Krippendorff's alpha [12] was 0.626. The percent agreement is considered over-optimistic, while the other two measures are known to be more conservative [14].

Table 2. Distribution of sentiment labels in our corpus

	Positive	Negative	Neutral
Frequency	641	292	103

4   Learning Sentiment from Students' Feedback

Using the 1036 labelled instances, we investigated the learning performance of different machine learning techniques: Naive Bayes (NB), Complement Naive Bayes (CNB), Maximum Entropy (ME) and Support Vector Machines (SVM). These methods are briefly described in the following subsections.

4.1   Naive Bayes and Complement Naive Bayes

Naive Bayes is a classifier that uses a probabilistic model; its origin is from Bayes theorem, which assumes independence between features. It has been found to perform well for sentiment analysis, e.g., [18,20]. Some advantages of Naive Bayes are that it only needs a small amount of training data to estimate parameters, it is fast and incremental, and can deal with discrete and continuous attributes.

Naive Bayes does not work well with uneven class sets. Complement Naive Bayes addresses this problem and has been proven to give higher results than Naive Bayes when the classes are uneven [10]. Complement Naive Bayes estimates the probability of a class using parameters of all the classes excluding the class itself. The NB algorithm was implemented in R[1], while for CNB Weka [29] was used.

---

[1] http://www.r-project.org/

4.2   Maximum Entropy

The Maximum Entropy classifier is similar to the Naive Bayes classifier, except that instead of the features acting independently, the model finds weights for the features that maximize the likelihood of the training data using search-based optimization. One advantage of maximum entropy is that it does not make assumptions about the relationships between features; consequently, in contrast to Naive Bayes and SVM, it could potentially perform better when conditional independence assumptions are not met.

One drawback is that it is not very realistic in many practical problems, as real datasets contain random errors or noise which create a less clean dataset [11]. For our experiments with Maximum Entropy, we use the R maxent package [4].

4.3   Support Vector Machines (SVM)

A Support Vector Machine (SVM) is a non-probabilistic binary linear classifier. It finds hyperplanes that separate the classes. SVM is highly effective at traditional text categorization and generally outperforms Naive Bayes. SVM is effective in high dimensional spaces and when the number of dimensions is greater than the number of samples. Moreover, it is memory efficient.

The effectiveness of the SVM can be affected by the kernel [6]. There are different types of kernels, of which the most common kernel methods are linear, polynomial, and radial basis functions. The linear kernel results in a simple classifier. It can work best with larger amounts of data and is graphed as a straight line. Non-linear kernels are more flexible and often give better performance [6]. From non-linear kernels, most common are polynomial kernel (SVM Poly) and radial basis kernel (SVM RB). The polynomial kernel works well with natural language processing [6] and is usually presented as a curved line. The radial basis kernel is popular [6] and flexible, and is graphed as a curved path. LibSVM in Weka [29] was used for our experiments.

5   Results and Discussion

To test the learning performance of the four models, 10-fold cross-validation was used. The results are displayed in Table 3, which includes the performance of the models without the neutral class, i.e., positive and negative, and with the use of the neutral class, i.e., positive, negative and neutral.

From the results we observe the following:

1. Two methods have a very good performance in terms of accuracy, precision and recall: Support Vector Machine with radial basis kernel and Complement Naive Bayes models;
2. Precision and recall are high in both Support Vector Machine and Complement Naive Bayes models, but low in Naive Bayes and Maximum Entropy models.

Table 3. Experiment results - without (W/O) and with (Neu) the neutral class

	Naive Bayes		CNB		ME		SVM Linear		SVM Poly		SVM RB	
	W/O	Neu	W/O	Neu	W/O	Neu	W/O	Neu	W/O	Neu	W/O	Neu
Accuracy	0.50	0.55	0.84	0.80	0.57	0.63	0.69	0.62	0.68	0.61	0.94	0.93
Precision	0.49	0.32	0.87	0.84	0.33	0.33	0.74	0.66	0.47	0.35	0.94	0.93
Recall	0.49	0.31	0.84	0.80	0.30	0.33	0.69	0.62	0.68	0.61	0.94	0.93
F-Score	0.48	0.28	0.84	0.81	0.31	0.32	0.57	0.48	0.56	0.47	0.94	0.92

3. Naive Bayes has a relatively poor performance despite being considered a good learning method for sentiment analysis;
4. When the neutral class is considered, performance decreases for most metrics and classifiers.

Our results show that SVM gave the highest accuracy, as opposed to the research of Ortigosa et al. [17] in the educational domain, and more specifically, e-learning. This could be due to the use of unigrams as opposed to Ortigosa et al. [17] who used pos (part of speech)-tagging as a feature.

Although our data is relatively clean, the Naive Bayes classifier had the lowest performance. This may be due to the uneven class sets, which could explain why the Complement Naive Bayes classifier had a high performance.

The recall values show that SVM RB is the most sensitive of the four models, i.e., it correctly identifies instances of all classes, while the Maximum Entropy is the least sensitive. Precision is highest for SVM RB and lowest for Naive Bayes with the neutral class. The best balance between precision and recall is achieved by SVM RB, making it the best classifier. This balance is also present for CNB as well, which is the second best performing method.

To investigate if the classifiers results are significantly different when the neutral class is not used compared with when the neutral class is used, we used two statistical tests: the paired t-test and the binomial test. The t-test is widely used for testing statistical differences on data mining methods [29]; however, some authors argue that it is not the best test for comparing the performance of different algorithms on the same data set and propose the use of the binomial test [21]. Consequently, we report the results for both of these tests, which are displayed in Table 4, where the t-test is represented as A and the binomial test as B. The significant values are marked in bold.

The significance tests show that the classifiers perform significantly better in terms of accuracy when the neutral class is not used for CNB and SVM with polynomial and radial basis kernels. Precision is significantly better when the neutral class is excluded for NB, CNB (just for the t-test; the binomial test indicated that the difference in not significant) and SVM with polynomial kernel. Recall is significantly better without the neutral class for NB, CNB and all versions of SVM; however, for SVM with linear kernel the t-test results indicate that the difference is significant, while the binomial test indicates that it is not. Finally, the F-scores are significantly better when the neutral class is excluded for NB, CNB (t-test only), SVM Poly and SVM RB.

Table 4. Level of significance (p-values) for differences between classifiers with the neutral class and without it

	Naive Bayes		CNB		ME		SVM linear		SVM Poly		SVM RB	
	A	B	A	B	A	B	A	B	A	B	A	B
Accuracy	0.01	0.00	0.00	0.02	0.00	0.00	0.05	0.10	0.00	0.00	0.00	0.00
Precision	0.00	0.00	0.01	0.10	0.91	1.00	0.05	0.34	0.00	0.00	0.106	0.109
Recall	0.00	0.00	0.00	0.00	0.07	0.10	0.01	0.10	0.00	0.00	0.00	0.00
F-score	0.00	0.00	0.00	0.10	0.26	0.75	0.06	0.34	0.00	0.00	0.00	0.00

The ME classifier performs significantly better when the neutral class is used in terms of accuracy, but with no significant difference in terms of precision, recall and F-score. The NB classifier has a significantly better accuracy when the neutral class is used, but significantly lower precision, recall and F-score.

Consequently, for most classifiers the evaluation metrics, i.e. accuracy, precision, recall and F-score, improve when the neutral class is not used. This may be due to the low number of training instances for the neutral class, i.e. 103 out of 1036, an aspect that has been pointed out in previous research, e.g., [27].

Given the results of our classifiers, arguments can be found for both using and disregarding the neutral class. On one hand, ignoring the neutral class seems to be consistent with people's tendency to give their opinions when they feel stronger about them, i.e., positive or negative, rather than when they do not have a particular view on the subject, i.e., neutral; consequently opinion mining often does not consider the neutral class as it is viewed as absence of opinion, e.g., [28].

Using the neutral class, on the other hand, may prevent problems such as overfitting [13]. It also provides a more complete picture of the data, where lack of sentiment is still important to be considered [13] as much as the positive and negative classes are.

Consequently, for our purposes, we will continue to investigate the use of neutral class for the educational domain, not just in terms of performance of classifiers, but also from the point of view of the users, i.e. lecturers, with regard to the usefulness of knowing how many students have a neutral view with regards to their teaching.

When looking at the t-test and the binomial test results, there is a disagreement between these tests only in 3 instances out of 48, with the t-test indicating a significant difference, while for the binomial test the difference in not significant.

6   Conclusions and Future Work

In this paper we investigated the learning capabilities of four machine learning methods for learning sentiment from students' textual feedback: Naive Bayes, Complement Naive Bayes, Maximum Entropy and Support Vector Machines (with three types of kernel).

A dataset of 1036 instances of teaching-related feedback was used, which was labelled by 3 experts. We experimented with the use of unigrams as features and a range of standard preprocessing techniques. Our experiments indicate that two methods in particular, i.e. SVM with radial basis kernel and CNB, give very good results; therefore, they could be used for real-time feedback analysis.

We also explored the use of the neutral class in the models and found that, in most cases, performance is better when the neutral class in not used. There are, however, arguments for using a neutral class from practical point of view, as it provides a more complete picture of a situation. Moreover, for the best performing method, i.e. SVM with radial basis kernel, the difference between using the neutral class and not using it, is 0.01 for accuracy, precision and recall. Consequently, one can argue that such a small loss is acceptable for having a more complete picture.

Future work includes an analysis of more preprocessing techniques and their impact on model performance, as well as experimentation with other features, such as bigrams, trigrams and pos(part of speech)-tagging. In addition, we will test the models using more real-time collected data.

References

1. Agarwal, A., Xie, B., Vovsha, I., Rambow, O., Passonneau, R.: Sentiment analysis of twitter data. In: Proceedings of the Workshop on Languages in Social Media, pp. 30–38. Association for Computational Linguistics, Stroudsburg (2011)
2. Altrabsheh, N., Gaber, M., Cocea, M.: SA-E: Sentiment Analysis for Education. In: International Conference on Intelligent Decision Technologies, vol. 255, pp. 353–362 (2013)
3. Barbosa, L., Feng, J.: Robust sentiment detection on twitter from biased and noisy data. In: International Conference on Computational Linguistics, vol. 23, pp. 36–44 (2010)
4. Bhargavi, P., Jyothi, S.: Applying naive bayes data mining technique for classification of agricultural land soils. International Journal of Computer Science and Network Security 9(8), 117–122 (2009)
5. Calders, T., Pechenizkiy, M.: Introduction to the special section on educational data mining. SIGKDD Explorations 13(2), 3–6 (2012)
6. Chang, Y.W., Hsieh, C.J., Chang, K.W., Ringgaard, M., Lin, C.J.: Training and testing low-degree polynomial data mappings via linear svm. Journal of Machine Learning Research 11, 1471–1490 (2010)
7. Fleiss, J.L.: Measuring nominal scale agreement among many raters. Psychological Bulletin 76(5), 378 (1971)
8. Gamon, M.: Sentiment classification on customer feedback data: Noisy data, large feature vectors, and the role of linguistic analysis. In: International Conference on Computational Linguistics, vol. 20, pp. 841–847 (2004)
9. Go, A., Huang, L., Bhayani, R.: Twitter sentiment analysis. CS224N Project Report, Stanford (2009), http://www-nlp.stanford.edu/courses/cs224n/2009/fp/3.pdf
10. Gokulakrishnan, B., Priyanthan, P., Ragavan, T., Prasath, N., Perera, A.: Opinion mining and sentiment analysis on a twitter data stream. Advances in ICT for Emerging Regions (ICTer) 13, 182–188 (2012)
11. de Groot, R.: Data mining for tweet sentiment classification. Master's thesis, Utrecht Univerity (2012)

12. Hayes, A.F., Krippendorff, K.: Answering the call for a standard reliability measure for coding data. Communication Methods and Measures 1(1), 77–89 (2007)
13. Koppel, M., Schler, J.: The importance of neutral examples for learning sentiment. Computational Intelligence 22(2), 100–109 (2006)
14. Lombard, M., Snyder-Duch, J., Bracken, C.C.: Practical resources for assessing and reporting intercoder reliability in content analysis research projects (2004), http://astro.temple.edu/~lombard/reliability/
15. Munezero, M., Montero, C.S., Mozgovoy, M., Sutinen, E.: Exploiting sentiment analysis to track emotions in students' learning diaries. In: Koli Calling International Conference on Computing Education Research, vol. 13, pp. 145–152 (2013)
16. Novak, J., Cowling, M.: The implementation of social networking as a tool for improving student participation in the classroom. In: ISANA International Academy Association Conference Proceedings, vol. 22, pp. 1–10 (2011)
17. Ortigosa, A., Martin, J.M., Carro, R.M.: Sentiment analysis in Facebook and its application to e-learning. Computers in Human Behavior 31, 527–541 (2014)
18. Pang, B., Lee, L.: A sentimental education: Sentiment analysis using subjectivity summarization based on minimum cuts. In: Annual Meeting on Association for Computational Linguistics, vol. 42, pp. 271–278 (2004)
19. Poulos, A., Mahony, M.J.: Effectiveness of feedback: the students perspective. Assessment & Evaluation in Higher Education 33(2), 143–154 (2008)
20. Prasad, S.: Micro-blogging sentiment analysis using bayesian classification methods. CS224N Project Report, Stanford (2010), http://nlp.stanford.edu/courses/cs224n/2010/reports/suhaasp.pdf
21. Salzberg, S.: On comparing classifiers: Pitfalls to avoid and a recommended approach. Data Mining and Knowledge Discovery 1(3), 317–328 (1997)
22. Song, D., Lin, H., Yang, Z.: Opinion mining in e-learning system. In: International Conference on Network and Parallel Computing Workshops, vol. 6, pp. 788–792 (September 2007)
23. Tan, S., Cheng, X., Wang, Y., Xu, H.: Adapting naive bayes to domain adaptation for sentiment analysis. In: Boughanem, M., Berrut, C., Mothe, J., Soule-Dupuy, C. (eds.) ECIR 2009. LNCS, vol. 5478, pp. 337–349. Springer, Heidelberg (2009)
24. Tian, F., Zheng, Q., Zhao, R., Chen, T., Jia, X.: Can e-learner's emotion be recognized from interactive Chinese texts? In: International Conference on Computer Supported Cooperative Work in Design, vol. 13, pp. 546–551 (April 2009)
25. Troussas, C., Virvou, M., Junshean Espinosa, K., Llaguno, K., Caro, J.: Sentiment analysis of facebook statuses using naive bayes classifier for language learning. Information, Intelligence, Systems and Applications (IISA) 4, 1–6 (2013)
26. Vohra, M.S., Teraiya, J.: Applications and challenges for sentiment analysis: A survey. International Journal of Engineering 2(2), 1–5 (2013)
27. Wang, W., Wu, J.: Emotion recognition based on cso&svm in e-learning. In: International Conference on Natural Computation (ICNC), vol. 7, pp. 566–570 (2011)
28. Wilson, T., Wiebe, J., Ilwa, R.: Just how mad are you? finding strong and weak opinion clauses. In: Proceedings of the 19th National Conference on Artifical Intelligence, pp. 761–767. AAAI Press (2004)
29. Witten, I.H., Frank, E., Mark, A.H.: Data Mining: Practical machine learning tools and techniques. Morgan Kaufmann (2011)

Decremental Rough Possibilistic K-Modes

Asma Ammar[1], Zied Elouedi[1], and Pawan Lingras[2]

[1] LARODEC, Institut Supérieur de Gestion de Tunis, Université de Tunis,
41 Avenue de la Liberté, 2000 Le Bardo, Tunisie
asma.ammar@voila.fr, zied.elouedi@gmx.fr
[2] Department of Mathematics and Computing Science, Saint Mary's University,
Halifax, Nova Scotia, B3H 3C3, Canada
pawan@cs.smu.ca

Abstract. This paper proposes decremental rough possibilitic k-modes (D-RPKM) as a new clustering method for categorical databases. It distinguishes itself from the conventional clustering method in four aspects. First, it can deal with uncertain values of attributes by defining possibility degrees. Then, it handles uncertainty when an object belongs to several clusters using possibilistic membership degrees. It also determines boundary regions through the computing of the approximation sets based on the rough set theory. Finally, it accommodates gradual changes in datasets where there is a decrease in the cluster number. Such a dynamically changing dataset can be seen in numerous real-world situations such as changing behaviour of customers, or popularity of products or when there is, for example, an extinction of some species or diseases. For experiments, we use UCI machine learning repository datasets with different evaluation criteria. Results highlight the effectiveness of the proposed method compared to different versions of k-modes method.

Keywords: Decremental learning, k-modes method, possibility theory, rough set theory, possibilistic membership, rough clusters.

1 Introduction

Clustering categorical datasets [12], [20], [21] allows the aggregation of similar objects to the same cluster. Decremental clustering is gaining importance in mining of dynamic datasets. The changes in datasets can be related to the number of clusters, attributes, or objects. The main advantage of the decremental clustering is that it reduces computational time and memory requirements by building on previous solutions. It overcomes the problem of re-clustering initial instances by allowing the use of the existing partitions. In addition, decremental clustering can improve the static clustering by providing better aggregation of objects. Originally, the decremental learning was proposed to deal with the gradually changing datasets. The number of clusters can evolve over time in many situations such as in medicine when some diseases are eradicated. Many researchers have used the dynamic learning aspect in their works including [3], [5], [6], [7]. In [4] a new method that dealt with uncertainty and decremental clustering was proposed.

A. Bouchachia (Ed.): ICAIS 2014, LNAI 8779, pp. 50–59, 2014.
© Springer International Publishing Switzerland 2014

The possibility theory has been shown to be effective for handling uncertainty. It handles imperfect data by representing each uncertain piece of information through a possibility degree. The wide use of possibility theory in a number of applications such as [1], [3] is an evidence of its effectiveness. Rough set theory was also proposed to handle imperfection [2] and more precisely the incomplete knowledge [22]. It offers a useful framework to represent rough clusters and detect the boundary regions. In this work, we propose the decremental rough possibilistic k-modes (D-RPKM) which aims to take advantages of possibility and rough set theories. It deals with uncertain attribute values and also with the uncertainty in the belonging of an object to several clusters. Furthermore, the D-RPKM uses the rough sets to detect clusters with rough boundary. The decremental clustering is handled, at the last step of our proposal, for removing non informative clusters.

The rest of the paper is structured as follows: Section 2 gives an overview of possibility and rough set theories. Section 3 provides a description of the k-modes method and its improvements. Section 4 details our proposal consisting of the decremental rough possibilistic k-modes. Section 5 shows the experimental results. Section 6 concludes the paper.

2 Possibility and Rough Set Theories

2.1 Possibility Theory

In [22], Zadeh proposed the well-known possibility theory in order to handle imperfect data. This theory of uncertainty has been widely used for clustering and classification [1], [2], [3] and to treat uncertainty in different areas such as data mining, medicine, and pattern recognition. It was also improved by several researchers including Dubois and Prade [10].

Assume we have the universe of discourse $\Omega = \{\omega_1, \omega_2, ..., \omega_n\}$ that presents the set of states ω_i, the possibility distribution function π associates a value from the scale $L = [0, 1]$ (quantitative setting in the possibility theory) to the state ω_i. Based on π, the normalization is defined by $max_i \{\pi(\omega_i)\} = 1$, the complete knowledge is defined in Equation (1), and the total ignorance is described by Equation (2).

$$\begin{cases} \exists \ a \ unique \ \omega_0, \ \pi(\omega_0) = 1, \\ \pi(\omega) = 0, \ otherwise. \end{cases} \tag{1}$$

$$\forall \omega \in \Omega, \pi(\omega) = 1 \tag{2}$$

In addition, the function π is used to define a well-known possibilistic similarity measure denoted by InfoAff to represent the information affinity [8]. This measure is applied between two normalized possibility distributions to compute the degree of similarity between them. The InfoAff is detailed in Equation (3).

$$InfoAff(\pi_1, \pi_2) = 1 - 0.5 [D(\pi_1, \pi_2) + Inc(\pi_1, \pi_2)]. \tag{3}$$

with $D(\pi_1, \pi_2) = \frac{1}{n} \sum_{i=1}^{n} |\pi_1(\omega_i) - \pi_2(\omega_i)|$, n the number of objects and $Inc(\pi_1, \pi_2) = 1 - \max(\pi_1(\omega) \, Conj \, \pi_2(\omega))$ and $\forall \omega \in \Omega$, $\Pi_{Conj}(\omega) = \min(\Pi_1(\omega), \Pi_2(\omega))$ where $Conj$ denotes the conjunctive mode.

2.2   Rough Set Theory

In [19], Pawlak proposed a new theory known as the rough sets for incomplete knowledge. This theory contributed to the improvement of different fields such as clustering [2], [13], [14], and [16]. In rough set theory, data is organized into an information table. This table contains instances in rows and attributes in columns. The information system IS is defined when the information table contains condition attributes and a decision attribute (considered as a class or a label).

Let us assume we have two finite and nonempty sets such that the universe U and the attribute set A such as $S = (U, A)$, the equivalence relation $(IND_S(B))$ for any $B \subseteq A$ is illustrated in Equation (4).

$$IND_S(B) = \{(x, y) \in U^2 | \forall a \in B \ a(x) = a(y)\}, \tag{4}$$

where $IND_S(B)$ is the B- indiscernibility relation and $a(x)$ and $a(y)$ present the attribute values relative to the instances x and y.

The approximation of sets known as the upper and lower sets can be also defined based on the IS as follows:

$$\overline{B}(Y) = \bigcup \{B(y) : B(y) \cap Y \neq \phi\}, \tag{5}$$

$$\underline{B}(Y) = \bigcup \{B(y) : B(y) \subseteq Y\}, \tag{6}$$

where $B \subseteq A$ and $Y \subseteq U$ is described through the attribute values from B.

The lower approximation of Y consists of objects that are members of Y. The upper approximation consists of objects that may be members of Y. Besides, the B-boundary region of Y is defined as $BN_B(Y) = \overline{B}(Y) - \underline{B}(Y)$.

3   The k-Modes Method under Uncertainty

3.1   The k-Modes Method

The k-modes clustering method was proposed in [11], [12] for categorical data. Using the same process as the k-means method [17], the k-modes was successfully applied to cluster large databases. It uses the modes to represent each cluster and a frequency based-function to update the modes. For the similarity measure, it uses the simple matching function d defined in Equation (7).

$$d(X_1, X_2) = \sum_{t=1}^{m} \delta(x_{1t}, x_{2t}), \tag{7}$$

where $X_1=(x_{11}, x_{12}, ..., x_{1m})$ and $X_2=(x_{21}, x_{22}, ..., x_{2m})$ are two objects with m categorical attributes.

$$\delta(x_{1t}, x_{2t}) = \begin{cases} 0 \text{ if } x_{1t} = x_{2t} \text{ i.e. values of } X_1 \text{ and } X_2 \text{ are completely similar,} \\ 1 \text{ if } x_{1t} \neq x_{2t} \text{ i.e. values of } X_1 \text{ and } X_2 \text{ are different.} \end{cases}$$
(8)

Assume that we have a set S of n objects to be clustered into k clusters C. $S = \{X_1, X_2, ..., X_n\}$ and $C = \{C_1, C_2, ..., C_k\}$ with their modes $Q = \{Q_1, Q_2, ..., Q_k\}$, $k \leq n$. The minimization problem of the clustering is defined in Equation (9).

$$\min \ D(W, Q) = \sum_{j=1}^{k} \sum_{i=1}^{n} w_{i,j} d(X_i, Q_j),$$
(9)

where W is an $n \times k$ partition matrix and $w_{i,j} \in \{0, 1\}$ is the membership degree of X_i in C_j.

As the standard k-modes method (SKM) was devoted to certain categorical datasets, different improvements were proposed. Various uncertain and soft versions of the SKM were developed [1], [3], [4] to overcome its drawbacks. The proposed approaches had the ability to perform clustering of uncertain datasets where values of attributes or the membership to different clusters were uncertain. In the following subsection, we briefly describe two proposed uncertain versions of SKM that provided important results in [2] and [4].

3.2   The Improvements of SKM Method

The rough possibilistic k-modes (RPKM) [2] and the decremental possibilistic k-modes (DPKM) are soft versions of the SKM. Both of them deal with uncertainty in the belonging of an object to several clusters (i.e. soft clustering). They combine advantages of the k-modes clustering method and possibility theory. As a result they improve the SKM. They avoid the SKM drawbacks mainly the non-uniqueness of cluster modes, inability to perform uncertain clustering, and ignoring all similarities that can exist between an object and multiple k clusters.

The possibility theory in DPKM was used to handle uncertain values of attributes. Each uncertain value was represented through a possibility degree. In addition, each object had a possibilistic membership degree that describes its similarity to the k clusters. The RPKM differs from the DPKM by having certain values of attributes and uses rough set theory. The rough set theory was used to detect boundary regions by computing the upper and lower approximations to indicate the rough clusters. The DPKM was useful for dynamic data. It can consider the changing in cluster numbers. In contrast to DPKM, the RPKM is an uncertain method used for static data where any modification in the cluster number leads to a re-clustering of the initial instances.

In this paper, we combine advantages of both RPKM and DPKM to propose the decremental rough possibilistic k-modes to cluster uncertain and dynamic data.

4 The Decremental RPKM Approach

4.1 Description

The decremental rough possibilistic k-modes (D-RPKM) keeps the advantages of the methods proposed in [2], [4] and overcomes their limitations. In fact, the D-RPKM builds k groups where objects share similar characteristics to the k clusters. Our proposal improves the RPKM by using the decremental learning when clustering and allows the update of cluster number over time. Besides, our proposal improves DPKM defined in [4] by applying the rough set theory and detecting peripheral objects. The D-RPKM combines the rough set and possibility theories with the k-modes method. First, it applies the possibility theory to handle uncertain values of attributes by defining a possibility distribution for each object. In addition, it is used to compute the similarity between each object and the k clusters using possibilistic membership degrees. Furthermore, the D-RPKM uses the rough set theory to calculate the boundary regions and indicates for each cluster the lower and upper sets. Finally, the D-RPKM takes into account of the dynamic evolution of the clusters. It allows the decrease of the number of clusters by improving the parameters of clustering of the SKM.

4.2 Parameters and Algorithm

The main parameters of the D-RPKM are:

1. An uncertain dataset: that is the input for the D-RPKM algorithm. The attributes could be uncertain and/or certain. They are represented through possibility distributions such that each value known with certainty is replaced by the degree 1 (the complete knowledge case in possibility theory). Each uncertain value is represented through a possibility degree from the interval $[0, 1]$.
2. Possibilistic similarity measure: is an improved version of the InfoAff measure. It is defined by $IA(X_1, X_2) = \frac{\sum_{j=1}^{m} InfoAff(\pi_{1j}, \pi_{2j})}{m}$, where m is the total number of attributes.
3. Possibilistic membership degrees $\omega_{ij} \in [0, 1]$: corresponding to the degree of belonging of each object i to the cluster j. More the value of ω_{ij} is close to 1, higher is the similarity. The ω_{ij} is computed based on the IA function.
4. Update of the cluster mode: The values of the modes are represented through possibility degrees. In order to update the mode, we use three steps as follows:
   - For each cluster j, determine the number of objects in the dataset having the highest ω_{ij} such as $NO_j = count_j(\max_i \omega_{ij})$.
   - Set a new coefficient Wt_j for the k' initial modes:

$$Wt_j = \begin{cases} \frac{NO_j}{total\ number\ of\ attributes} & \text{if } NO_j \neq 0, \\ \frac{1}{total\ number\ of\ attributes\ +1} & \text{otherwise.} \end{cases} \quad (10)$$

   - Multiply the computed weight Wt by the initial values of the k' modes to get the new modes M'_j such as $\forall j \in k', M'_j = Wt_j \times Mode_j$.

5. Compute boundary regions: For each cluster j, compute the lower and upper approximations and deduce the boundary regions. To this end, for each object, calculate the ratio R [9], [15] using ω_{ij} such as $R_{ij} = \frac{\max \omega_i}{\omega_{ij}}$. Set a threshold $T \geq 1$ then, compare it to R and interpret the results. If $R_{ij} \leq T$, the object i is a part of the upper bound of the cluster j. If the object i is a member of the upper bound of exactly one cluster j, it is necessarily a member of the lower bound of j. However, if it belongs to the upper bound of, at least, two clusters it means that it does not belong to any lower bounds. The object i can only belong to the lower bound of one cluster.

6. Decrease the cluster number: It is possible to remove c clusters using one of these ways. The user randomly chooses a cluster to be removed or the program suggests the cluster with the lowest membership degree such as $1 \leq j \leq k$, *Suppressed Cluster* $= \min_j \sum_{i=1}^{n} \omega_{ij}$ to be removed. In both situations, the ω_{ij} of the remaining $(n-c)$ clusters and the boundary regions have to be updated.

The D-RPKM algorithm is shown in Figure 1.

---

1. *Randomly select ($k' = k + c$) initial modes, one mode for each cluster.*
2. *Calculate the possibilistic similarity measure IA between instances and modes. Calculate ω_{ij} of each object to the k' clusters.*
3. *Assign each object to the k' clusters based on ω_{ij}.*
4. *Update the cluster mode.*
5. *Retest the similarity between objects and modes. Reallocate objects to clusters using ω_{ij} then, update the modes.*
6. *Repeat (5) until all clusters are stable.*
7. *Compute the upper and lower approximations for each cluster. Assign each object to the upper or the lower region of the rough cluster.*
8. *Remove c clusters and compute the possibilistic similarity measure IA between the objects and the remaining clusters. Update the ω_{ij} and the modes.*
9. *Repeat (5) until all clusters are stable then, compute rough clusters and deduce boundary region.*

Fig. 1. The D-RPKM algorithm

5 Experiments

5.1 The Framework

We run our D-RPKM algorithm using different databases from UCI machine learning repository [18]. The databases consist of *Balloons (Bal)*, *Soybean (S)*, *Post-Operative Patient (POP)*, *Balance Scale (BS)*, *Solar-Flare (SF)*, and *Car Evaluation (CE)*. We have used possibility theory to represent the uncertainty. The artificial creation of the uncertain datasets is described as follows:

1. To represent the certain case i.e. certain attributes' values: The complete knowledge in possibility theory is used where only the known values takes the degree 1. Remaining values are represented by the possibility degree 0.
2. To represent the uncertain case i.e. uncertain attributes' values: We use different possibility degrees from $]0,1[$ for attributes except true values which have the possibility degree of 1.

5.2 Evaluation Criteria

The D-RPKM was tested using four evaluation criteria. First, we apply the accuracy [11] $AC = \frac{\sum_{j=1}^{k} a_j}{T}$ where a_j is the correctly classified objects from the total number of objects T. From the AC, the error rate ER is calculated as $ER = 1 - AC$. High value of AC implies better clustering results. Then, we compute the iteration number (IN) and the execution time (ET).

5.3 Experimental Results

In this section, we report all results provided when applying the real-world UCI datasets to our proposal followed by a comparison between the D-RPKM and SKM, RPKM, and DPKM. We run our algorithm ten times then, we calculate the average of results relative to the evaluation criteria.

Certain Case. Table 1 shows the results of D-RPKM compared to other certain and uncertain methods.

Initially, we test our proposal using a number of clusters $k' = k + 1$ where k is the number of classes in [18]. We notice that D-RPKM considerably improves the results of the certain k-modes since, it avoids its drawbacks such as the non-uniqueness of clusters' modes. In addition, the D-RPKM produces the same results as the RPKM because they use the same principal. In addition, our results are very close to the DPKM results based on the different evaluation criteria. By removing c clusters, the SKM and RPKM re-cluster the datasets from the beginning. However, the D-PKM and D-RPKM use the last results that is why they saves execution time and hence, memory. For the Soybean dataset, for example, both of the ET (16.08) and ER (0.4) of the SKM are higher than our proposal which has an ET equals to 0.9 and ER equals to 0.13.

Uncertain Case. Each value of the dataset is represented through a possibility degree from the interval $]0,1]$. As the RPKM and SKM perform clustering with certain values and cannot represent these values through possibility degrees, in this part we compare our proposal to only the DPKM. Table 2 describes the average of the error rates for our proposal compared to DPKM, where A is the percentage of uncertain values in the dataset and d is possibilistic degree.

In Table 2, we notice that the D-RPKM improves over DPKM by decreasing the error rate. This is obvious for the different databases. By applying the decremental clustering and removing one cluster, the D-PRKM again proves its efficiency by keeping the lowest ER compared to the DPKM for the Car Evaluation database.

Table 1. The results of D-RPKM vs. SKM, RPKM, and DPKM in the certain case

		Bal	S	POP	BS	SF	CE
k'		3	5	4	4	4	5
SKM	ER	0.58	0.56	0.47	0.38	0.29	0.35
	IN	5	8	8	10	10	9
	ET/s	11.85	12.69	14.08	31.71	1810.21	2593.17
RPKM	ER	0.3	0.26	0.2	0.15	0.08	0.18
	IN	2	2	3	2	4	4
	ET/s	3.34	2.82	1.1	5.11	30.64	72.37
DPKM	ER	0.28	0.24	0.2	0.11	0.09	0.15
	IN	2	2	3	4	4	2
	ET/s	1.2	1.17	1.33	4.1	29.57	71.31
D-RPKM	ER	0.3	0.26	0.2	0.15	0.08	0.18
	IN	2	2	3	2	4	4
	ET/s	3.34	2.82	1.1	5.11	30.64	72.37
k		2	4	3	3	3	4
SKM	ER	0.48	0.4	0.32	0.22	0.13	0.2
	IN	9	10	11	13	14	11
	ET/s	14.55	16.08	17.23	37.81	2661.634	3248.613
RPKM	ER	0.32	0.27	0.23	0.12	0.06	0.08
	IN	4	6	8	2	12	12
	ET/s	13.14	15.26	16.73	35.32	95.57	209.68
k= k'-n				n=1			
DPKM	ER	0.2	0.19	0.14	0.09	0.07	0.09
	IN	2	2	4	2	2	4
	ET/s	0.72	0.91	0.95	4.15	22.81	35.11
D-RPKM	ER	0.21	0.13	0.14	0.08	0.07	0.09
	IN	2	2	3	2	2	2
	ET/s	0.7	0.9	0.93	4.1	20.7	36.31

Table 2. Average of error rates of D-RPKM vs. DPKM in the uncertain case

		Bal	S	PO	BS	SF	CE
k'		3	5	4	4	4	5
A < 50% and 0<d<0.5	D-RPKM	0.4	0.25	0.3	0.3	0.2	0.10
	DPKM	0.39	0.24	0.3	0.32	0.19	0.12
A < 50% 1 and 0.5≤d≤ 1	D-RPKM	0.4	0.35	0.29	0.25	0.12	0.15
	DPKM	0.4	0.32	0.3	0.28	0.11	0.16
A ≥ 50% and 0<d<0.5	D-RPKM	0.2	0.22	0.22	0.15	0.10	0.10
	DPKM	0.21	0.25	0.27	0.13	0.09	0.12
A ≥ 50% and 0.5≤d≤ 1	D-RPKM	0.3	0.3	0.31	0.21	0.15	0.15
	DPKM	0.27	0.3	0.3	0.25	0.19	0.15
n=1 k=k'-n		2	4	3	3	3	4
A < 50% and 0<d<0.5	D-RPKM	0.13	0.15	0.15	0.15	0.10	0.08
	DPKM	0.15	0.11	0.16	0.12	0.07	0.1
A < 50% 1 and 0.5≤d≤	D-RPKM	0.21	0.18	0.19	0.14	0.10	0.10
	DPKM	0.2	0.17	0.16	0.13	0.07	0.11
A > 50% and 0<d<0.5	D-RPKM	0.12	0.12	0.15	0.07	0.09	0.07
	DPKM	0.11	0.12	0.15	0.07	0.08	0.07
A > 50% and 0.5≤d≤ 1	D-RPKM	0.20	0.20	0.15	0.1	0.09	0.08
	DPKM	0.22	0.2	0.16	0.1	0.08	0.1

Table 3 illustrates the IN and ET of our proposal compared to the DPKM. From Table 3, we remark that the proposed approach provides a low IN and ET. However, it needs little more time to find the rough clusters and calculate

Table 3. The IN and ET of D-RPKM vs. DPKM in the uncertain case

		Bal	S	PO	BS	SF	CE
k'		3	5	4	4	4	5
The IN of the main program	D-RPKM	3	3	6	3	6	2
	DPKM	2	4	6	2	4	2
The elapsed time in seconds	D-RPKM	0.25	0.4	0.45	5.01	32.82	60.12
	DPKM	0.21	0.38	0.42	4.71	32.17	68.09
n=1 k=k'-n		2	4	3	3	3	4
The IN of the main program	D-RPKM	4	3	4	2	4	2
	DPKM	3	2	3	2	4	2
The elapsed time in seconds	D-RPKM	0.22	0.33	0.41	4.31	28.10	50.12
	DPKM	0.2	0.31	0.4	4.43	30.12	53.24

the ratio of each objects. We can also remark that for Car evaluation dataset the D-RPKM still provides the best results. Generally, the D-RPKM has many advantages by essentially reducing the execution time and providing accurate results.

6 Conclusion

In this paper, we have proposed a new uncertain decremental method (D-RPKM) that handles uncertainty using both possibility and rough set theories. Our proposal detects objects that can share similarities with numerous clusters belonging to the boundary regions. In addition, it considers the decremental learning aspect by offering the possibility to reduce the number of cluster over time. Our proposal was tested using real-world UCI machine learning databases based on different evaluation criteria. Results show the improvement from our method when considering uncertainty and decremental learning aspect.

References

1. Ammar, A., Elouedi, Z.: A New Possibilistic Clustering Method: The Possibilistic K-Modes. In: Pirrone, R., Sorbello, F. (eds.) AI*IA 2011. LNCS (LNAI), vol. 6934, pp. 413–419. Springer, Heidelberg (2011)
2. Ammar, A., Elouedi, Z., Lingras, P.: RPKM: The Rough Possibilistic K-Modes. In: Chen, L., Felfernig, A., Liu, J., Raś, Z.W. (eds.) ISMIS 2012. LNCS, vol. 7661, pp. 81–86. Springer, Heidelberg (2012)
3. Ammar, A., Elouedi, Z., Lingras, P.: Incremental Rough Possibilistic K-Modes. In: Ramanna, S., Lingras, P., Sombattheera, C., Krishna, A. (eds.) MIWAI 2013. LNCS, vol. 8271, pp. 13–24. Springer, Heidelberg (2013)
4. Ammar, A., Elouedi, Z., Lingras, P.: Decremental Possibilistic K-Modes. In: Proceedings of the 12th Scandinavian Artificial Intelligence Conference, SCAI, pp. 15–24 (2013)
5. Langford, T., Giraud-Carrier, C., Magee, J.: Detection of infectious outbreaks in hospitals through incremental clustering. In: Quaglini, S., Barahona, P., Andreassen, S. (eds.) AIME 2001. LNCS (LNAI), vol. 2101, pp. 30–39. Springer, Heidelberg (2001)

6. Lin, J., Vlachos, M., Keogh, E.J., Gunopulos, D.: Iterative Incremental clustering of time series. In: Bertino, E., Christodoulakis, S., Plexousakis, D., Christophides, V., Koubarakis, M., Böhm, K. (eds.) EDBT 2004. LNCS, vol. 2992, pp. 106–122. Springer, Heidelberg (2004)
7. Charikar, M., Chekuri, C., Feder, T., Motwani, R.: Incremental clustering and dynamic information retrieval. In: Proceedings of the 29th Annual ACM Symposium on Theory of Computing, pp. 626–635 (1997)
8. Jenhani, I., Ben Amor, N., Elouedi, Z., Benferhat, S., Mellouli, K.: Information Affinity: A new similarity measure for possibilistic uncertain information. In: Mellouli, K. (ed.) ECSQARU 2007. LNCS (LNAI), vol. 4724, pp. 840–852. Springer, Heidelberg (2007)
9. Joshi, M., Lingras, P., Rao, C.R.: Correlating Fuzzy and Rough Clustering. Fundamenta Informaticae 115(2-3), 233–246 (2011)
10. Dubois, D., Prade, H.: Possibility theory: An approach to computerized processing of uncertainty. Plenum Press (1988)
11. Huang, Z.: Extensions to the k-means algorithm for clustering large datasets with categorical values. Data Mining and Knowledge Discovery 2, 283–304 (1998)
12. Huang, Z., Ng, M.K.: A note on k-modes clustering. Journal of Classification 20, 257–261 (2003)
13. Lingras, P., Peters, G.: Rough clustering. In: Wiley Interdisciplinary Reviews: Data Mining and Knowledge Discovery, vol. 1, pp. 64–72. John Wiley & Sons, Inc. (2011)
14. Lingras, P., Hogo, M., Snorek, M., Leonard, B.: Clustering Supermarket Customers Using Rough Set Based Kohonen Networks. In: Zhong, N., Raś, Z.W., Tsumoto, S., Suzuki, E. (eds.) ISMIS 2003. LNCS (LNAI), vol. 2871, pp. 169–173. Springer, Heidelberg (2003)
15. Lingras, P., Nimse, S., Darkunde, N., Muley, A.: Soft clustering from crisp clustering using granulation for mobile call mining. In: Proceedings of the International Conference on Granular Computing, pp. 410–416 (2011)
16. Lingras, P., West, C.: Interval Set Clustering of Web Users with Rough K-means. Journal of Intelligent Information Systems 23, 5–16 (2004)
17. MacQueen, J.B.: Some methods for classification and analysis of multivariate observations. In: Proceedings of the Fifth Berkeley Symposium on Mathematical Statistics and Probability. Statistics, vol. 1, pp. 281–297 (1967)
18. Murphy, M.P., Aha, D.W.: UCI repository databases (1996), http://www.ics.uci.edu/mlearn
19. Pawlak, Z.: Rough Sets. International Journal of Information and Computer Science 11, 341–356 (1982)
20. Rezankova, H.: Cluster analysis and categorical data. Statistika, roc. 89, 216–232 (2009) ISSN 0322-788X
21. Rezankova, H., Loster, T., Husek, D.: Evaluation of Categorical Data Clustering. In: Mugellini, E., Szczepaniak, P.S., Pettenati, M.C., Sokhn, M. (eds.) AWIC 2011. AISC, vol. 86, pp. 173–182. Springer, Heidelberg (2011)
22. Zadeh, L.A.: Fuzzy sets as a basis for a theory of possibility. Fuzzy Sets and Systems 1, 3–28 (1978)

A Dynamic Bayesian Model
of Homeostatic Control

Will Penny[1] and Klaas Stephan[2]

[1] Wellcome Trust Centre for Neuroimaging,
University College London, 12 Queen Square, UK
w.penny@ucl.ac.uk
http://www.fil.ion.ucl.ac.uk/~wpenny
[2] Translational Neuromodeling Unit,
Institute for Biomedical Engineering, University of Zurich and ETH Zurich,
Wilfriedstrasse 6 CH-8032 Zurich

Abstract. This paper shows how a planning as inference framework
with discrete latent states can be used to implement homeostatic control
by providing an agent with multivariate autonomic set points as goals.
Before receiving these goals the agent navigates according to the 'Prior
Dynamics' which embody a cognitive map of the environment. Given the
goals, optimal value functions are implicitly computed using a forward
and backward message passing algorithm, which is then used to construct
the 'Posterior Dynamics'. We propose that this formalism provides a
useful description of computations in the mammalian Hippocampus.

Keywords: Planning as Inference, Homeostasis, Hippocampus.

1 Introduction

In previous work we have shown how an autonomous agent can be specified using a Hidden Markov Model, and that probabilistic inference in that model can be used to instantiate the operations of localisation and planning [12]. Importantly, both of these operations rely on the same underlying algorithm; belief propagation using forward and backward message passing. The only difference is that sensory inputs are upregulated during localisation whereas goal inputs are upregulated during planning.

The operations of localisation and planning are naturally addressed together as both require access to the same underlying environmental model or 'cognitive map'. Our inference approach naturally allows uncertainty from localisation to be incorporated into planning. Moreover, localisation and planning are both thought to engage the hippocampus [11,7,14].

Our overall approach conforms to a 'planning as inference' perspective in which sequential decision making problems that have previously been the domain of Reinforcement Learning (RL) and dynamic programming, have been recast as problems of statistical inference [1]. More specifically, our HMM agent uses a cognitive map of its environment and its decisions are based on this model. This

A. Bouchachia (Ed.): ICAIS 2014, LNAI 8779, pp. 60–69, 2014.

is to be contrasted with the state-action mappings that are learnt in RL. The two approaches to decision making may more generally be referred to as model-based and model-free control [13] and are thought to have different neuronal substrates [4].

One interesting recent development in RL has been the replacement of scalar reward signals with homeostatic goals [9]. This incorporates the simple notion that an agent's behavioral objective is dependent on its current autonomic state. Thus, food rewards are more important when an agent is hungry. In this paper we show how the HMM framework can be used to implement homeostatic control [3] by providing an agent with multivariate autonomic set points, rather than binary goals. Our overall approach thus provides a mechanism for model-based homeostatic control.

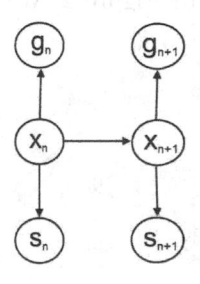

Fig. 1. The agent's generative model. This corresponds to an HMM with two sets of observations; goals, g_n, and sensory inputs, s_n.

2   Methods

We consider a dynamical system evolving over time points $n = 1..N$ with discrete latent states x_n, goals g_n and sensory states s_n. The overall generative model is shown in Figure 1 and is fully specified via the definition of three probability distributions (i) the state transition density $p(x_{n+1}|x_n)$, (ii) the sensory observation density $p(s_n|x_n)$ and (iii) the goal observation density $p(g_n|x_n)$.

Inference is implemented in two separate phases (i) planning and (ii) localisation. In the planning phase, goals are provided and the posterior distribution over latent states is computed. At this time sensory states are either not provided or their influence on planning is eliminated, for example, by reducing sensory precision.

In the localisation phase, sensory observations are provided and the posterior distribution over latent states is computed. In this phase goals are either not provided or their influence on localisation is eliminated, for example, by reducing goal precision. This paper focusses on planning, as localisation has been dealt with in a previous publication [12].

In what follows each of the $k = 1..K$ discrete latent states is associated with a location in a 2D environment, l_k, and $N(x; \mu, \Sigma)$ denotes a multivariate Gaussian distribution over x with mean μ and covariance Σ.

2.1   Prior Dynamics

In the planning phase the agent is given information about task goals. Prior to observing these goals the hidden states evolve according to Markovian dynamics

$$p(x_{n+1} = i | x_n = j) = A_{ij} \tag{1}$$

where A is a $K \times K$ state transition matrix. Although high-dimensional this matrix is sparse, reflecting the spatial structure of an environment and allowed transitions within it, as shown in Figure 2. We refer to the above equation as describing the 'Prior Dynamics'.

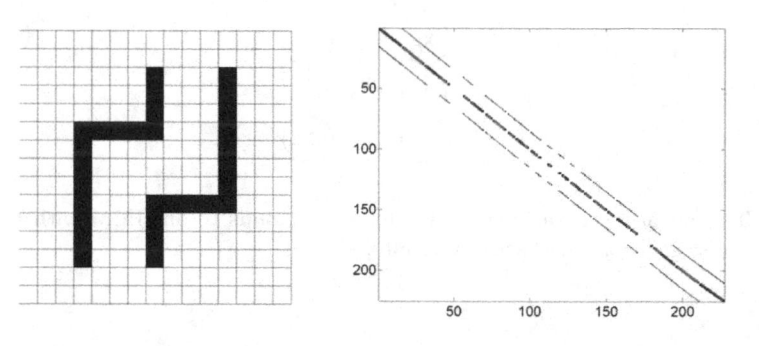

Fig. 2. Left Panel: The environment contains $K = 15 \times 15 = 225$ discrete states, with black squares denoting forbidden locations. At each time step agents may move to cardinal neighbours or remain in the same position but cannot transit across edges of the domain (eg top to bottom). Right Panel: The prior dynamices are embodied in a state transition matrix A of dimension 225×225 having a highly sparse structure reflecting the allowed transitions in an environment.

2.2   Probabilistic Goals

The probability of observing goal g_n given state x_n is given by the density $p(g_n | x_n)$. This formulation has many interesting properties. First, goals are inherently probabilistic; one specifies the likelihood of obtaining a goal at a given location. The simplest instantiation of this is the case of binary goals

$$p(g_n | x_n = k) = r_k \tag{2}$$

where r_k denotes the probability of reward at location k.

More interestingly, the goal signal g_n can be multivariate, allowing an agent to have multiple simultaneous goals. Here, the observed goal signal can be used to specify set points and thereby implement a system for instantiating homeostatic control. For example, if we have

$$p(g_n|x_n = k, a) = \mathsf{N}(g_n; a + a_k, C) \tag{3}$$

where g_n is the homeostatic set point (the multivariate goal), C encodes the allowed (co-)variance around that set point, a is the agent's autonomic state, and a_k denotes the change in autonomic state (per unit time) that will accrue from visiting state k.

If the autonomic variables (eg. body water, glucose, temperature) have their own dynamics, the posterior dynamics, q, (see below) will need to be recomputed to account for this. The posterior dynamics could be updated at satiety, at every time point, or according to some other regime. In this paper, we choose to update them periodically, after a fixed number of time points. We consider linear autonomic dynamics

$$a_n = Ba_{n-1} + a_k \tag{4}$$

where B encodes the relevant time scales and a_k is the change accrued from visiting state k. This dynamical process is external to the HMM agent (loosely speaking, it is instantiated in the agent's body).

2.3   Posterior Dynamics

We now consider an agent being in receipt of a goal signal g. In order to specify to the agent that this goal is to be reached within a 'time horizon' of N steps we set the sequence of observation variables $g_n = g$ for $n = 1..N$. We denote this sequence as $G_N = \{g_1, g_2, ..., g_N\}$.

The dynamics of the agent after receiving the goal signal, or the 'Posterior Dynamics', are defined as

$$q_{ij} \equiv p(x_{n+1} = i|x_n = j, a, G_N) \tag{5}$$
$$= \frac{p(x_{n+1} = i|x_n = j)p(x_n = j|a, G_N)}{\sum_{i'=1}^{K} p(x_{n+1} = i'|x_n = j)p(x_n = j|a, G_N)}$$

Note also the dependence on the autonomic state, a. In this paper we set a to the autonomic state observed just prior to computing the posterior dynamics (but see Discussion). An agent following the posterior dynamics implements goal-directed navigation, whilst one following the prior dynamics merely obeys the physics of a given environment, and its motion within it.

2.4   State Posterior

The posterior dynamics constitute a reweighting of the prior dynamics by the density $p(x_n = j|a, G_N)$. This density can be computed using standard inference algorithms such as the alpha-beta recursions [2]. This requires a forward sweep to compute

$$\alpha(x_n) = p(g_n|x_n, a) \sum_{x_{n-1}} p(x_n|x_{n-1})\alpha(x_{n-1}) \tag{6}$$

with $\alpha(x_1 = k) = p(x_1 = k)p(g_1|x_1 = k, a)$, and a backward sweep to compute

$$\beta(x_n) = \sum_{x_{n+1}} p(g_{n+1}|x_{n+1}, a)p(x_{n+1}|x_n)\beta(x_{n+1}) \tag{7}$$

with $\beta(x_N = k) = 1$. We then have

$$p(x_n = j|a, G_N) = \frac{\alpha(x_n = j)\beta(x_n = j)}{\sum_k \alpha(x_n = k)\beta(x_n = k)} \tag{8}$$

To avoid numerical underflow [2] we scale the forward and backward messages by $\sum_k \alpha(x_n = k)$. The forward 'alpha' recursions embody the prior distribution and provide a normalisation factor for the backward 'beta' recursions. It is also worth noting that both the alpha and beta recursions implicitly make use of prediction errors, as the Gaussian goal densities take on higher values with smaller prediction errors between the set point and predicted autonomic state. In equations 6 to 9, n is a virtual time index that organises the planning computations. We hypothesise that these are instantiated within a hippocampal ripple (see Discussion).

2.5   Trajectories

A known state at time n is equivalent to a probability distribution $p(x_n)$ with unit mass at $x_n = k$ and zero elsewhere. A probabilistic planning trajectory can then be found by integrating the posterior dynamics from this initial distribution. The probability mass at time point $n + 1$ is

$$p(x_{n+1} = i) = \sum_{k=1}^{K} q(x_{n+1} = i|x_n = k)p(x_n = k) \tag{9}$$

The state density at subsequent time points can be computed as

$$p(x_{n+m} = i) = \sum_{k=1}^{K} q(x_{n+m} = i|x_{n+m-1} = k)p(x_{n+m-1}) \tag{10}$$

or in matrix form as

$$p(x_{n+m+1}) = Q^m p(x_{n+1}) \tag{11}$$

Iteration of this equation produces 'goal-directed flows' and individual paths to goal are produced by sampling from these flows.

2.6   KL Control

The state posterior can alternately be expressed as

$$p(x_n = j|a, G_N) = \frac{p(G_N|x_n = j, a)p(x_n = j)}{\sum_{j'=1}^{K} p(G_N|x_n = j', a)p(x_n = j')} \tag{12}$$

Given a uniform prior $p(x_n = j)$ the equation for the Posterior Dynamics reduces to

$$q_{ij} = \frac{p(x_{n+1} = i|x_n = j)p(G_N|x_n = j, a)}{\sum_{i'=1}^{K} p(x_{n+1} = i'|x_n = j)p(G_N|x_n = j, a)} \tag{13}$$

Equation 13 corresponds to the 'Active Dynamics' of KL control, and $\log p(G_N|x_n = j, a)$ to the 'Optimal Value' function [16]. The 'Passive Dynamics' of KL control then correspond to our 'Prior Dynamics'. The scaling of the beta recursions in the HMM implementation (see above) is analogous to the normalisation used in the power method for computing the Optimal Value function [16].

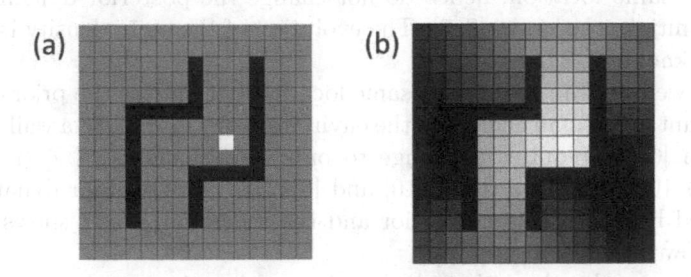

Fig. 3. Time to Goal *The figure shows the state posterior, $p(x_1|G_N)$, for four different times to goal (a) $N = 1$, (b) $N = 1024$. The goal location is $[10, 8]$. Under a uniform prior, $p(x_1)$, these plots correspond to the exponent of the Optimal Value function of KL control.*

3   Results

This section refers to videos showing goal directed flows. These are available from http://www.fil.ion.ucl.ac.uk/~wpenny/icais14_movies/.

3.1   Binary Goals

Figure 2 shows an example 2D environment and the state transition matrix, A, corresponding to the prior dynamics associated with it. Here A_{ij} has been set to $1/N_j$ if a transition is allowed from j to i, with N_j being the number of allowable transitions from j (fewer next to boundaries and corners). This includes transitions from a state to itself. Transitions are not allowed to or from wall or edge locations (we set $0/0 = 0$, as per usual).

Figure 3 (a) now superimposes a binary goal onto this environment. The goal observation density $p(g_n|x_n)$ is set so that the probability density is 1 at the goal (white square in Figure 3a) and zero elsewhere. We then computed the state posterior for different values for the time to goal N. This computation is implemented using the alpha-beta recursions in equations 6 to 8. For $N = 1$ the state posterior has a single peak at the goal. The spatial gradient of the posterior at sites remote from the goal is zero for $N = 1$, but increases with N. This gradient informs the posterior dynamics via equation 5, allowing a path to be found from remote sites to the goal. The posterior dynamics, q, were then computed from equation 5 using $N = 1024$ with the goal at $[10, 8]$. Note that for large N, we have $p(x_1|G_N) \approx p(x_2|G_N) \approx p(x_3|G_N)$ etc., so we can simply use $p(x_1|G_N)$ in equation 5.

The movie `known_15_1.avi` shows the state density evolving according to the posterior dynamics. The initial state density is a delta function with unit probability mass at location $[15, 1]$ and zero elsewhere. The state density at subsequent time points has been computed using equation 11. We now keep the goal at the same location, hence do not change the posterior dynamics q, but move the initial position to $[2, 8]$. The evolution of the state density is shown in the movie `known_2_8.avi`.

Finally, we keep the goal at the same location but update the prior dynamics, A, to account for a small change to the environment. This hole in a wall appearing at location $[6, 10]$ requires a change to only four elements of A (reciprocally between $[6, 10]$ and $[6, 9]$, and $[6, 10]$ and $[6, 11]$). The posterior dynamics were recomputed based on this new prior and the movie `hole.avi` shows the goal-directed flow from position $[2, 8]$.

The above results show that changes in goal location are accommodated by recomputing the posterior dynamics, q. Small changes in the environment are readily accommodated by small changes in the prior dynamics (and updating q). These nonstationarities are less gracefully accommodated in RL which requires extensive relearning of state-action mappings.

3.2   Homeostatic Goals

This simulation considers three autonomic variables reflecting the levels of body glucose, water and temperature. The set point is given by $g = [10, 10, 10]$ with covariance $C = 0.5I_3$. Here the autonomic dynamics are set by specifying a diagonal transition matrix, B, with entries $0.99, 0.97, 0.95$. These numbers reflect the rate at which body water, food and temperature levels are depleted. The changes in autonomic state (per unit time) afforded by visiting state k are set as follows

$$a_k(i) = \exp(-0.5||s_k - \mu(i)||^2) \qquad (14)$$

where s_k is the location of the kth latent variable (place cell) and $\mu(i)$ denote the spatial locations with maximal affordance for increases in water, glucose and temperature respectively. This implements affordances as a continuous but local function of space; other eg. discrete forms are of course possible. We set

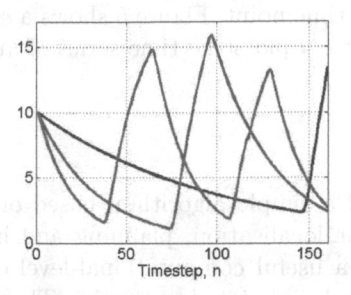

Fig. 4. Autonomic Variables *Body temperature (red), glucose (green) and water (blue). The state is initialised to the set point* [10, 10, 10]. *Increases correspond to the agent visiting locations which afford increases in body temperature, glucose, temperature and water respectively. Decreases reflect the time scales of depletion encoded in matrix B.*

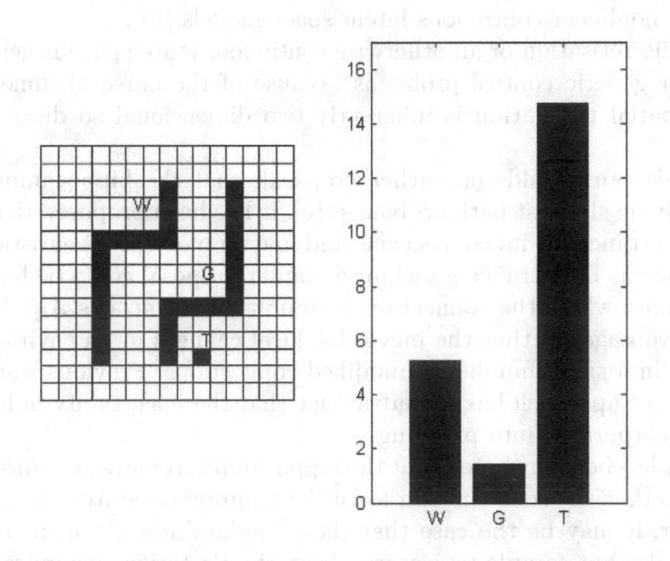

Fig. 5. Agent State *The state of the agent at time step n = 65. Left Panel: The letters W, G and T denote locations which afford maximal increases in body water, glucose and temperature, respectively. The location of the agent is marked with the black square (close to T). Right Panel: Levels of autonomic variables, a_n. At this time point the agent has sufficiently warmed itself and is now leaving location T and heading towards G, as its glucose level is far from set point.*

$\mu(1) = [6, 12]^T$, $\mu(2) = [10, 8]^T$ and $\mu(3) = [10, 4]^T$. Thus, for example, the agent receives a unit increase in glucose at location [10, 8] and a smaller amount at neighbouring locations.

The movie `auto.avi` shows the agent navigating according to the posterior dynamics, which are recomputed every 32 steps. This requires a forward and backward pass to compute the posterior state density, based on the autonomic state of the agent at that time point. Figure 5 shows a snapshot of this movie at time step $n = 65$ and figure 4 plots the time series of autonomic state variables over all time points.

4   Discussion

This paper has described a simple algorithm, based on inference in an HMM, that an agent can use for localisation, planning and homeostatic control. We propose that it provides a useful computational-level description of aspects of Hippocampal function and associated networks. There are several appealing features.

First, the use of a discrete rather than a continuous latent space allows multimodal posteriors to be supported using simple, exact inference. This is necessary for solving the problem of localisation, as shown in previous work [12]. This is to be contrasted with the approximate inference procedures (particle filtering etc.) required for nonlinear continuous latent space models [13].

Second, discretisation of an otherwise continuous state space is generally unworkable for generic control problems because of the curse of dimensionality. However, spatial navigation is inherently two dimensional so discretisation is tenable.

Third, this work builds on earlier proposals that the hippocampus itself is suited to solving shortest path problems [10]. It has been proposed that CA3 encodes path distances in its connections and may implement a heuristic planning approach such as Dijkstra's algorithm. A similar proposal could be based on the Prior Dynamics where the connection from unit j to i encodes A_{ij}. This shares previous advantages in that the inevitable local changes in an environment can be reflected in a small number of modified connections. Previous work [12] has shown that our approach has the advantage that the uncertainty in localisation is readily incorporated into planning.

Fourth, it has been proposed that the hippocampus replays goal-directed state sequences so that the striatum can learn the appropriate state-action mappings [8]. However, it may be the case that these 'replays' are not memories of successful episodes but sample trajectories from the Posterior Dynamics.

Fifth, the two phases of inference we have proposed may map onto two distinct modes of hippocampal function, differentiated by the degree of theta activity. Mammalian localisation is accompanied by a high theta state [5], whereas planning related replay activity [14] is accompanied by high frequency ripples in a low theta state. In rats, planning related ripple activity is observed to occur after reaching a goal.

We have shown that homeostatic control can be instantiated using a probabilistic goal model in which the goals are autonomic set points. By endowing autonomic variables with their own dynamics, and periodically reactivating the agent's planning algorithm, the agent has been shown to exhibit rather complex autonomous behaviour.

The resulting system is similar to, and inspired by, the free-energy principle which is founded on the concepts of active inference and homeostasis [6]. Our approach is marked out by its use of discrete latent variables and backwards message passing, and we have previously proposed that these messages are instantiated in ripple activity [13].

In this paper, planning is based on the agent's autonomic state just prior to computation of the posterior dynamics. Its homeostatic control mechanism is therefore reactive rather than predictive. However, if the agent were also endowed with a predictive autonomic model (cf. equation 4) planning could be based on these predicted autonomic states [15].

References

1. Attias, H.: Planning by probabilistic inference. In: Bishop, C., Frey, B. (eds.) Proceedings of the 9th International Conference on Artificial Intelligence and Statistics (2003)
2. Bishop, C.M.: Pattern Recognition and Machine Learning. Springer, New York (2006)
3. Cannon, W.: Organization for Physiological Homeostasis. Physiol Rev. 9, 399–431 (1929)
4. Daw, N., Niv, Y., Dayan, P.: Uncertainty-based competition between prefrontal and dorsolateral striatal systems for behavioral control. Nat. Neurosci. 8(12), 1704–1711 (2005)
5. Foster, D., Wilson, M.: Hippocampal theta sequences. Hippocampus 17(11), 1093–1099 (2007)
6. Friston, K., Kilner, J., Harrison, L.: A free energy principle for the brain. J. Physiol. Paris 100(1-3), 70–87 (2006)
7. Hassabis, D., Maguire, E.: The construction system of the brain. Philosophical Transactions of the Royal Society London B 364, 1263–1271 (2009)
8. Johnson, A., Redish, A.: Hippocampal replay contributes to within session learning in a temporal difference reinforcement learning model. Neural Netw. 18(9), 1163–1171 (2005)
9. Keramati, M., Gutkin, B.: A reinforcement learning theory for homeostatic regulation. In: Neural Information Processing Systems (2011)
10. Muller, R., Stead, M.: Hippocampal place cells connected by Hebbian synapses can solve spatial problems. Hippocampus 6, 709–719 (1997)
11. O'Keefe, J., Nadel, L.: The Hippocampus as a Cognitive Map. Oxford University Press (1978)
12. Penny, W.: Simultaneous localisation and mapping. In: 4th International Workshop on Cognitive Information Processing, Copenhagen, Denmark (2014)
13. Penny, W., Zeidman, P., Burgess, N.: Forward and Backward Inference in Spatial Cognition. PLoS CB 9(12), e1003383 (2013)
14. Pfeiffer, B., Foster, D.: Hippocampal place-cell sequences depict future paths to remembered goals. Nature 497, 74–79 (2013)
15. Sterling, P.: Allostasis: a model of predictive regulation. Physiology and Behaviour 106, 5–15 (2012)
16. Todorov, E.: Efficient computation of optimal actions. Proceedings National Academy of Sciences 106(28), 11478–11483 (2009)

ICALA: Incremental Clustering and Associative Learning Architecture

Matthias U. Keysermann

Robotics Laboratory, School of Mathematical and Computer Sciences,
Heriot-Watt University, Edinburgh, UK
muk7@hw.ac.uk
http://www.macs.hw.ac.uk/~muk7

Abstract. I propose a learning and memory architecture which can incrementally learn and associate an increasing number of patterns. The approach consists of the integration of two methods – a topology learning algorithm to perform incremental clustering, and an associative memory model to learn relationships based on the co-occurrence of input patterns. The approach supports online learning, is tolerant to noise, and generally applicable to any kind of real-valued vector data. I tested the proposed architecture on an incremental associative learning task with visual patterns. Evaluations were performed both in a simulated setup and with a real robot. Results showed that the architecture could learn nearly all presented patterns but in some cases the recall rate decreased as these patterns were retrieved. I suggest ways to overcome this effect and also discuss future work aimed at achieving a better performance.

Keywords: Incremental Learning, Clustering, Associative Learning.

1 Introduction

Working with robots requires incremental learning methods that work online [17, 2, 20, 11, 3]. A benefit of online incremental learning techniques is the opportunity to learn smaller amounts of data and directly recall the stored knowledge during the ongoing learning process. Incremental methods are also more efficient in terms of learning time because only additional instances need to be incorporated to update the stored knowledge.

Existing methods for incremental topology learning include the *Growing Neural Gas* (GNG) [6], the *Growing Neural Gas with Utility measure* (GNG-U) [7], the *evolving Self-Organizing Map* (eSOM) [5], the *Self-Organizing Incremental Neural Network* (SOINN) [8] and the *Enhanced Self-Organizing Incremental Neural Network* (E-SOINN) [9]. These approaches are suitable for clustering the received inputs by similarity into different categories. By applying associative learning methods like Hebbian learning [12, 16] it is possible to learn relationships between these categories. Advancements of the mentioned algorithms incorporate ways for associating different inputs, such as the *Self-Organizing Incremental Associative Memory* (SOIAM) [21], a multi-layer variant of the SOIAM [22] and

A. Bouchachia (Ed.): ICAIS 2014, LNAI 8779, pp. 70–79, 2014.

the *General Associative Memory* (GAM) [10]. However, these approaches are limited in the way they must be trained, e.g. the algorithms must receive the data in a strict order and only specific types of associations can be learned. I aim to provide a more flexible approach without these restrictions.

I incorporated methods of the listed topology learning techniques into a novel architecture for incremental and online learning (Section 2). By combining different machine learning techniques the architecture fulfils the tasks of generalisation and learning by association. I tested the architecture in an incremental learning task (Sections 3 and 4). Corresponding results are discussed in Section 5 and Section 6 presents the conclusions.

2   Incremental Clustering and Associative Learning Architecture

The *Incremental Clustering & Associative Learning Architecture* (ICALA) combines methods of incremental clustering and associative learning (Figure 1). I employ a modified version of the SOINN, named the *Modified Self-Organizing Incremental Neural Network* (M-SOINN), for clustering the incoming data and an associative memory model, the *Temporal-Order Sensitive Associative*

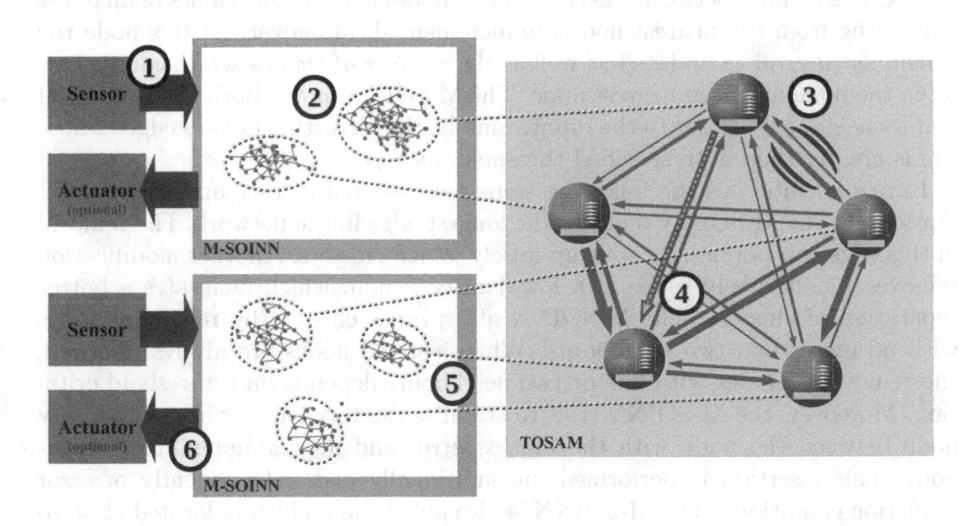

Fig. 1. The structure of the ICALA consisting of M-SOINN modules and the TOSAM. From a sensor a data vector is read (1) by an M-SOINN module where a topology of the inputs is learned and the data is clustered (2). Each cluster corresponds to a unit in the TOSAM. The TOSAM learns an association between each pair of activated units (3). Upon reception of an input into a cluster, the corresponding unit gets activated. Activation spreads and activates other units (4). The activation levels of all units corresponding to a module's clusters are passed back to the respective module (5). Based on these levels and the cluster centroids the module generates a data vector which can be used to influence an actuator (6).

Memory (TOSAM), based on previously formulated desiderata [13]. All components use short processing cycles and run at frequencies independent of each other.

2.1 Modified Self-organizing Incremental Neural Network

The *Modified Self-Organizing Incremental Neural Network* (M-SOINN) is based primarily on the SOINN and stores a topology of the inputs in one layer in a network of nodes and edges. When an input is received the algorithm determines the two nearest nodes and calculates *similarity thresholds* for these nodes. This threshold is the maximum distance to the node's neighbours (connected nodes) or the minimum distance to any other node if the node has no neighbours. The M-SOINN allows to set a fixed similarity threshold for all nodes [18, 15].

The algorithm calculates the distances from the input to the two nearest nodes. If any of the distances exceeds the respective similarity threshold, a new node is created. Then the M-SOINN can create an edge if the new node is close enough to the nearest node [18], based on two conditions: first, the new node must be further away from the cluster mean than the determined nearest node; second, the distance between new node and nearest node must be greater than the average node distance in the corresponding cluster.

If both distances are within the corresponding similarity thresholds, then a new edge is created between the two nearest nodes and the *age* values of all edges emanating from the nearest node are incremented. Moreover, for this node the *accumulated error* is updated as well as the *number of signals* which counts how often the node has been nearest node. The M-SOINN moves both the node itself and its neighbours closer to the input. Finally, the algorithm deletes edges whose age is greater than a prespecified threshold age_{dead}.

In regular intervals the following steps are executed to tidy up the topology. Optionally, the M-SOINN removes the longest edge in the network. The removal of this edge can potentially split up falsely joined clusters. Another modification removes a node likely to be in a low-density region, which facilitates a better separation of clusters. The M-SOINN also prunes clusters by removing nodes with no more than two neighbours. While isolated nodes are always removed, the removal of nodes with one or two neighbours depends on a threshold criterion. Moreover, the M-SOINN tries to stabilise the topology by inserting a new node between the node with the highest error and its maximum error neighbour. This insertion is performed unconditionally and independently of error reduction conditions. The M-SOINN is also able to join clusters located close to each other to better generalise over similar inputs. The distance-based threshold criterion for cluster joining can be adjusted by either a relative or an absolute join tolerance value. These refinement criteria are in favour of lower computational cost; enhanced concepts for splitting and merging of clusters can be found in [14, 4].

The complete M-SOINN algorithm listing is available online[1].

---

[1] http://www.macs.hw.ac.uk/~muk7/ICALA/supplementary.pdf

2.2 Temporal-Order Sensitive Associative Memory

The *Temporal-Order Sensitive Associative Memory* (TOSAM) stores assoca-
tions between incoming perceptions based on the co-occurrence of inputs. The
TOSAM recalls associated information depending on the strength of the learned
association. The TOSAM consists of a network of information units which store
different patterns of information. As a part within the ICALA the TOSAM
does not receive actual sensory data but only unique cluster identifiers from the
M-SOINN. If no unit with the incoming identifier exists, such a unit is created.

Each information unit has an *input load* and an *activation level*. The input
load models the perceptional strength of the respective input and drives the
learning process. The activation level indicates how strongly the corresponding
information can be recalled. When receiving an input both input load and activation level are raised immediately but otherwise underlie a fast decay. The
TOSAM maintains a fully connected network with two directed connections between any pair of units. A *connection weight* represents the associative strength
between the connected units and influences how much activation can be spread
over the corresponding connection.

The TOSAM learns associations by modifying connection weights between
units with input load. An asymmetric Hebbian learning rule allows the weights
to encode sequential information. A strong increase in weight can only occur
when the input load of the respective destination unit is high. The change in
weight is smaller the closer the weight value is to its maximum [19]. Our rule
also implements the effect of extinction [1]: unlearning occurs when a stimulus is
present but a previously associated response is not observed. This further allows
connections to develop negative weights and become inhibitory.

During the spreading process, activation is removed from the source unit and is
transferred to the destination unit. The exact amount is calculated based on the
activation level of the source unit and the connection weight to the destination
unit. A highly activated destination unit will attract less activation, resulting in
a smaller amount being spread. Additionally, low values are weakened and high
values are strengthened to provide a clearer recall. A unit cannot spread more
activation than it has – the available amount is distributed proportionally over
all outgoing connections.

Equations and details of the described processes are available online[1].

2.3 Synchronisation of M-SOINN and TOSAM

The units in the TOSAM reflect the cluster structure present in the M-SOINN
modules. The M-SOINN maintains identifiers for all clusters which must remain
consistent even if the topological structure changes. In such a case, the TOSAM
needs to make adjustments to its network.

Whenever a node is created, also a cluster with a new identifier is created
for this node; whenever a node is removed, the corresponding cluster, if empty,

must be removed; the corresponding unit in the TOSAM has no representation anymore and must be removed as well. Whenever an edge is created, two clusters may merge into one; the cluster with more nodes incorporates the nodes of the smaller cluster which is then removed; in the TOSAM, the corresponding units and connections must be merged as well; the input load, activation level and association strengths are, in each case, updated to store the maximum of the merged values. Whenever an edge is removed, a cluster may be split into two; the M-SOINN maintains the cluster identifier for the majority of nodes and creates a new cluster for the remaining nodes; the TOSAM creates a new unit for the new cluster as well as corresponding connections; input load, activation level and weight values are copied from the existing unit and connections, respectively.

To avoid excessive synchronisation operations each M-SOINN module defines a minimum number of nodes required to activate a cluster. The module does not inform the TOSAM about the activation of clusters with fewer nodes.

3   Methods

A dataset for an incremental learning task should be reasonably large but also allow the architecture to generalise over similar inputs. I used the *AT&T database of faces*[2] which contains greyscale images of 40 different people. For each of these persons 10 images exist which show variations of facial expression, head rotation, etc. Each image is 92 by 112 pixels in size.

I tested the incremental learning capabilities of the ICALA in both simulated and real robot scenarios. One person after the other was presented as an input, accompanied with a corresponding label to learn associations. Each person was learned for 240 seconds while every 4 seconds the current image randomly changed to another image of this person. After learning each person, the architecture had to recall the labels of all presented images so far. The images were presented in a random permutated order and each image was shown for 12 seconds, preceded by a blank image for 12 seconds. After each recall phase I measured for how many images the correct person was identified.

Table 1. Parameters of the M-SOINN module *FacesATT*

input dimensions	value range	cluster activation threshold	remove minimum density node	λ	age_{dead}	join clusters	relative join tolerance
10304	[0,1]	2	no	50	50	yes	-
cycle time	connect new nodes	fixed similarity threshold	reduce local error	c_1	c_2	remove longest edge	absolute join tolerance
2000 ms	no	-	yes	0.01	0.001	yes	0.1

In the simulated scenario the ICALA included the TOSAM and two M-SOINN modules: one for clustering the face images (*FacesATT*) and one for storing the text labels (*TextLabel*). The TOSAM was running at 1 Hz; parameters of the

[2] http://www.cl.cam.ac.uk/research/dtg/attarchive/facedatabase.html

Table 2. Parameters of the M-SOINN module *NAOCamera*

input dimensions	value range	cluster activation threshold	remove minimum density node	λ	age_{dead}	join clusters	relative join tolerance
4800	[0,1]	2	no	50	50	yes	-

cycle time	connect new nodes	fixed similarity threshold	reduce local error	c_1	c_2	remove longest edge	absolute join tolerance
2000 ms	yes	0.07	yes	0.01	0.001	yes	0.07

FacesATT module are listed in Table 1. For the *TextLabel* module the cycle time was 2000 ms and the threshold for activating clusters was 2; other parameters were set to $age_{dead} = 1000$, $\lambda = 100$, $c_2 = 0.0$ and $c_1 = 0.0$; none of the introduced modifications were active for this module; an incremental numbering scheme was used to map the labels to numeric values.

The robot setup involved a NAO T14 robot[3] and the images were displayed on a screen which was captured by the robot's front camera (Figure 2). The recalled label was spoken out by the NAO's built-in text-to-speech system. The ICALA included a module for processing the inputs from the NAO's camera (*NAOCamera*), a module for providing and speaking out the labels (*NAOText-ToSpeech*), as well as the TOSAM. The cycle time of the TOSAM was 1000 ms. The *NAOTextToSpeech* was configured exactly as the *TextLabel* module. Table 2 lists parameters of the *NAOCamera* module. I applied minor transformations to the images on the screen to create a more realistic setup where actual people would stand in front of the robot: as a person would never place their head in exactly the same position, a translation between 0 and +/-10 pixels randomly displaced each image along both axes and randomly scaled it by a factor between -1% and +1%; also each image was randomly rotated by an angle of up to 1 degree.

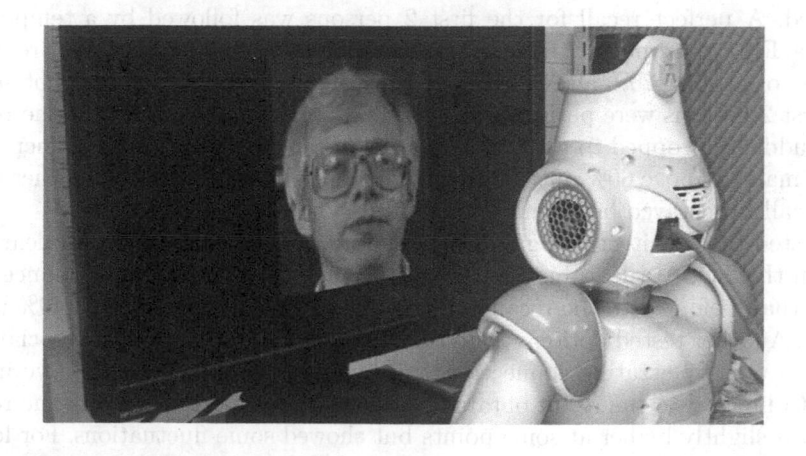

Fig. 2. The NAO robot observes the image of a person's face on a screen

---

[3] http://www.aldebaran.com/en/humanoid-robot/nao-robot

4   Results

The ICALA could incrementally learn up to 37 people in the simulated setup and up to 36 people in the robot setup. For the remaining persons no clusters were created in the respective M-SOINN module for the visual inputs. The *FacesATT* module had to process 2045 nodes, 1927 edges and 118 clusters, the topology of the *NAOCamera* contained 672 nodes, 689 edges and 115 clusters.

The cluster counts steadily increased as more people were introduced (Figure 3). Although the topologies contained always more clusters than persons, the number of clusters generated remained reasonably low but always stayed far below the total number of presented faces. In both setups the algorithm created ca. 3 or 4 clusters per person on average (instead of ideally 1 cluster per person).

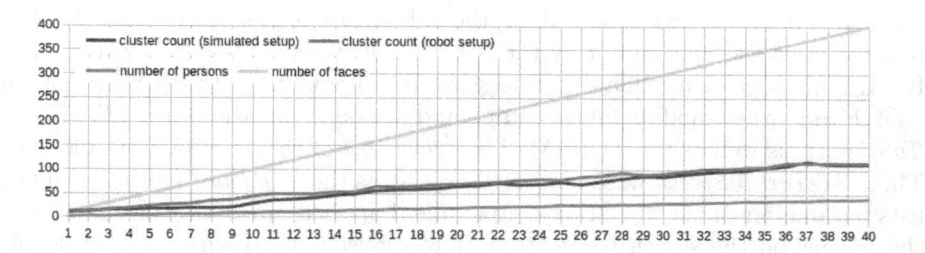

Fig. 3. Topology development for the *FacesATT* module (simulated setup) and *NAO-Camera* module (robot setup)

Figure 4 shows the ratio of correctly identified faces. In the simulated setup the recall rate started high and gradually decreased as more people had to be recalled. A perfect recall for the first 2 persons was followed by a temporary decline. For 6 to 13 people the recall rate was higher than 70% but finally reached a value of around 20% after having learned 36 people. Also in the robot setup the first 2 persons were perfectly recalled and immediately afterwards the recall rate suddenly dropped to ca. 40%. When recalling 10 people, the rate increased and remained above 60% until 22 people had been presented. After another drop the recall rate stayed between 20% and 40%.

I tested the architecture again in the simulated setup without the unlearning part in the TOSAM learning rule. With this change the recall performance was worse than before with the recall rate being mostly between 20% and 40% (Figure 5). Another tested option was to reduce the number of outgoing associations for each unit by creating connections only between units with a positive input load. Compared to the result obtained with a fully connected network the recall rate was slightly higher at some points but showed some fluctuations. For lower numbers of persons the recall rate was very low but stabilised from 14 people onwards (Figure 5).

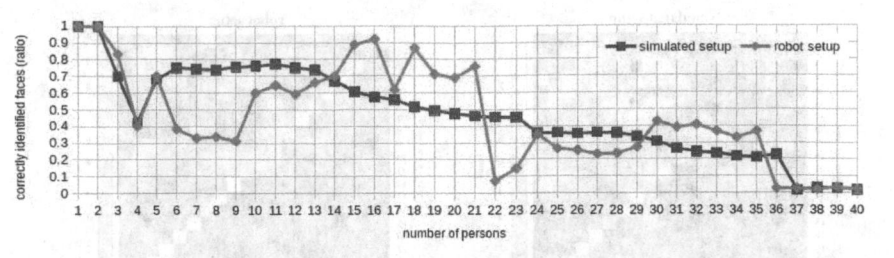

Fig. 4. The ratio of correctly identified faces plotted against the number of persons learned incrementally for the simulated setup and the robot setup

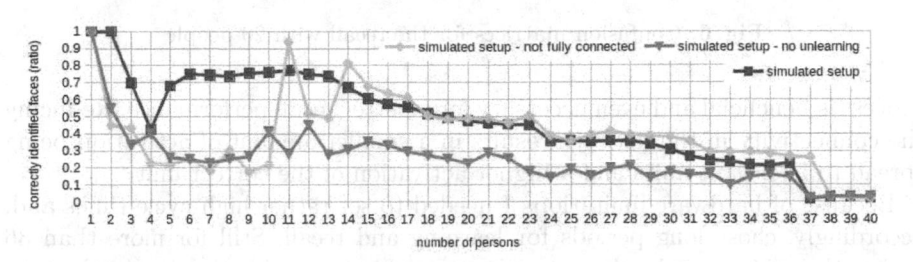

Fig. 5. The ratio of correctly identified faces plotted against the number of persons learned incrementally for the simulated setup with changes in the TOSAM

5   Discussion

The ICALA showed limited recall performance in the given incremental learning task. Already for a small number of patterns no perfect recall was possible. For 20 people almost half of the learned faces could be identified correctly in the simulated setup. In the robot setup the architecture temporarily achieved higher recall performances but the recall rate fluctuated including sudden drops. In the confusion matrices I could observe that mainly persons learned earlier could not be identified correctly (Figure 6). For these people the system tends to predict the label of a more recently learned person.

If the topology does not contain all face variations of a person, certain faces cannot be recalled. However, by looking at the actual topologies, I could not notice any significant lack in face variations. For all people most of the face variations were represented in the topology.

If the association from an image to the corresponding label is too weak, then not enough activation can be spread to highly activate the respective unit. During recall the unlearning process of the TOSAM decreases the weight values. Eventually negative weights can predominate in the spreading process and the major amount of activation is spread over these connections. The amount spread over the positively-weighted connection to the correct label becomes tiny.

Without unlearning, the connection weights do not decrease during recall and no negative weights can develop for connections to other units. These negative weights would normally suppress the activation of other units and lead to a cleaner recall of the associated information. It seems that such a competitive

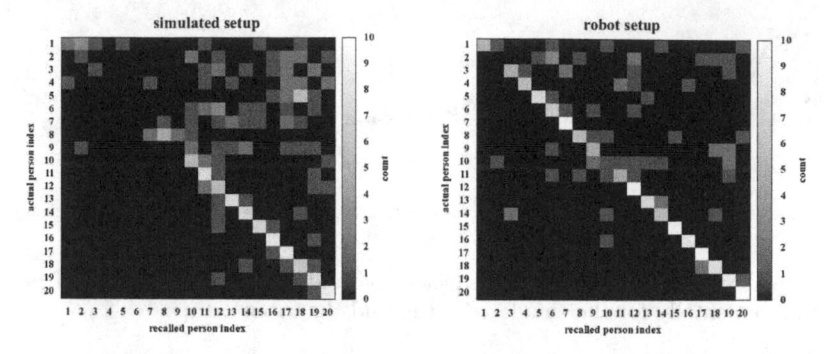

Fig. 6. Confusion matrices for the recall with 20 people

process is beneficial and even necessary for a better recall performance. Reducing the connectivity in the network results in a smaller amount of activation being spread to irrelevant units and a higher activation of the correct unit.

Because of hardware limitations I needed to set rather high cycle times and, accordingly, chose long periods for learning and recall. Still for more than 36 people the underlying hardware was not capable to process the data within the demanded time frame. However, given faster hardware, all time-related parameters could be decreased to provide a more realistic setup.

6   Conclusions

I introduced the ICALA, a novel architecture for incremental associative learning. The performance of the architecture was evaluated in an incremental learning task in both simulated and real robot scenarios. Despite being able to learn nearly all presented inputs, the associated label could not always be retrieved correctly. In the simulated setup the ratio of correctly recalled information decreased while the number of patterns increased. Previously learned patterns became harder to retrieve the more often they were recalled. In the robot setup the recall performance was partially better but very inconsistent due to fluctuations in the recall rate. I discussed possible causes for the decrease in recall rate and reassessed modified versions of the architecture. The tested variants could not lead to a strictly better recall performance. Without using a fully connected network, however, the recall performance could be partially improved by a small margin. To stabilise the incremental recall performance of the ICALA further investigations into the topology development in the M-SOINN are needed.

References

1. Balkenius, C., Morén, J.: Computational models of classical conditioning: A comparative study. Tech. rep., Lund University Cognitive Science (1998)
2. Bouchachia, A.: Evolving clustering: An asset for evolving systems. IEEE SMC – eNewsletter (36) (September 2011)

3. Bouchachia, A., Lughofer, E., Sayed-Mouchaweh, M.: Editorial to the special issue: Evolving soft computing techniques and applications. Applied Soft Computing 14, 141–143 (2014)

4. Bouchachia, A., Vanaret, C.: Incremental learning based on growing gaussian mixture models. In: Proceedings of the 10th International Conference on Machine Learning and Applications (ICMLA 2011), pp. 47–52 (2011)

5. Deng, D., Kasabov, N.: On-line pattern analysis by evolving self-organizing maps. Neurocomputing 51, 87–103 (2003)

6. Fritzke, B.: A growing neural gas network learns topologies. In: Advances in Neural Information Processing Systems 7, pp. 625–632. MIT Press (1995)

7. Fritzke, B.: A self-organizing network that can follow non-stationary distributions. In: Gerstner, W., Hasler, M., Germond, A., Nicoud, J.-D. (eds.) ICANN 1997. LNCS, vol. 1327, pp. 613–618. Springer, Heidelberg (1997)

8. Furao, S., Hasegawa, O.: An incremental network for on-line unsupervised classification and topology learning. Neural Networks 19, 90–106 (2006)

9. Furao, S., Ogura, T., Hasegawa, O.: An enhanced self-organizing incremental neural network for online unsupervised learning. Neural Networks 20, 893–903 (2007)

10. Furao, S., Ouyang, Q., Kasai, W., Hasegawa, O.: A general associative memory based on self-organizing incremental neural network. Neurocomputing 104, 57–71 (2013)

11. Gama, J.: Knowledge Discovery from Data Streams. Data Mining and Knowledge Discovery Series. Chapman & Hall/CRC (2010)

12. Hebb, D.O.: The Organization of Behavior – A Neuropsychological Theory. John Wiley & Sons (1949)

13. Keysermann, M.U., Vargas, P.A.: Desiderata for a memory model. In: Proceedings of the 12th UK Workshop on Computational Intelligence, pp. 37–44 (2012)

14. Lughofer, E.: A dynamic split-and-merge approach for evolving cluster models. Evolving Systems 3(3), 135–151 (2012)

15. Marsland, S., Shapiro, J., Nehmzow, U.: A self-organising network that grows when required. Neural Networks 15(8), 1041–1058 (2002)

16. O'Reilly, R.C., Munakata, Y.: Computational Explorations in Cognitive Neuroscience - Understanding the Mind by Simulating the Brain. MIT Press (2000)

17. Pfeifer, R., Scheier, C.: Understanding Intelligence. MIT Press (1999)

18. Prudent, Y., Ennaji, A.: An incremental growing neural gas learns topologies. In: Proceedings of the 2005 IEEE International Joint Conference on Neural Network (IJCNN 2005), vol. 2, pp. 1211–1216 (2005)

19. Rescorla, R.A., Wagner, A.R.: A theory of pavlovian conditioning: Variations in the effectiveness of reinforcement and nonreinforcement. In: Classical Conditioning II: Current Theory and Research, pp. 64–99. Appleton-Century-Crofts (1972)

20. Sayed-Mouchaweh, M., Lughofer, E.: Learning in Non-Stationary Environments – Methods and Applications. Springer, New York (2012)

21. Sudo, A., Sato, A., Hasegawa, O.: Associative memory for online learning in noisy environments using self-organizing incremental neural network. IEEE Transactions on Neural Networks 20(6), 964–972 (2009)

22. Tangruamsub, S., Kawewong, A., Tsuboyama, M., Hasegawa, O.: Self-organizing incremental associative memory-based robot navigation. IEICE Transactions on Information and Systems E95-D(10), 2415–2425 (2012)

Context Identification and Exploitation in Dynamic Data Mining – An Application to Classifying Electricity Price Changes

Lida Barakat

Department of Management Science, Lancaster University, UK
l.barakat@lancaster.ac.uk

Abstract. Adapting classification models to concept changes is one of the main challenges associated with learning in dynamic environments, where the definition of the target concept may change over time under the influence of varying contextual factors. Existing adaptive approaches, however, are limited in terms of the extent to which such contextual factors are *explicitly* identified and utilised, despite their importance. In response, we propose an information-theoretic-based approach for systematic context identification, aiming to learn from data the contextual characteristics of the domain by identifying the context variables contributing to concept changes. Such explicit identification of context enables capturing the causes of drift, and hence facilitating more effective adaptation. We conduct experimental analyses to demonstrate the effectiveness of the approach on both simulated datasets with various change scenarios, and on an actual benchmark dataset from an electricity market.

Keywords: Classification, Concept Drift, Context.

1 Introduction

In supervised classification problems, available historical labeled examples (input-output pairs) are normally utilised in order to learn a target concept (i.e. learn the underlying function between the variable to be predicted and the respective input data). In many real world applications, however, target concepts are not static and may change over time (a phenomenon referred to as concept drift) under the influence of varying *context* [15]. Generally, there are many definitions for the term context. A commonly used one is "any information that can be used to characterise the situation of an entity" [3]. Here, by context, we refer to the underlying situation and environmental conditions of the target concept [2]. For example, in electricity price prediction, potential context may include season, weather, and time of the week, which may affect the electricity consumption habits. In probabilistic terms, concept drift can be described as changes in the conditional distribution of the target variable over time. That is, $P_t(Y|X)$ may not be equal to $P_{t+1}(Y|X)$, where Y represents the target variable, and X the vector of input data. In the presence of such drift, adapting the classification model (re-estimating the model parameters) is essential to produce more

A. Bouchachia (Ed.): ICAIS 2014, LNAI 8779, pp. 80–89, 2014.

accurate and reliable classification decisions. Yet, this task is far from trivial since drift can occur at any time, and its type (gradual, abrupt, etc.) cannot be known in advance. This poses a challenge on how to select relevant training data to adapt the model, which is a vital issue since the ability of the classification model to make accurate decisions is highly dependent on the data used for the learning process.

Many adaptive learning approaches have been proposed in the literature to address concept drift [6, 10, 12, 16], but these mostly do not account for the contextual factors under which the training examples are collected, despite their importance in determining the relevance of the examples for the current situation. Recently, learning with respect to context started to receive increasing attention [7, 15, 17]. Yet, these approaches mostly rely on monitoring the *implicit* context, via clustering with respect to the prediction accuracy of the classifier [7], monitoring the predictive ability of the primary variables [15], and other methods [17], and remain limited in terms of the extent to which the contextual aspects are *explicitly* identified and utilised. Explicit identification and monitoring of the contextual aspects of the application enables capturing the causes of drift, and hence facilitating more effective adaptation (faster drift detection and selection of more relevant training examples), as opposed to existing adaptive learning strategies, which mostly rely on monitoring the effects of drift (in terms of the degradation of the classifier's performance). Although Gomes et al [5] present an attempt towards explicit context utilisation (for selecting the classifier relevant for the current situation among a number of candidates), the contextual variables are assumed to be known a priori, with no identification method being suggested.

In response, we propose an information-theoretic-based approach for systematic context identification, aiming to learn from data the contextual characteristics of the domain by identifying the context variables contributing to concept changes. The context variables identified are then utilised in selecting more relevant training data for the classification model. A simple realisation of an adaptive classifier (Naïve Bayes classifier) is presented for this purpose. Alternatively, the context variables identified could be incorporated as additional input variables into the classification model. This, however, may unnecessarily increase the problem dimensionality, and achieve lower prediction accuracy compared to the external utilisation proposed (as demonstrated by our results), especially that context variables are not relevant for prediction during periods of concept stability (potentially long periods). Thorough experimental analyses are conducted on simulated datasets and a realistic dataset concerning electricity price prediction, to validate our approach.

The rest of the paper is organised as follows. Section 2 introduces the problem of context identification. Section 3 and Section 4 present the proposed context learning solution and a corresponding context-aware training example weighting, respectively. Experimental results are reported in Section 5, while Section 6 concludes the paper.

2   Problem Formulation

The context knowledge for an application domain of interest can be represented as a tuple (C, vl, wt), where: $C = \{C_1, C_2, ..., C_m\}$ is the initial set of candidate context variables (which are not all necessarily relevant for the underlying concept); function $vl(C_j, t)$ is a context instantiation function, associating candidate context variable $C_j \in C$ with its value at a particular time step $t \in T$; and finally function $wt(C_j) \in \mathbb{R}^+$ is a context weighting function, which maps candidate context variable $C_j \in C$ to a weighting factor reflecting its importance in distinguishing concept changes. Weights wt provide indication of the actual contextual characteristics of the domain (and facilitate controlling the contribution of classification training examples, as we illustrate later), with $wt(C_j) = 0$ indicating that candidate C_j has no effect regarding concept drift (i.e. it is not an actual contextual variable for the concept of interest).

Since candidate context variables C can be usually derived from the background knowledge about the domain, and assuming the ability to access values vl, our problem of context identification reduces to that of assessing weights wt. We propose to learn such weights from the historical data available on the concept of interest, as detailed in the next section.

3   Context Learning

Our approach for the actual context recognition is inspired by the definition of context variables proposed by Turney [13], who was among the first to recognise the issue of context in supervised learning and to give a formal definition for context variables. According to this definition, an actual contextual variable C_j affects the discrimination ability of the input (primary) variables, i.e. $P(Y|X, C_j) \neq P(Y|X)$, where $X = (X_1, X_2, \dots, X_p)$ represents the vector of input data in a p-dimensional feature space, and Y represents the target class label.

We extend this definition to allow measuring the influence degree that C_j has on X (and consequently facilitating the calculation of weights wt), as follows: the degree of influence of a candidate context variable $C_j \in C$, on the discrimination ability of the primary variable(s) X, is proportional to the difference between the conditional probabilities $P(Y|X, C_j)$ and $P(Y|X)$. This can be quantified by measuring the additional information that C_j has about Y, and that is not already provided by X. In other words, we are interested in measuring the degree to which knowledge of the candidate context variable reduces the uncertainty in the target variable, given the primary variables. Shannon's Information Theory [11], which measures uncertainty and information content (the quantities of interest), thus provides a good formalisation for this purpose. It is introduced next, followed by the respective context weighting approach, and a corresponding computational realisation.

3.1   Information Theoretic Measures

The measures of Information Theory of interest for our model are: *Conditional Entropy*, $H(Y|X)$, quantifying the amount of uncertainty about random variable Y, given knowledge of variable(s) X; and *Conditional Mutual Information*, $I(C_j; Y|X)$, quantifying the reduction in uncertainty (information content) about random variable Y with respect to random variable C_j, given the knowledge already provided by variable(s) X. These measures are defined as follows [1]:

$$H(Y|X) = \sum_x p(x) H(Y|X = x) \tag{1}$$

$$I(C_j; Y|X) = \sum_x \sum_{c_j} \sum_y p(c_j, y, x) \log \frac{p(c_j, y|x)}{p(c_j|x)p(y|x)} \tag{2}$$

where $p(.)$, $p(.,.,..)$, and $p(.|.)$ represent the probability mass function, joint probability mass function, and conditional marginal probability mass function of the corresponding random variables, respectively; and the entropy $H(Y)$ of a random variable Y is given by $H(Y) = -\sum_y p(y) \log p(y)$, with log being the natural logarithm. Note that above definitions assume the random variables are discrete. For continuous cases, the summation over the states of possible values is replaced by the integral.

Conditional mutual information (or shortly CMI), $I(C_j; Y|X)$, satisfies three properties [1]: *non-negativity*, i.e. $I(C_j; Y|X) \geq 0$; *measure of independence*, where CMI equals zero *if and only if* variables Y and C_j are independent, i.e. $I(C_j; Y|X) = 0 \Leftrightarrow P(Y|X, C_j) = P(Y|X)$; and *boundedness*, where $I(C_j; Y|X) \leq H(Y|X)$.

3.2   Context Variable Identification

Based on above, a candidate context variable $C_j \in C$ is considered to be actually contextual if there is a dependency between C_j and the target variable Y, i.e. $I(C_j; Y|X) \neq 0$, indicating that C_j reduces uncertainty about Y. The weight of variable C_j is calculated according to its corresponding degree of uncertainty reduction, as follows:

$$wt(C_j) = \begin{cases} \frac{I(C_j; Y|X)}{H(Y|X)} & \text{if } I(C_j; Y|X) \neq 0 \\ 0 & \text{otherwise} \end{cases} \tag{3}$$

Note that $wt(C_j) \in [0,1]$, which can be easily concluded from the properties of CMI.

3.3   Computational Solution

In discrete systems, the probability mass functions for estimating CMI can be computed using the relative frequencies from the observed examples. However, unlike the discrete case, computing CMI for continuous variables requires estimating probability density functions (pdf) from the available data samples, which is not a straightforward task, and in fact, considered as one of the main problems associated with applying this measure. With this regard, different possible non-parametric approaches exist in the literature, of which we select the k-nearest neighbour estimator [9, 14]. Unlike many other approaches, this estimator allows accommodating high variable dimensionality (the estimator of the CMI for context variables must be able to work well with higher dimensions) and produces more accurate results.

4   Training Example Weighting

In supervised classification problems, the classification model is normally derived based on the previously observed labeled examples $\{(x(i), y(i))\}_{i=1}^{t}$, where $x(i) = (x_1, x_2, \ldots, x_p)$ represent the value vector of primary characteristics and $y(i)$ is the target class label, at time step i. In the presence of concept drift, the examples may not remain relevant, and hence the contribution of each example in estimating the classification model should be governed by its relevance for the situation at hand (the current concept). To achieve this, we propose a context-aware example weighting, assessing importance of each example based on the similarity degree between the example's context and the current context. That is, each example, $u(i) = (x(i), y(i))$, is associated with a weighting factor, $exm\_wt(u(i))$, that reflects its relevance:

$$exm\_wt(u(i)) = sim\big(ctx(i), ctx(t)\big) \tag{4}$$

where $ctx(i) = \big(vl(C_1, i), vl(C_2, i), \ldots, vl(C_m, i)\big)$ is the context instance (the value vector of the candidate context variables) at time step i, under which example $u(i)$ is collected; $ctx(t) = \big(vl(C_1, t), vl(C_2, t), \ldots, vl(C_m, t)\big)$ is the context instance at the current time step t; and sim is a similarity measure between two context instances, and is based on their weighted distance, given as follows:

$$\sum_{C_j \in C} wt(C_j) \times diff\big(vl(C_j, i), vl(C_j, t)\big) \tag{5}$$

with function $diff\big(vl(C_j, i), vl(C_j, t)\big)$ measuring the difference between values $vl(C_j, i)$ and $vl(C_j, t)$ (an example of this function is presented in Section 5).

5   Evaluation

In this section, we conduct empirical evaluation of the proposed approach. Specifically, we focus on testing the effectiveness of the proposed context identification method, and on demonstrating the positive influence of exploiting the identified context (in terms of example weighting) on classification results. Both are detailed next.

5.1   Context Identification

Our first aim is to test the following two hypotheses. *Hypothesis 1*. The proposed context identification method is able to correctly identify the actual contextual characteristics of the domain, and to rank these according to their importance. *Hypothesis 2*. Hypothesis 1 holds under varying factors, including sample size, noise level, type of concept change (abrupt or gradual), and type of context variable (discrete or continuous). The corresponding experimental setup and results are discussed in what follows.

Experimental Design. *Dataset:* Since evaluation here requires pre-existing knowledge about the actual contextual characteristics of the problem (not the case with real-world data), we base this evaluation on an artificial dataset, allowing us to study the behavior of the approach under different conditions. For this purpose, and inspired by SEA concepts [12], we generate an artificial dataset defined in terms of 3 independent and normally distributed primary variables, $x_i \sim N(0,1)$, i=1:3, and a binary class label, $y \in \{0,1\}$. The target concept is defined by equation $\sum_{i=1}^{3} x_i \leq a$, where a is a threshold value distinguishing the two classes for a given concept. That is, examples satisfying $\sum_{i=1}^{3} x_i \leq a$ could be labelled as positive, and as negative otherwise. Concept changes can thus be simulated by varying the value of parameter a. In total, we generate 3000 examples, divided among three different concepts, Concept 1, Concept 2, and Concept 3, corresponding to $a = -1.5$, $a = 0$, and $a = 1.5$, respectively. For the context model, we introduce three candidate contextual variables $C = \{C_1, C_2, C_3\}$. The importance of these variables is assumed to be as follows: variable C_1 has the highest importance, perfectly distinguishing among the three concepts; variable C_2 is of less importance due to inability to discriminate between Concept 2 and Concept 3; and finally variable C_3 has no discrimination ability between the three concepts (i.e. has no contextual importance). The value distribution of these variables, for the two cases of discrete and continuous context variables, is presented in Table 1.

Table 1. Value distribution of candidate context variables for each concept

	Discrete Context Variables			Continuous Context Variables		
Concept 1	$C_1 = 1$	$C_2 = 1$	$C_3 \in \{1,3\}$	$C_1 \in [0,1]$	$C_2 \in [0,1]$	$C_3 \in [0,3]$
Concept 2	$C_1 = 2$	$C_2 \in \{2,3\}$	$C_3 \in \{1,3\}$	$C_1 \in [1,2]$	$C_2 \in [1,3]$	$C_3 \in [0,3]$
Concept 3	$C_1 = 3$	$C_2 \in \{2,3\}$	$C_3 \in \{1,3\}$	$C_1 \in [2,3]$	$C_2 \in [1,3]$	$C_3 \in [0,3]$

Strategies: In the evaluation, we refer to the following strategies for the purpose of context identification: *conditional mutual information (CMI)*, representing the identification method proposed in this paper; and *mutual information (MI)*, a commonly used method in the literature for assessing the importance of candidate variables with respect to the target variable, and which we utilise as a baseline.

Performance Measure: We compare the weights produced for candidate context variables by the detection strategy against their ranking preferences assumed above.

Results. Figure 1 reports the results (averaged over 30 runs) of the considered identification strategies, for the two cases of discrete (Figure 1(a)) and continuous (Figure 1(b)) context variables, with sudden concept changes (as described above). The sample size (i.e. the number of examples generated) for each concept occurrence is varied between 50 and 1000 examples, and a 5% class noise is added to each concept (i.e. 5% of the examples have incorrect class labels). Note that other noise levels (including 10% and 20% class noise) have been also considered, and they exhibit similar trends, but are omitted due to space limitation. We can see that the conditional mutual information measure is able to recognise the relative importance among the candidate context variables, and outperform the mutual information measure, in all cases.

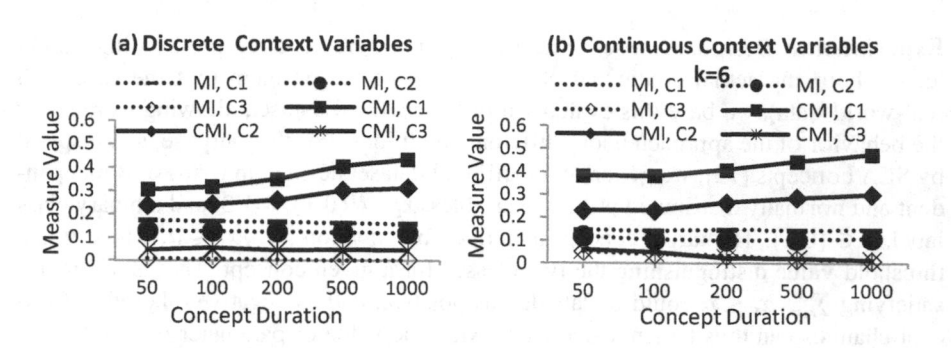

Fig. 1. Evaluation of context identification strategies (sudden concept changes)

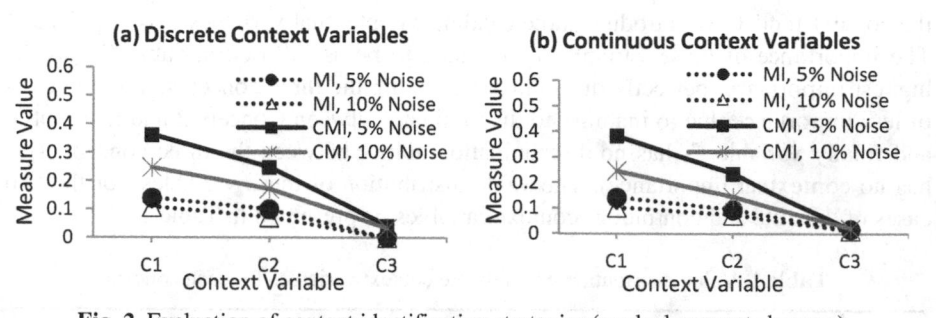

Fig. 2. Evaluation of context identification strategies (gradual concept changes)

Further analysis is provided in Figure 2, considering gradual concept changes. To simulate such changes, we fix the duration of each of the three concepts at 1000 examples, and gradually change the threshold (i.e. parameter a) at each time step by a step of $\frac{mg}{1000}$, where mg represents the magnitude of change during one concept (in our case, $mg = 1.5$). We add $n\%$ class noise to each concept, with $n \in \{0.05, 0.10\}$. The results show that, although context variables C_1 and C_2 get lower values in comparison with the results achieved in the previous experiment, these variables are still correctly ranked according to their importance, across all noise levels. Again, conditional mutual information achieves better results than the mutual information approach.

5.2   Context Exploitation

Our second aim is to test the following hypothesis. *Hypothesis 3.* Applying the proposed context-aware example weighting approach results in a positive effect on the classifier's accuracy. Experimental setup and results are presented next.

Experimental Design. *Dataset:* Here, we utilise a real-world dataset consisting of 45312 records about electricity price changes, obtained from the Australian New South Wales Electricity Market between May 1996 and December 1998. Each record represents a period of 30 minutes, with a binary class label and the following input (primary) variables: the time stamp, the New South Wales electricity demand,

Victoria (adjacent area) demand, and the scheduled electricity transfer between states. The class label refers to the price change (up/down) with respect to a moving average of the last 24 hours. This dataset exhibits drifts due to changes in consumption habits corresponding to various candidate contextual characteristics such as season and time of the week [5, 8]. In our analysis, we regard the following variables as candidate context variables: day of the week, season, and three randomly generated noisy variables. The value domain for each of these variables is given in Table 2. Note that, since the actual contextual characteristics of this data are not known in advance, the effectiveness of the approach here can only be assessed in terms of the improvement in the prediction ability of the classification model when utilising the identified context variables. Moreover, due to the dependencies among the labels in this dataset [18] (which cause even the simplest classifier predicting the next label based only on the previously seen label to achieve very high accuracy), we subsample the data to break such dependencies [16]. Specifically, we take every 20th observation at regular intervals, resulting in a total of 2265 records utilised for classifier evaluation.

Table 2. Candidate context variables for Electricity dataset

Variable	Value Domain
Day of the week	$\in \{Mon, Tue, Wed, Thu, Fri, Sat, Sun\}$
Season	$\in \{winter, spring, summer, autumn\}$
Noise	$N \in \{0,1\}$

Strategies: Three classification strategies are compared. The first strategy is a standard Naïve Bayes classifier. It is re-estimated based on all the examples observed so far, assigning equal weights to all examples (without any context utilisiation). The second strategy is similar to the first, but it incorporates the identified context variables as additional input variables. Finally, the third strategy is a weighted Naïve Bayes classifier utilising the proposed example-weighting scheme (see Equation 4). Specifically, each appearance of a variable value is multiplied by the weight exm_wt of the corresponding example. Since the contextual variables are categorical here, the value difference function, $diff$, is given as follows: $diff(v_1, v_2) = 0$ if $v_1 = v_2$; $diff(v_1, v_2) = 1$, otherwise.

Performance Measure: Here, we are interested in measuring the predictive accuracy of the classification strategy, computed as the ratio between the number of correctly classified examples and the total number of classified examples (with 1265 records out of the total number being utilised for testing the classifiers' accuracy in the experiments).

Results. First, we apply the proposed context identification approach to deduce the actual contextual variables for the electricity dataset. The results, in Table 3, indicate that both day of the week and season are relevant for characterising context (both get CMI values greater than zero), while the noisy variables are irrelevant (all get values close to zero). To test the significance of these results, we apply a non-parametric permutation test with the following idea [4]: randomly shuffle (reorder) the data to generate independent series and then compare the estimated value of the test statistic (here CMI) from the original data with the distribution of this value from the permuted data. We perform 1000 such permutations, and report the corresponding p-value, obtained by counting the number of times the value of CMI in the permuted data is at least as extreme as that of the observed value in the actual data, divided by the number of permutations. As can be seen from Table 3, the permutation test confirms the significance of the obtained CMI values for both day of the week and season, and the insignificance for the noisy variables.

Table 3. Conditional mutual information estimates for the candidate context variables of the Electricity dataset

Variable	CMI	Permutation Test (p-value)
Day of the Week	0.1615	0
Season	0.1124	0
N1	0.0299	1
N2	0.030	1
N3	0.0288	1

Based on this, Table 4 reports the results of the three classification strategies considered. As can be seen, employing the context-aware example weighting improves the accuracy of the standard classifier from 63% to 67%. It also outperforms the classifier that includes context variables as input variables, with the latter being only slightly better than the standard classifier (increasing accuracy from 63% to 64%).

Table 4. Accuracies of different classifiers on the Electricity dataset

Classification Model	Prediction Accuracy
Naïve Bayes Classifier	0.63
Naïve Bayes Classifier with context as input variables	0.64
Weighted Naïve Bayes Classifier	0.67

6   Conclusions and Future Work

The paper presented a conditional mutual information based approach for systematic context identification, which learns the contextual characteristics of the domain from available historical data. The knowledge learned is then incorporated into a classification model, facilitating the weighting of training examples according to their relevance. Experimental results demonstrated the feasibility of the approach for both discrete and continuous contextual variables, and its ability to improve the prediction accuracy of the classification model. The main focus of the paper is on relevant context identification, and therefore only a very basic form of an adaptive classifier was outlined for validation purposes. Future work involves improving this for a more efficient version (e.g. trigger data re-weighting only when necessary), and comparing it thoroughly against relevant adaptation strategies in the literature (e.g. [5]).

References

1. Cover, T.M., Thomas, J.A.: Elements of Information Theory. Wiley, New York (2006)
2. Chen, A.: Context-Aware Collaborative Filtering System: Predicting the User's Preference in the Ubiquitous Computing Environment. In: Strang, T., Linnhoff-Popien, C. (eds.) Lo-CA 2005. LNCS, vol. 3479, pp. 244–253. Springer, Heidelberg (2005)
3. Dey, A.: Understanding and Using Context. Personal and Ubiquitous Computing 5(1), 4–7 (2001)
4. Francois, D., Wertz, V., Verleysen, M.: The Permutation Test for Feature Selection by Mutual Information. In: Proc. of the 14th European Symposium on Artificial Neural Networks, pp. 239–244 (2006)
5. Gomes, J.B., Sousa, P.A., Menasalvas, E.: Tracking Recurrent Concepts Using Context. Intelligent Data Analysis 16(5), 803–825 (2012)
6. Gama, J., Medas, P., Castillo, G., Rodrigues, P.: Learning with Drift Detection. In: Bazzan, A.L.C., Labidi, S. (eds.) SBIA 2004. LNCS (LNAI), vol. 3171, pp. 286–295. Springer, Heidelberg (2004)
7. Harries, M., Sammut, C., Horn, K.: Extracting Hidden Context. Machine Learning 32(2), 101–126 (1998)
8. Harries, M.: Splice-2 Comparative Evaluation: Electricity Pricing. Technical report, University of New South Wales (1999)
9. Kraskov, A., Stögbauer, H., Grassberger, P.: Estimating Mutual Information. Physics Review E 69(6), 66138–66154 (2004)
10. Pavlidis, N.G., Tasoulis, D.K., Adams, N.M., Hand, D.J.: Adaptive Consumer Credit Classification. Journal of the Operational Research Society 63(12), 1645–1654 (2012)
11. Shannon, C.: A Mathematical Theory of Communication. The Bell System Technical Journal 27(7), 379–423 (1948)
12. Street, W.N., Kim, Y.S.: A Streaming Ensemble Algorithm (SEA) for Large-Scale Classification. In: Proc. of the 7th ACM SIGKDD International Conference on Knowledge Discovery and Data Mining, pp. 377–382. ACM, New York (2001)
13. Turney, P.: The Identification of Context-Sensitive Features: A Formal Definition of Context for Concept Learning. In: Proc. of the ICML Workshop on Learning in Context-Sensitive Domains, Bari, Italy, pp. 53–59 (1996)
14. Tsimpiris, A., Vlachos, I., Kugiumtzis, D.: Nearest Neighbor Estimate of Conditional Mutual Information in Feature Selection. Expert Systems with Applications 39, 12697–12708 (2012)
15. Widmer, G.: Tracking Context Changes through Meta-Learning. Machine Learning 27(3), 259–286 (1997)
16. Zliobaite, I., Kuncheva, L.: Determining the Training Window for Small Sample Size Classification with Concept Drift. In: Proc. of the IEEE International Conference on Data Mining Workshop, pp. 447–452. IEEE, Washington, DC (2009)
17. Žliobaitė, I.: Identifying Hidden Contexts in Classification. In: Huang, J.Z., Cao, L., Srivastava, J. (eds.) PAKDD 2011, Part I. LNCS, vol. 6634, pp. 277–288. Springer, Heidelberg (2011)
18. Zliobaite, I.: How Good is the Electricity Benchmark for Evaluating Concept Drift Adaptation. CoRR, abs/1301-3524 (2013)

Towards a Better Understanding of the Local Attractor in Particle Swarm Optimization: Speed and Solution Quality

Vanessa Lange, Manuel Schmitt, and Rolf Wanka

Department of Computer Science, University of Erlangen-Nuremberg, Germany
{vanessa.lange,manuel.schmitt}@fau.de, rolf.wanka@cs.fau.de

Abstract. Particle Swarm Optimization (PSO) is a popular nature-inspired meta-heuristic for solving continuous optimization problems. Although this technique is widely used, the understanding of the mechanisms that make swarms so successful is still limited. We present the first substantial experimental investigation of the influence of the local attractor on the quality of exploration and exploitation. We compare in detail classical PSO with the social-only variant where local attractors are ignored. To measure the exploration capabilities, we determine how frequently both variants return results in the neighborhood of the global optimum. We measure the quality of exploitation by considering only function values from runs that reached a search point sufficiently close to the global optimum and then comparing in how many digits such values still deviate from the global minimum value. It turns out that the local attractor significantly improves the exploration, but sometimes reduces the quality of the exploitation. The effects mentioned can also be observed by measuring the potential of the swarm.

1 Introduction

The Particle Swarm Optimization Algorithm. Particle Swarm Optimization (PSO) is a popular metaheuristic designed for solving optimization problems on continuous domains. It has been introduced by Kennedy and Eberhart [9,3]. In contrast to evolutionary algorithms, the particles of a swarm cooperate and share information about the search space rather than competing against each other. PSO has been applied successfully to a wide range of optimization problems, e. g., in Biomedical Image Processing [19], Geosciences [12], Mechanical Engineering [4], and Materials Science [15]. The popularity of the PSO framework in these scientific communities is due to the fact that it on the one hand can be realized and, if necessary, adapted to further needs easily, but on the other hand empirically shows good performance results with respect to the quality of the solution found and the speed needed to obtain it. By adapting its parameters, users may in real-world applications easily and successfully control the swarm's behavior with respect to "exploration" ("searching where no one has searched before") and "exploitation" ("searching around a good position").

A. Bouchachia (Ed.): ICAIS 2014, LNAI 8779, pp. 90–99, 2014.

A thorough discussion of PSO can be found in [13]. To be precise, let a fitness function (also called objective function) $f : \mathbb{R}^D \to \mathbb{R}$ on a D-dimensional domain be given that (w. l. o. g.) has to be minimized. A population of *particles*, each consisting of a *position* (the candidate for a solution), a *velocity* and a *local attractor* (also referred to as *private guide*), moves through the search space $\mathbb{R}^D$. The local attractor of a particle is the best position with respect to f this particle has encountered so far. Additionally, the swarm has a common memory, the *global attractor* (also referred to as *local guide*), which is the best position any particle has found so far. The movement is governed by the so-called *movement equations*.

Many variants of PSO have been developed and empirically proven to be efficient. Most of them extend the classical PSO algorithm by additional operations. As just one example out of many, van den Bergh/Engelbrecht [1] substantially modify the movement equations, enabling the particles to count the number of times they improve the global attractor and use this information.

Although the efficiency of PSO is widely known, the understanding of the mechanisms that make the swarm so successful is still limited. A theoretical analysis of the particles' trajectories can be found in [2]. Parameter selection guidelines guaranteeing the convergence of the swarm under the assumption of fixed attractors have been developed in [6]. Additional guidelines, for which the classical swarm in the 1-dimensional case and a slightly modified PSO in the D-dimensional case finds provably at least a local optimum of any sufficiently smooth function can be found in [16]. In [16], also the notion of the *potential* of a particle swarm has been introduced. The potential, which we will use also in this paper, is a measure for the swarm's capability to reach search points far away from the current global attractor.

In this paper, we investigate the influence of the local attractor on the speed of convergence and the quality of the found solution.

In [11], the authors prove that a swarm consisting of only a single particle does, with positive probability, not converge towards a local optimum. Therefore, the importance of the global attractor is beyond doubt since without it, the swarm would act like many completely independent 1-particle swarms. But to the best of our knowledge, the exact influence of the local attractor has not yet been formally addressed. Closest to that direction, Kennedy [8] applied, among other simplified versions of PSO, the so-called "social-only model," which consists of a particle swarm without local attractors, to an artificial neuronal network learning problem. He already noticed a "slight susceptibility to be captured by local optima." Pedersen and Chipperfield [14] proposed a Meta-Optimizer for finding good parameter choices of both classical PSO and again the variant with disabled local attractors, which they call Many Optimizing Liaisons. However, the question of the benefit from using the local attractor remains unsolved. That is why this paper is dedicated to the particles' local attractors.

Our Contribution. Our main goal is to better understand the influence of the local attractor on the swarm's behavior. In order to measure the benefit of the local attractor, we compare classical PSO with social-only PSO where we ignore the local attractors. We explain, why the local attractor is important for exploration and for improving the chances of finding not only an arbitrary local optimum, but often the global optimum of the fitness function (it helps to leave 'traps' of local optima). Additionally, we give empirical evidence that the influence of the local attractors is significant. However, sometimes the price of this improved exploration is a delay in the convergence. Here, we only consider those runs of both variants that actually (after some fixed time has been expired) come close to the global optimum and compare which results come closer to this optimum. The experiments show that on some fitness functions and with fixed time budget, classical PSO performs worse than social-only PSO. That means: The local attractor directs 'in general' the swarm to better regions, and without the local attractor the swarm finds better solutions in such a region. We also explain the observations in terms of the swarm's potential.

The paper is organized as follows: In Section 2, we state the relevant definitions of the PSO algorithm and the notion of potential we use for our experiments. In Section 3, the general setting of the performed experiments is described. In Section 4, the results of the comparison between the classical and the social-only PSO are presented, as well as the potential-based explanation. For an extended version of this paper, containing additional experimental results, see the arXiv Technical Report [10].

2   Preliminaries

Let D be the dimension of the fitness function f that should be (w. l. o. g.) minimized. A particle swarm consists of N particles. At every time, each particle i has a position $\vec{x}_i \in \mathbb{R}^D$, representing a point in the search space (being a possible solution) and a velocity $\vec{v}_i \in \mathbb{R}^D$. Additionally, particle i has a local attractor $\vec{p}_i \in \mathbb{R}^D$, the best point it has visited so far. Finally, the swarm shares the global attractor $\vec{p}_{\text{glob}} \in \mathbb{R}^D$, the best point *any* particle has visited so far. Algorithm 1 provides an overview over the classical PSO algorithm. In particular, the movement of the swarm is governed by the so called *movement equations* in lines 6 and 7. Here, $\odot$ denotes entrywise multiplication (Hadamard product), and $\vec{r}_{\text{glob}}$ and $\vec{r}_{\text{loc}}$ are random vectors with entries chosen u. a. r. from $[0, 1]$ at each occurrence. Moreover, a, b_{glob} and b_{loc} are constant weights, the so-called *PSO parameters*. As recommended in [2], we choose $a = 0.72984$ and $b_{\text{loc}} = b_{\text{glob}} = 1.496172$.

Since we are interested in the benefit the local attractor has for the algorithm, we also study a version that has been called the social-only PSO ([8]) and is obtained by setting $b_{\text{loc}} = 0$ and therefore making the particles ignore their personal memory. For a fair comparison, since a lot of effort has been put into finding good parameters for the classical PSO, we tested several parameter settings for the social-only PSO. Experiments have shown that using $a = 0.72984$, $b_{\text{glob}} = 1.496172$ is continuing to be reasonable.

For our investigations, we will also use the notion of the so-called potential $\vec{\Phi}$ of the swarm as a measure for its movement in the different dimensions

---

Algorithm 1. Classical PSO

---

   input : $f : \mathbb{R}^D \to \mathbb{R}$, number N of particles, maxiter
   output: $\vec{p}_{\text{glob}} \in \mathbb{R}^D$
1 **for** $i = 1 \to N$ **do**
2   Initialize $\vec{x}_i$ randomly;   Initialize $\vec{v}_i := 0$;   Initialize $\vec{p}_i := \vec{x}_i$;
3 Initialize $\vec{p}_{\text{glob}} := \arg\min\{f(\vec{p}_i) \mid i = 1 \ldots N\}$;
4 **for** $k = 1 \to$ maxiter **do**
5   **for** $i = 1 \to N$ **do**
6         $\vec{v}_i := a \cdot \vec{v}_i + b_{\text{glob}} \cdot \vec{r}_{\text{glob}} \odot (\vec{p}_{\text{glob}} - \vec{x}_i) + b_{\text{loc}} \cdot \vec{r}_{\text{loc}} \odot (\vec{p}_i - \vec{x}_i)$;
7         $\vec{x}_i := \vec{x}_i + \vec{v}_i$;
8   **for** $i = 1 \to N$ **do**
9   **if** $f(\vec{x}_i) \le f(\vec{p}_i)$ **then** $\vec{p}_i := \vec{x}_i$;
10   **if** $f(\vec{x}_i) \le f(\vec{p}_{\text{glob}})$ **then** $\vec{p}_{\text{glob}} := \vec{x}_i$;

$d \in \{1, \ldots, D\}$ as introduced in [16]. Since there are different ways to measure the potential, we use the following formulation:

$$(\vec{\Phi})^d := \sqrt{\sum_{i=1}^{N} a_\Phi \cdot |(\vec{v}_i)^d| + |(\vec{p}_{\text{glob}})^d - (\vec{x}_i)^d|} \, ,$$

where $(.)^d$ means the dth entry of the vector and a_Φ is set to 2.5, a value of the same order as the ones suggested in [16], to emphasize the influence of the velocity. Additionally, to measure the potential of a single particle i instead of the potential of the complete swarm, we use $(\vec{\Psi}_i)^d := a \cdot |(\vec{v}_i)^d| + b_{\text{glob}} \cdot |(\vec{p}_{\text{glob}})^d - (\vec{x}_i)^d| + b_{\text{loc}} \cdot |(\vec{p}_i)^d - (\vec{x}_i)^d|$.

3 Setting

Our experiments were performed with the following setting:

- The swarm size was N set to 100, the number of iterations maxiter to 500.
- We investigated the functions ACKLEY, GRIEWANK, RASTRIGIN, ROSENBROCK, SCHWEFEL, SPHERE (for a description of these functions, see, e. g., [5, p. 94ff]), and the non-shifted, non-rotated High Conditioned ELLIPTIC [18].
- For all functions, we tested all dimensionalities $D \in \{1, 2, 3, 4, 5, 10\}$.
- Since every considered function has a bounded search space $\mathcal{I}$, we used the bound handling method *Random* ([20]), i. e., if in dimension d a particle leaves the search space, the dth entry of its position is set randomly to a value inside the search boundaries.
- The particles' positions were initialized u. a. r. over $\mathcal{I}$, the velocities were initialized with 0.
- Every run of Algorithm 1 was repeated 50 times.

The reason for the comparatively high swarm size combined with the rather low number of search space dimensions is that finding the global optimum for highly multi-modal functions is difficult. For smaller swarm sizes or search spaces with more dimensions, none of the studied PSO variants would have found the global optimum, preventing any meaningful comparison. We used the following criteria to classify the obtained solution on the benchmark functions as a 'local optimum' or even the 'global optimum.'

Global Optimum (G). For all functions except for SCHWEFEL and ROSEN-BROCK, we categorize a result as 'global optimum' if each dimension differs by at most $0.0015 \cdot |\mathcal{I}|$ from the known position of the global minimum. This value guarantees that no other local optimum than the global optimum itself is detected as the global minimum even for the highly multi-modal functions.

For SCHWEFEL and ROSENBROCK, the value was set to $0.005 \cdot |\mathcal{I}|$ instead, since with the value above too many results were falsely classified 'O' (see below).

Local Optimum (L). Since the information about the positions of all local optima is generally unavailable, a result is classified as a 'local minimum' if it is not classified as the global optimum and the absolute value of the derivative of the function is ≤ 0.1 in each dimension. Tests showed that only the low-dimensional ($D \leq 3$) ROSENBROCK function has regions flat enough to lead to a wrong classification. Therefore, here the classification explicitly uses the fact that ROSENBROCK has only one local optimum for $D \leq 3$ ([17]).

Otherwise (O). The obtained solution is classified 'O' otherwise because it is still far away from the global and any local optimum.

This classification serves as a measure for the exploration capability of the swarm, i.e., the better the swarm explores, the more results should be classified as (G). Additionally to the classification, we collected for each fitness function f all fitness values of the results that were classified as global optimum and calculated their average in order to measure the quality of the exploitation on f. The obtained value will be referred to as *precision*.

4   Results on the Social-Only PSO Algorithm

We examined our results under two different aspects. First, we focused on the exploration behavior of the PSO and measured how frequently the obtained result could be classified as (G). Afterwards, we studied the exploitation capabilities by comparing how close the results that were categorized as global optimum came to the actual global minimum.

4.1   Impact of the Local Attractor on Exploration

We wanted to examine the influence of the local attractor on the capability of the PSO to converge towards the global optimum of our benchmark functions.

Table 1 shows the results for 50 runs with $D = 3$ and, for reasons to be stated later in this section, also for the 4-dimensional RASTRIGIN. As one can see, with

Table 1. Comparison of the classification results from the classical and the social-only PSO processing various 3-dimensional and a 4-dimensional function. For GRIEWANK, RASTRIGIN and SCHWEFEL, classical PSO shows a significantly better exploration.

Function	Classical PSO			Social-only PSO		
	G	L	O	G	L	O
ACKLEY	50	0	0	50	0	0
GRIEWANK	**25**	25	0	2	48	0
H. C. ELLIPTIC	50	0	0	50	0	0
RASTRIGIN (3-dim.)	**50**	0	0	28	22	0
ROSENBROCK	47	0	3	50	0	0
SCHWEFEL	**50**	0	0	36	3	11
SPHERE	50	0	0	50	0	0
RASTRIGIN (4-dim.)	**50**	0	0	10	40	0

respect to the behavior of the PSOs, two essentially different classes among the fitness functions can be distinguished.

Within the first group, consisting of ACKLEY, High Conditioned ELLIPTIC, ROSENBROCK and SPHERE, the global optimum was easily found. The social-only as well as the unmodified PSO algorithm brought good results, finding the global minimum in every or almost every run. Since the High Conditioned ELLIPTIC, the (3-dimensional) ROSENBROCK and the SPHERE function are unimodal, the importance of exploring the search space and therefore of the local attractor itself is comparatively small. Although the ACKLEY function is not unimodal, there are major differences in location and function value between the global optimum and the other local optima. Therefore, even the limited exploration capability of social-only PSO is still sufficient. Manual checks on the ROSENBROCK runs revealed that the results classified as 'O' usually were close to the bound for being classified as global optimum, but had a precision slightly too poor. Therefore, these results are not caused by a weakness in exploration but in exploitation.

In the second group, consisting of GRIEWANK, RASTRIGIN and SCHWEFEL, the outputs of social-only PSO were considerably worse. While the unmodified, i. e., classical PSO algorithm could still solve the optimization problems in most cases, the social-only algorithm often failed to find the global optimum. As a matter of fact, these functions all have a large number of local optima around the global optimum, some of them with values close to the global minimum. Therefore, exploring the search space is vital for finding the global optimum and without the local attractors, social-only PSO gets trapped into local optima more easily.

For an explanation of the much better success rate of unmodified PSO in finding the best among many similar local optima, consider a function with unique global optimum $\vec{x}_*$ and many local optima with function values close to $f(\vec{x}_*)$ around $\vec{x}_*$. This is the case, e. g., on the GRIEWANK function. Since the particles are uniformly distributed over the search space, there is a certain probability for the global attractor $\vec{p}_{\text{glob}}$ to be closer to a local optimum $\vec{x}_L$ than to $\vec{x}_*$. On the other hand, there is a good chance for some particle i to have at least its local attractor $\vec{p}_i$ close to $\vec{x}_*$. Figure 1 presents such a situation. While the probability for such a con-figuration to occur does not depend much on the use of the local attractor, we will see that the probability for the global attractor to enter the valley of the global optimum after the occurrence of such a situation indeed does. Let A_* denote the region around $\vec{x}_*$ consisting of all points better than $\vec{p}_{\text{glob}}$, and let A_L denote the region of all points around $\vec{x}_L$ better than $\vec{p}_i$. One can think of A_* as the region that after entering allows particle i

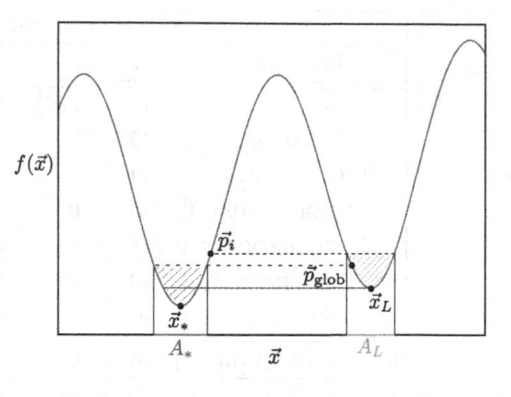

Fig. 1. Pathological situation of a particle with lo-cal attractor near the global optimum and global attractor near a non-global but local optimum; in order to convince the swarm for the global optimum, the particle must hit A_*.

to update the global attractor and therefore convince the whole swarm to start searching in this region. Similarly, A_L can be thought of as the region which upon entering makes particle i update its local attractor and consequently for-get about the valley of the global minimum. For social-only PSO, i. e., when the swarm is not influenced by the local attractor, for hitting A_* a particle needs in every dimension d potential $(\vec{\Psi})^d$ of order $|(\vec{x}_*)^d - (\vec{p}_i)^d|$ to overcome the distance between $\vec{p}_i$ and $\vec{x}_*$. Consequently, even with sufficiently high potential, the probability of hitting A_* is of order at most $\approx |A_*|/(|Q(\vec{x}_*, \vec{x}_L)|)$ where $Q(\vec{a}, \vec{b}) = [(\vec{a})^1, (\vec{b})^1] \times \ldots \times [(\vec{a})^D, (\vec{b})^D]$ is the smallest paraxial box containing $\vec{a}$ and $\vec{b}$. Under the assumption that meanwhile the global attractor is not altered substantially by the remaining swarm, the potential drops and after some iter-ations it falls below a certain bound. Then $\vec{x}_*$ is out of reach and particle i has no chance to lure the swarm towards $\vec{x}_*$ anymore.

On the other hand, if the local attractor is present, the chance of the particle hitting A_* is also of order $\approx |A_*|/(Q(\vec{x}_*, \vec{x}_L))$, but since the distance of both attractors maintains the necessary potential level and therefore prevents $\vec{x}_*$ from getting out of reach, the probability for hitting A_* does not vanish until particle i updates its local attractor by hitting A_L. The overall chance of hitting A_* before hitting A_L is of order $|A_*|/(|A_*| + |A_L|)$. For small values of $|A_*|$ and $|A_L|$, this success probability is considerably larger than $|A_*|/|Q(\vec{x}_*, \vec{x}_L)|$. Furthermore, even if the unmodified particle hits A_L before A_*, then in the next iteration after the respective local attractor update, particle i is likely to have still a sufficient potential to reach x_* and is therefore in a situation not worse than the situation of the social-only particle was already in the beginning.

4.2   Impact of the Local Attractor on Exploitation

After having analyzed how often the global optimum was found by the social-only PSO algorithm, we now focus on the precision of the results. We calculated the arithmetic mean of the function values of the PSOs' results subtracted by the known function value of the global minimum , taking only the runs into account which actually found the global optimum. The calculations were done using Java 1.7 and Python 2.7.3 which work with double precision on the chosen architecture. For our examination this was sufficiently precise. The results are shown in Table 2.

Since both PSO versions reached the limit of double precision when processing the 3-dimensional RASTRIGIN, we added the results of the 4-dimensional RASTRIGIN to make the differences in precision visible. One can see that the precision of the results the social-only PSO algorithm returned was often better and never extremely worse than the precision of the unmodified algorithm. It is noticeable that sometimes (GRIEWANK, ROSENBROCK, RASTRIGIN for at least 4 dimensions) the precision was even significantly better. Manual checks confirmed that this significance is not an artifact of the functions' shapes but that the obtained positions were significantly closer to the optimum. Since the presence of the local attractor improves exploration, it is natural to assume that it harms exploitation by a certain amount, so disabling the local attractors might result in a higher precision of the result.

Table 2. Comparison of the precision of the classical PSO and the social-only PSO processing various 3-dimensional and a 4-dimensional function. For GRIEWANK, ROSENBROCK and RASTRIGIN (4-dim.), classical PSO shows a significantly worse precision.

	Classical PSO	Social-only PSO
Function	Precision	Precision
ACKLEY	4.4409e-16	1.2967e-15
GRIEWANK	3.6068e-12	**0.0**
H. C. ELLIPTIC	4.0877e-37	8.2328e-40
RASTRIGIN (3-dim.)	0.0	0.0
ROSENBROCK	0.0011	**8.5184e-20**
SCHWEFEL	0.0776	0.8312
SPHERE	6.0717e-42	7.2010e-44
RASTRIGIN (4-dim.)	4.6544e-07	**0.0**

In order to further illustrate that the local attractor indeed improves exploration at the cost of exploitation and that there is indeed a measurable effect, we analyzed the potential of the swarm. If the potential of a swarm tends towards zero, the swarm converges ([16]). We measured the course of the potential for both algorithms over the iterations. The obtained measurements have in common that the swarms of the social-only PSO algorithm lost their potential faster. The difference to the unmodified swarm was sometimes very close, but in many cases clearly visible or even considerably big. For example, Figure 2 shows the course

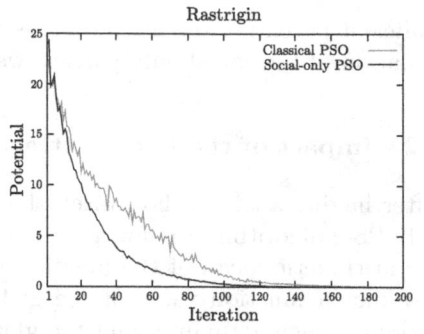

Fig. 2. Course of the potential of the first 200 iterations obtained from a sample run for both the classical and the social-only PSO, processing the 1-dimensional RASTRIGIN function.

of the potential obtained from a sample run of both classical and social-only PSO, processing 1-dimensional RASTRIGIN.

5   Concluding Remarks

From our experiments, it is clearly evident that the local attractor supports exploration and to a certain degree helps to avoid being trapped in a local optimum. The price of the local attractor is a sometimes reduced quality of the exploitation due to a slower convergence rate. For future work, one can form a hybrid PSO variant between the social-only PSO and the classical PSO. For one attempt of doing so, see the extended version of this paper (arXiv Report [10]), where we propose a PSO version that uses the local attractor during the first half of the iterations and sets b_{loc} to zero afterwards. Although this is just one first step, the experiments already indicate that in this way the exploitation can be significantly improved without worsening the exploration too much.

References

1. van den Bergh, F., Engelbrecht, A.P.: A new locally convergent particle swarm optimiser. In: Proc. IEEE Int. Conf. on Systems, Man and Cybernetics (SMC), vol. 3, pp. 94–99 (2002), doi:10.1109/ICSMC.2002.1176018
2. Clerc, M., Kennedy, J.: The particle swarm – explosion, stability, and convergence in a multidimensional complex space. IEEE Transactions on Evolutionary Computation 6, 58–73 (2002), doi:10.1109/4235.985692
3. Eberhart, R.C., Kennedy, J.: A new optimizer using particle swarm theory. In: Proc. 6th International Symposium on Micro Machine and Human Science, pp. 39–43 (1995), doi:10.1109/MHS.1995.494215
4. Gnezdilov, A., Wittmann, S., Helwig, S., Kókai, G.: Acceleration of a relative positioning framework. International Journal of Computational Intelligence Research 5, 130–140 (2009), doi:10.5019/j.ijcir.2009.176

5. Helwig, S.: Particle Swarms for Constrained Optimization. Ph.D. thesis, Department of Computer Science, University of Erlangen-Nuremberg, Germany (2010), urn:nbn:de:bvb:29-opus-19334
6. Jiang, M., Luo, Y.P., Yang, S.Y.: Particle swarm optimization – stochastic trajectory analysis and parameter selection. In: Chan, F.T.S., Tiwari, M.K. (eds.) Swarm Intelligence – Focus on Ant and Particle Swarm Optimization, pp. 179–198 (2007), http://www.intechopen.com/download/books/books_isbn/978-3-902613-09-7, corrected version of [7]
7. Jiang, M., Luo, Y.P., Yang, S.Y.: Stochastic convergence analysis and parameter selection of the standard particle swarm optimization algorithm. Information Processing Letters 102, 8–16 (2007), doi:10.1016/j.ipl.2006.10.005, corrected by [6]
8. Kennedy, J.: The Particle Swarm: Social Adaptation of Knowledge. In: Proc. IEEE International Conference on Evolutionary Computation (ICEC), pp. 303–308 (1997), doi:10.1109/ICEC.1997.592326
9. Kennedy, J., Eberhart, R.C.: Particle swarm optimization. In: Proc. IEEE International Conference on Neural Networks, vol. 4, pp. 1942–1948 (1995), doi:10.1109/ICNN.1995.488968
10. Lange, V., Schmitt, M., Wanka, R.: Towards a better understanding of the local attractor in particle swarm optimization: Speed and solution quality (2014),arXiv:1406.1691
11. Lehre, P.K., Witt, C.: Finite first hitting time versus stochastic convergence in particle swarm optimisation (2011), arXiv:1105.5540
12. Onwunalu, J.E., Durlofsky, L.J.: Application of a particle swarm optimization algorithm for determining optimum well location and type. Computational Geosciences 14, 183–198 (2010), doi:10.1007/s10596-009-9142-1
13. Panigrahi, B.K., Shi, Y., Lim, M.H. (eds.): Handbook of Swarm Intelligence — Concepts, Principles and Applications. Springer (2011), doi:10.1007/978-3-642-17390-5
14. Pedersen, M.E.H., Chipperfield, A.J.: Simplifying particle swarm optimization. Applied Soft Computing 10(2), 618–628 (2010), doi:10.1016/j.asoc.2009.08.029
15. Ramanathan, K., Periasamy, V.M., Pushpavanam, M., Natarajan, U.: Particle swarm optimisation of hardness in nickel diamond electro composites. Archives of Computational Materials Science and Surface Engineering 1, 232–236 (2009), http://archicmsse.org/vol09_4/0945.pdf
16. Schmitt, M., Wanka, R.: Particle swarm optimization almost surely finds local optima. In: Proc. 15th Genetic and Evolutionary Computation Conference (GECCO), pp. 1629–1636 (2013), doi:10.1145/2463372.2463563
17. Shang, Y.W., Qiu, Y.H.: A note on the extended Rosenbrock function. Evolutionary Computation 14(1), 119–126 (2006), doi:10.1162/106365606776022733
18. Suganthan, P.N., Hansen, N., Liang, J.J., Deb, K., Chen, Y.P., Auger, A., Tiwari, S.: Problem definitions and evaluation criteria for the CEC 2005 special session on real-parameter optimization. Tech. rep., KanGAL Report Number 2005005 (Kanpur Genetic Algorithms Laboratory, IIT Kanpur) (2005)
19. Wachowiak, M.P., Smolíková, R., Zheng, Y., Zurada, J.M., Elmaghraby, A.S.: An approach to multimodal biomedical image registration utilizing particle swarm optimization. IEEE Transactions on Evolutionary Computation 8, 289–301 (2004), doi:10.1109/TEVC.2004.826068
20. Zhang, W., Xie, X.F., Bi, D.C.: Handling boundary constraints for numerical optimization by particle swarm flying in periodic search space. In: Proc. IEEE Congress on Evolutionary Computation (CEC), vol. 2, pp. 2307–2311 (2004), doi:10.1109/CEC.2004.1331185

A Models@run.time Approach
for Multi-objective Self-optimizing Software

Sebastian Götz, Thomas Kühn, Christian Piechnick,
Georg Püschel, and Uwe Aßmann

Technische Universität Dresden, Software Technology Group
sebastian.goetz@acm.org,
{thomas.kuehn3,christian.piechnick,georg.pueschel,
uwe.assmann}@tu-dresden.de

Abstract. This paper presents an approach to operate multi-objective self-optimizing software systems based on the models@run.time paradigm. In contrast to existing approaches, which are usually specific to a single or selected set of objectives (e.g., performance and/or reliability), the presented approach is generic in that it allows the software architect to model the relevant concerns of interest to self-optimization. At runtime, these models are interpreted and used to generate optimization problems. To evaluate the applicability of the approach, a scalability analysis is provided, showing the approach's feasibility for at least two objectives.

1 Introduction

A central, required characteristic of future software systems is their ability to adjust themselves to changing environments. Notably, such adjustments fulfill a certain purpose: they reduce or eliminate the deviance of the system from it's desired state. Often, this desired state is an interpretation of *multiple goals* (i.e., objectives) in the context of the current system state. Hence, to compute the required adjustments to reconfigure the system to its desired state, multi-objective optimization (MOO) approaches are required.

Systems capable of reconfiguring themselves with the aim to be operate optimally with regard to specified goals are called self-optimizing systems [1], where the term *self* refers to the ability of the system to autonomously react to changes in the environment. The goals usually span various non-functional properties (NFPs) of the system. For example, performance, energy consumption, reliability and availability to name but a few. The need for MOO approaches arises when multiple, potentially competing, NFPs shall be optimized together.

Two general classes of MOO can be distinguished: a-priori and a-posteriori approaches [2]. The first type tries to unify all objectives into a single objective. Such approaches often use utility-theory, but have the problem that not all NFPs are comparable with each other and, thus, a unification of the objectives is semantically wrong [3]. Hence, a-posteriori approaches, which do not unify the objectives, but are know to be very time-consuming [2], are required.

In our previous work, we proposed [4] a model-driven approach for single-objective self-optimizing systems enabling the developer to model structural

A. Bouchachia (Ed.): ICAIS 2014, LNAI 8779, pp. 100–109, 2014.

and behavioral aspects of the system, and extract runtime information from the system into runtime models used to automatically generate optimization problems for standard problem solvers. The solution presented in this paper extends this approach, to allow for the operation of a-posteriori multi-objective self-optimizating systems.

This paper is structured as follows. The next section introduces a running example. Section 3 briefly outlines our previous work. Section 4 then describes our solution for the operation of multi-objective self-optimizing systems. The approach is evaluated in terms of its scalability in Section 5. Finally, Section 6 covers related work and Section 7 concludes the paper.

2 Running Example: Confidential Sorting

A confidential sort is to be performed whenever the list subject to sorting contains confidential data. This data, in consequence, has to be encrypted. A typical approach to encryption is the use of a pair of public and private keys (e.g., SHA-2 [5]). The bigger the keys used for encryption are, the more effort is required for an attacker to decrypt the data. But, the bigger the keys, the more time is required to encrypt the data. Typically, users intend to get their lists sorted as fast as possible, but encrypted as much as possible. Listing 1.1 shows such a user request for a list with 200.000 elements. The request is formulated against the structure model shown in Figure 1(b). The list, subject to sorting, is encrypted prior to sorting. This way the sort algorithm can be placed on any available machine, even if it is not considered safe (due to its encryption).

3 Single-objective Self-optimization

In previous work [4], we presented a component-based metamodel and quality contract language to be used by developers of self-optimizing software systems. Moreover, we proposed a model-driven approach [4] utilizing these models to automatically generate optimization problems and, thereby, overcome the limitations of related approaches. This section recapitulates the specifications for the single objective case, which serve as a base for the multi-objective case. Due

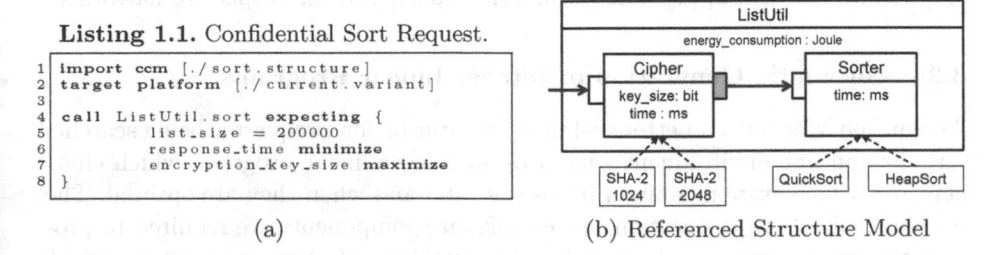

Listing 1.1. Confidential Sort Request.

```
1  import ccm [./sort.structure]
2  target platform [./current.variant]
3
4  call ListUtil.sort expecting {
5        list_size = 200000
6        response_time minimize
7        encryption_key_size maximize
8  }
```

(a)   (b) Referenced Structure Model

Fig. 1. Request and Model for the Confidential Sort Example

```
 1   contract SHA−2 implements Cypher.encrypt {
 2     mode secure {
 3       requires resource RAM { free_size min: 5 * message_size }
 4       requires software RandomGen { value_range min: 100 }
 5       provides key_size = 4096
 6       provides runtime max: f1(message_size)
 7     }
 8     mode fast {
 9       requires resource RAM { free_size min: 1 * message_size }
10       requires software RandomGen { value_range min: 25 }
11       provides key_size = 256
12       provides runtime max: f2(message_size)
13     }
14   }
```

Listing 1.2. An Example QCL Contract for an Encryption Implementation

to space limitations, we cannot fully recapitulate the approach, but focus on the specification of quality contracts and the generation of optimization problems.

3.1 The Quality Contract Language (QCL)

Implementations and devices can be characterized in terms of their behavior and dependencies to each other by contracts, which are a special type of Quality-of-Service contract [6] and are comprised of assumptions and guarantees on properties defined in structural models. Listing 1.2 depicts an example contract for an encryption implementation and illustrates the mentioned concepts.

QCL contracts define different modes, representing levels of satisfaction for users of the system. For example, a contract for an encryption implementation could define the modes *secure* and *fast*, representing a variant with large encryption key (4096 bit), which will take more time and memory compared to the second variant, which has a small encryption key (512 bit), but will be much faster. For the processing of highly confidential data the first mode will be prefered, whereas for less critical data the second mode is more likely to be prefered.

Each mode specifies a set of assumptions (**requires**). These assumptions are either tight to the properties of the implementation itself or to those of other system constituents. For example, an encryption implementation requires an implementation of a random number generator and has requirements on memory. In addition, each mode defines a set of guarantees for the properties of the respective implementation (**provides**). For example, the *maximum* **response time**, which is characterized as a function, which is replaced at runtime by an empirically derived, approximated function specific to the respective hardware.

3.2 Automatic Generation of Integer Linear Programs

At runtime, whenever a better system configuration for a request is being searched for, the runtime environment generates an integer linear program, which characterizes which system configurations are valid and when they are optimal. The problem solved is the question, *which* software components are required to process the user request and *which* implementations of them running on *which* resources ensure the non-functional requirements of the user best.

```
1  /* objective functions */
2  min:  25 x2 +  35 x3 + 180 x0 + 240 x1;  //response time
3  max:   0 x2 +   0 x3 + 512 x0 + 4096x1;  //encryption key size
4  /* architectural constraints */
5  x0 + x1  = 1;
6  x2 + x3  = 1;
7  /* Resource negotiation */
8  12 x3 + 22 x1 <= 84;
9  12 x2 + 22 x0 <= 48;
10 /* NFP negotiation */
11 97 x2 + 97 x3 >= 52 x0 + 52 x1;
12 /* binary constraint */
13 bin x2, x3, x0, x1;
```

Listing 1.3. Generated ILP for Confidential Sort Example.

Thus, the decisions to be made comprise the selection of implementations and their mapping to resources. Such a problem can be expressed as an integer linear program (ILP), which is comprised of a set of variables, an objective function and a set of constraints. As shown in our previous work, it suffices to encode all possible decisions as variables. For example, the Boolean variable b#cypher#sha2#server2 denotes the decision to run the SHA-2 implementation of the encryption component on a server called *server2*.

An example ILP for the running example (cf. Sect. 2) is shown in Listing 1.3. The variables x_0 and x_1 represent the decision for the SHA-2 algorithm with a 512 bit key or a 4096 bit key respectively. The variables x_2 and x_3 represent the decision for QuickSort or HeapSort. To keep the number of variables low, the example comprises only one server.

The first objective function describes the effect of each decision on the overall response time w.r.t. the current user request. It resamples the fact that QuickSort is faster than HeapSort and encryption with a 512 bit key is faster than with a 4096 bit key. The second objective function shows, explicitly, the effect of using a 1024 or a 2048 bit key and, by this, allows to consider the key size as separate dimension of the Pareto front.

The constraints of the generated ILP denote which combinations of decisions lead to a valid system configuration. There are three types of constraints:

1. Architectural constraints (cf. line 4&5): denote which components are required to serve the user request and the need to select at least one implementation of these components.
2. Negotiation of resources (cf. line 7&8): denote the impact of the decisions on resource properties, which are physically limited (e.g., maximum memory).
3. Negotiation of non-functional properties (cf. line 10): denote the interplay between guarantees and assumptions on NFPs as stated in QCL contracts by each decision.

Finally, the decision variables are constrained to be Boolean (cf. line 13).

In previous work, we showed the applicability of the approach to compute an optimal configuration for a single user objective only. In this paper, we investigate the case of multiple, potentially competing objectives.

4   Multi-objective Self-optimization

This section covers our approach to identify a set of Pareto-optimal system configurations using multiple objective integer linear programming (MOILP). This set of configurations is then presented to the user, who can select his preferred alternative. Pareto-optimality denotes that each configuration presented to the user is the best in all but one objective.

The approach to generate MOILP does not deviate from the approach to generate single-objective ILPs except for the generation of multiple objective functions, where each objective function is associated to a non-functional property defined by the user to be of his interest. Integer variables are required to cover clear yes/no decisions. In the following, we show how the resulting MOILP can be efficiently solved.

To determine a Pareto-optimal set of solutions for a MOILP, a variety of approaches have been developed in the past decades. An appropriate MOILP approach has to be able to scale and has to support multiple objectives of free form. We decided to apply the approach introduced by Klein and Hannan in 1982 [7], which fulfills these requirements [8]. As basis for explaining their approach, firstly 0-1 MOLIPs are defined as shown in Equation 1. C is a (p,n)-matrix covering p objective functions over n decision variables denoted by the vector x of size n. A is an (m,n)-matrix covering the left hand side of m constraints over n variables. The vector b of size m denotes the right hand side of these constraints.

$$min\{Cx : Ax \geq b, x \geq 0, x \in \mathbb{B}^n\}$$

In each iteration of the approach, a set of single objective ILPs is to be solved. The ILPs of iteration i are denoted by P_i. As a starting point P_0 is to be derived. Here one of the p objective functions is randomly selected denoted by $0 \leq s \leq p$. All other objective functions are omitted from P_0. This leads to a single-objective ILP, which can be handled by standard ILP solvers like LP Solve [9]. The solution of P_0 is the first solution being part of the Pareto front and used to compute the succeeding ILPs.

In general the construction of ILPs of P_i for $i > 0$ depends on the solutions found until solving the last ILP (i.e., P_{i-1}). The variable r denotes the number of solutions found until P_{i-1}. Klein and Hannan formalized the construction as follows:

$$min : z_s = c^s x$$

$$subject\ to : Ax \geq b, x \geq 0, x \in \mathbb{B}^n \quad and \quad \bigcap_{i=1}^{r} \bigcup_{k=1 \wedge k \neq s}^{p} c^k x \leq c^k y^i - f_k$$

Thus, all ILPs to be solved have a single objective function, namely, the objective function selected for P_0. The additional constraints added to the ILP depend on the number of solutions found until P_{i-1}, denoted by r, and the number of objective functions excluding objective function s selected in P_0. For each objective function, except for s, a disjunctive set of constraints is added. Additionally, for each found solution these disjunctive sets of constraints are conjunctivly added to the ILP. The constraint term $c^k x \leq c^k y^i - f_k$ describes that the kth objective function has to have a value lower or equal to the value of the kth objective function for solution y^i minus a constant f_k. If this constant is set to $f_k = 1$ the approach is guaranteed to provide the complete Pareto front [7, p. 380]. For $f_k > 1$ a subset of the Pareto front is determined.

A crucial detail of the approach is the use of the operators $\cup$ and $\cap$. Standard ILP solvers implicitly assume a conjunction over all constraints. Disjunction ($\cup$-operator) is not supported, but can be handled by solving multiple alternative ILPs instead. This practically leads to a combinatorial explosion of ILPs to be solved. As in Klein and Hannan's approach all disjunctions have the same size $(p - 1)$, the number of ILPs to be solved in P_i can be computed as r^{p-1}.

In summary, the basic principle of Klein and Hannan's approach is to successively exclude solutions by enriching an initial ILP with constraints. The original objective functions are used to iteratively restrict the feasible area of an initially selected single-objective ILP. In each iteration the solutions found are added to the Pareto front. The algorithm terminates when all ILPs of P_i are infeasible, i.e., no additional solutions are found. Applying this approach to compute an optimal system configuration for a given user request deviates from the approach for a single objective function only in the number of solutions presented to the user, who has to select the most suitable solution from the Pareto front.

5   Evaluation

This section evaluates the application of Klein and Hannan's approach to MOILP for the computation of an optimal system configuration.

5.1   Approach and Methodology

We randomly generated $C \times S$ pipe-and-filter systems capturing C component types to be mapped on S servers, where each component type has 2 implementations. Due to the combinatorial explosion of ILPs to be solved only 2×2 to 30×30 systems have been measured for systems with more than 2 objectives. The bi-objective case has been evaluated against systems up to 100×100. We refer the interested reader to [4] for the single objective case.

Measurements were taken for 841 systems with 3 and 4 objective functions to analyze the impact of a growing number of objectives. All of these measurements have been conducted on a DELL Alienware X51, Intel i7-2600, 8 GB RAM, 64bit Windows 7 with LP Solve 5.5.20. A notable fact about the special case of two objective functions is the lack of or-constraint-blocks in the generated ILPs of P_i where $i > 0$. This is because the number of constraints per or-block equals the number of objective functions minus one, i.e., one in the case of two objective functions. In consequence, there is no combinatorial explosion of ILPs to be solved. Instead, as many ILPs are to be solved as solutions are found (and a final ILP, which is infeasible).

As complex MOILPs can require several days to be solved, the measurements taken for MOILPs were limited to 2 minutes for practical reasons. Due to the combinatorial explosion of ILPs to be solved, MOILPs with more than 2 objective functions, a second reason for failing is to be considered: lack of memory. For all measurements 4 GB of main memory are reserved. But, as will be shown in the following, this does not suffice for MOILPs having a big Pareto front. Thus, a MOILP can fail by timeout or by running out of memory.

The generation time of MOILPs is similar to the single objective case [4], because the generation process is almost the same, except for the generation of multiple objective functions. Hence, we do not separately analyze the generation time, but focus on the overall runtime of the approach.

5.2   Results

Figure 2(a) shows the runtime for 2x2 to 100x100 systems with 2 objective functions. As can be seen, the number of servers has a stronger impact than the number of components. The runtime grows very fast per server (approximately 60 seconds already at 5 servers), but slower per additional component (below 1 second until 10 components). Only 27,12% of all MOILPs timed out (2658 of 9801). Notably, no bi-objective MOILP run out of memory. The mean runtime across all systems showed up to be at 36,54 s, the median runtime at 60,12 s only. The 3rd quantile is at 62,92s.

Two further properties are of interest to interpret the behavior of the MOILP solver: the number of ILPs generated for each MOILP and the size of their Pareto front. Figure 2(c) depicts the correlation between the number of components and servers to the size of the Pareto front. For the bi-objective case, the size of the Pareto front almost equals the number of solved ILPs.

Another insight from Figure 2(c) is the high number of solutions in the Pareto front for relatively small systems. For systems as small as 10x10 more than 50 solutions are part of the Pareto front. This poses a challenge to user interaction. The question is how to present this high amount of solutions to the user so he can make an educated decision, but this is out of this paper's scope.

An investigation of 3 objective MOILPs shows, as to expect, considerably worse performance. In each iteration an additional or-block of two constraints is added, leading to a quadratic increase in ILPs to be solved. With a mean runtime of 79,391 s and its third quantile at the timeout limit of 2 minutes its more than 4 times worse than the bi-objective measurements. In contrast to the bi-objective case many more MOILPs timed out and ran out of memory. In total 305 MOILPs (36,27%) timed out and 195 MOILPs (23,19%) ran out of memory, where both sets do not overlap. Hence, for 500 MOILPs (59.45%) no solution could be found. Interestingly, these ≈60% of failed MOILPs are not concentrated on bigger systems, but range from small to big systems as can be seen in Figure 2(b).

Moreover, Figure 2(b) shows that most MOILPs, which do not timeout or run out of memory are solved very fast as there are more points on the bottom plane than between the bottom and top plane. An investigation of the successful MOILPs

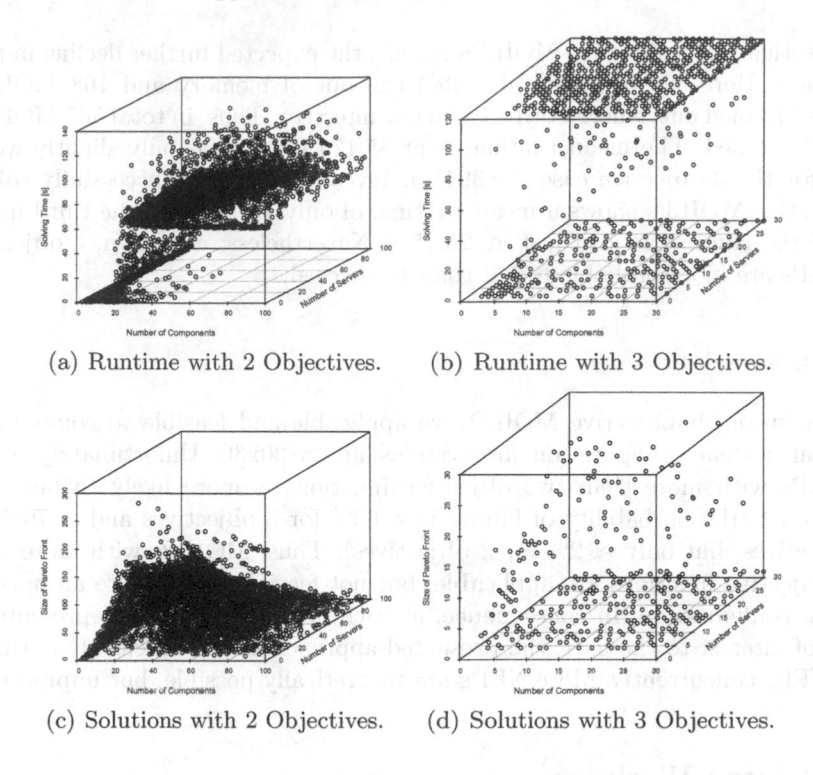

(a) Runtime with 2 Objectives.   (b) Runtime with 3 Objectives.

(c) Solutions with 2 Objectives.   (d) Solutions with 3 Objectives.

Fig. 2. Runtime of MOILP and size of Pareto Front

shows a mean runtime of 19,55 s (compared to 20,49 s in the bi-objective scenario) and a third quantile of just 8.3 s. Thus, if the MOILPs do not fail, they perform comparably good. Unfortunately, it is impossible to predict whether a MOILP will fail without solving it. Thus, the high probability of failure revealed in this analysis renders the approach infeasible for more than 2 objective functions.

The reason for MOILPs running out of memory is the combinatorial explosion of ILPs to be solved. Notably, the size of the Pareto fronts in the 3-objective case is very small as Figure 2(d) depicts. It comprises only up to 30 solutions. The number of ILPs to be solved is much higher, but most ILPs are infeasible. Small systems can have comparably large Pareto fronts (e.g., a generated 3x4 system had a Pareto front with 16 solutions) and large systems can have small Pareto fronts (e.g., a generated 29x24 system had a Pareto front with 4 solutions only). An interesting contrast is the larger size of Pareto fronts in the 2-objective case ($\approx$200) compared to the 3-objective case ($\approx$30). A possible explanation is that the more objective functions exist, the constraint qualifying a solution as being non-dominated (i.e., being part of the Pareto front) is stressed, as such a solution has to be best in all but one objective. The maximum number of solutions in a Pareto front corresponds to the largest objective function (i.e., the objective function comprising the most different values).

Investigating 4-objective MOILPs reveals the expected further decline in performance. Here 399 MOILPs (47,44%) run out of memory and 168 MOILPs (19,98%) timed out, where both sets do not intersect. Thus, in total 567 MOILPs (67,42%) failed. The mean runtime is at 85,174 s, which is only slightly worse than for the 3-objective case (79,391 s). Investigating only successfully solved 4-objective MOILPs shows a mean runtime of only 13,11 s and the third quantile of the runtime is also just at 25,75 s. Nevertheless, as shown, 4-objective MOILPs are more probable to fail than to succeed.

5.3 Discussion

In conclusion, bi-objective MOILP are applicable and feasible to compute an optimal system configuration for systems up to 30x30. Unfortunately, using MOILPs with more than two objective functions is more likely to fail than to succeed (the probability of failing is $\approx$ 60% for 3 objectives and $\approx$ 70% for 4 objectives, but only $\approx$ 2% for 2 objectives). Thus, MOILPs with more than two objective functions are applicable, but not feasible to compute an optimal system configuration. In consequence, as each objective function represents an NFP of interest to the user, the presented approach allows to feasibly optimize two NFPs concurrently. More NFPs are theoretically possible, but impractical.

6 Related Work

In [10], de Roo et al. introduce an architectural style (MO2) for software systems as an extension to the component and connector style [11]. According to MO2, the basic elements constituting software are adaptable components (AC), multi-objective optimization components (MOO-C) and transformation components (TC). These three types of components are connected by relations with each other. In comparison to the expressiveness of CCM and QCL, the MO2 style has three major drawbacks: (1) global optimization is hard to express, (2) no means to express contextual dependencies exist and (3) no distinction between software and hardware exists.

In [12], Calinescu et al. present a generic architecture for adaptive service-based systems (SBS). The central constituents of the approach are formal specifications of QoS requirements including the specification of dependencies between QoS requirements, and reasoning techniques, based on high-level, user-specified goals and multi-objective utility functions. In contrast to the approach presented in this paper, the approach by Calinescu et al. applies a-priori multi-objective optimization by combining the different objectives as a weighted sum.

The aggregation of individual objective functions to apply single objective optimization methods has been used in many other approaches, too (e.g., in [13, 14]). Nevertheless, as pointed out by Poladian et al. [3], NFPs with different characteristics cannot be unified. In consequence, a-posteriori approaches to multi-objective optimization as presented in this paper are required.

7   Conclusion

In this paper, an a posteriori approach to multi-objective optimization to determine an optimal system configuration has been presented. We showed how to apply and evaluated Klein and Hannan's approach [7] for this purpose. The evaluation showed the general applicability, but revealed the feasibility for the bi-objective case only. Notably, this assessment is based on the used measurement environment. More powerful resources could render 3- and 4-objective MOILPs feasible in the future. In future work, an investigation of when a subset of all objective functions can be unified should be conducted.

References

[1] Salehie, M., Tahvildari, L.: Self-adaptive software: Landscape and research challenges. ACM TAAS 4, 14:1–14:42 (2009)

[2] Marler, R., Arora, J.: Survey of multi-objective optimization methods for engineering. Structural and Multidisciplinary Optimization 26(6), 369–395 (2004)

[3] Poladian, V., Butler, S., Shaw, M., Garlan, D.: Time is not money: The case for multi-dimensional accounting in value-based software engineering. In: Proceedings of EDSER-5 (2003)

[4] Götz, S., Wilke, C., Richly, S., Püschel, G., Assmann, U.: Model-driven self-optimization using integer linear programming and pseudo-boolean optimization. In: Proceedings of ADAPTIVE, pp. 55–64. XPS Press (2013)

[5] Eastlake, D., Hansen, T.: RFC 6234: US Secure Hash Algorithms (SHA and SHA-based HMAC and HKDF), IETF Std. (2011)

[6] Beugnard, A., Jézéquel, J.-M., Plouzeau, N.: Contract aware components, 10 years after. Proceedings of Theoretical Computer Science 37 (2010)

[7] Klein, D., Hannan, E.: An algorithm for the multiple objective integer linear programming problem. European Journal of Operational Research 9(4), 378–385 (1982)

[8] Rasmussen, L.M.: Zero-one programming with multiple criteria. European Journal of Operational Research 26, 83–95 (1986)

[9] Eikland, K., Notebaert, P.: LP Solve 5.5 reference guide, http://lpsolve.sourceforge.net/5.5/ (access on November 26, 2012)

[10] de Roo, A., Sözer, H., Aksit, M.: An architectural style for optimizing system qualities in adaptive embedded systems using multi-objective optimization. In: Proceedings of WICSA/ECSA, pp. 349–352. IEEE (2009)

[11] Clements, P., Garlan, D., Bass, L., Stafford, J., Nord, R., Ivers, J., Little, R.: Documenting Software Architectures: Views and Beyond. Pearson (2002)

[12] Calinescu, R., Grunske, L., Kwiatkowska, M., Mirandola, R., Tamburrelli, G.: Dynamic QoS Management and Optimization in Service-Based Systems. IEEE Transactions on Software Engineering 37(3), 387–409 (2011)

[13] Bratskas, P., Paspallis, N., Kakousis, K., Papadopoulos, G.A.: Applying utility functions to adaptation planning for home automation applications. In: Information Systems Development, pp. 529–537. Springer (2010)

[14] Zeller, M., Prehofer, C., Weiss, G., Eilers, D., Knorr, R.: Towards self-adaptation in real-time, networked systems: Efficient solving of system constraints for automotive embedded systems. In: Proceedings of SASO, pp. 79–88. IEEE (2011)

Reference Architecture for Self-adaptive Management in Wireless Sensor Networks

Jesús M.T. Portocarrero[1], Flavia C. Delicato[1], Paulo F. Pires[1], and Thais V. Batista[2]

[1] PPGI-iNCE/DCC-IM/Federal University of Rio de Janeiro, Rio de Janeiro, Brazil
{jesus140,fdelicato,paulo.f.pires}@gmail.com
[2] DIMAp, Federal University of Rio Grande do Norte, Natal, Brazil
thaisbatista@gmail.com

Abstract. Self-adaptive component-based architectures facilitate the building of systems able of dynamically adapting to varying execution contexts. Such a dynamic adaptation is particularly relevant in the domain of wireless sensor networks (WSNs), where numerous and unexpected changes of the execution context prevail. In this paper, we introduce a reference architecture for WSNs in order to contribute to middleware development for enabling self-adaptive behavior in service-oriented WSNs. This reference architecture follows the autonomic computing model MAPE-K, for making decisions aiming to attend self-adaptive WSN requirements. At the end of this paper, we present a case study to explain how instantiate our reference architecture in order to create a specific concrete middleware for WSN.

Keywords: Autonomic computing, sensor network, reference architecture.

1 Introduction

Wireless sensor networks (WSN) consist of networks composed of devices equipped with sensing, processing, storage, and wireless communication capabilities. Each node of the network can have several sensing unit, which is able to perform measurements of physical variables. The nodes in a WSN have limited computing resources, and are usually powered by batteries; thus energy saving is a key issue in these networks in order to prolong their operational lifetime. WSN nodes operate collaboratively, extracting environmental data, performing same simple processing and transmitting them to one or more exit points of the network called sink nodes, to be analyzed and further processed.

There is currently a wide range of applications for WSN, ranging from environmental monitoring to structural damage detection. The first WSN applications had simple requirements that did not demand complex software infrastructures. Typically WSN were designed to attend requirements of a unique target application. However, the rapid evolution in this area and the increasing of complexity of sensors and applications involved the need of specific middleware platforms for these networks. Furthermore, typically WSN are used in highly dynamic and hostile environments, without human participation, and therefore, they should have an autonomous behavior, able to be fault-tolerant coverage and connectivity. Sensor nodes must be smart to recover

A. Bouchachia (Ed.): ICAIS 2014, LNAI 8779, pp. 110–120, 2014.

autonomously from failures with minimal human intervention; in other words, WSN should be able to self-manage and to adapt itself to the context dynamically.

According to [1], autonomic computing, also known as self-adaptive computing, is a capacity of an infrastructure for adapting itself according to policies and business goals. Autonomic computing just tries to help IT professionals to focus in higher value tasks, turning technological work more intelligent, with business rules oriented to self-management. These rules also known as self-* properties are: (i) Self-Configuration, it is the ability to adapt itself to the environment changing according to high-level policies, aligned with business goals and defined by system administrators; (ii) Self-Healing, it is the ability to recover after a system disturbance and to minimize interruptions to maintain the software available for the user, even in the presence of individual failure of components; (iii) Self-Optimization, it is the system ability to improve its operation continuously and (iv) Self-Protection, it is the ability to predict, detect, recognize and protect from malicious attacks and unplanned cascade failures.

A highlight approach to develop autonomic systems is the architecture to autonomic computing proposed by IBM [2] that defines an abstract framework for self-managing IT systems. In this framework an autonomic system is a collection of autonomic elements. Each element consists of an autonomic manager and a managed resource. In the context of WSN, an autonomic manager can be a middleware system and the own sensor network represents the managed resource. The autonomic manager allows adaptation through four activities: monitoring, analyzing, planning and executing, with support from a knowledge base. In monitoring activity, elements collect relevant data via sensors to reflect the current state of the system – the managed resource (and thus, grant it context awareness). In analyzing activity, the collected data are analyzed in search of symptoms relating the current and desired behavior. The planning activity decides whether is necessary to adapt the system to attend the goals defined previously. In execution activity are instrumented the desired adaptation acts by actuators or effectors. In order to implement these activities to allow self-adaptation of software feedback loops are required, with explicit functional elements and interactions between them for managing the dynamic adaptation. These elements are known as MAPE-K model (Monitor, Analyze, Plan, Execute and Knowledge Base). Feedback control loops are considered a key issue in pursuing self-adaption for any system, because they support the four above-mentioned activities. They play an integral role in adaptation decisions. Thus, key decisions about a self-adaptive system's control depend on the structure of the system and the complexity of the adaptation goals. Control loops can be composed in series, parallel, multi-level (hierarchical), nested, or independent patterns. We refer the interested readers to [3] which have further discussed the choices and impact of control loops on the design of self-adaptive systems. In this context, Autonomic Computing is presented as an interesting option to meet basic requirements in WSN design. Thus, autonomic computing principles can be applied to WSN in order to optimize network resources, facilitate their operations and achieve desired functionality in the wide field of sensing-based applications and providing conditions for this type of network manage itself without involve human operators. So, a WSN becomes an autonomous WSN. The MAPE-K model described above provides conceptual guidelines about the autonomic systems conception; in practice, this information model needs to be mapped to an implementable architecture for managing and control of autonomic WSNs.

Hence, this work proposes a middleware reference architecture for self-adaptive management of WSN. Middleware for WSN [4] assists the development of WSN applications, providing services and abstractions that hide details about underlying hardware devices and low-level software mechanisms. Reference architectures are created based on reference models and architectural patterns [5]. Our reference architecture adopts the MAPE-K model and a component-based and service-oriented approach. The main purpose of a reference architecture is to facilitate and guide [6] (i) the design of concrete architectures for new systems; (ii) the extensions of systems of neighbor domains of a reference architecture (iii) the evolution of systems that were derived from the reference architecture and (iv) the improvement in the standardization and interoperability of different systems. These play a dual role in relation to specific software architectures, the first role generalizes and extracts common functions and configurations, and the second role provides a base for instantiating target systems. In other words, reference architectures can be seen as a repository of a given knowledge area, contributing towards software development, since the reuse of knowledge and improvements of productivity are promoted. Thus, the proposed middleware reference architecture aims to satisfy this dual role in WSN domain. This middleware reference architecture has been designed applying a service-based approach [7], in which the WSN is seen as a service provider for user applications. The service provided by the WSN is data collection and delivery. The services provided by the middleware are the interpretation of the application requirements and the selection of the best initial network configuration and network reconfiguration based on those requirements.

The rest of the paper is organized as follows: Section 2 introduces the self-adaptive WSN requirements addressed in the work. Section 3 details the proposed approach. An instance of our reference architecture is described and analyzed in Section 4. Section 5 draws conclusions and related work.

2   Self-adaptive WSN Requirements

Considering WSN singularities, especially with regard to resource constraints, there are some requirements of design in WSN applications that also must be considered in the middleware design for WSN:

— **Hardware resources:** the advent in microelectronics technology made it possible to design miniaturized devices on the order of one cubic centimeter. These tiny devices could be deployed in hundred or even thousands in harsh and hostile environments, where in some situations a physical contact to maintain or replace these devices is impossible and wireless media is the only way for remote accessibility.
— **Scalability and dynamic network topology:** the network topology is subject to frequent changes due to diverse factors as devices failures, mobile obstacles, mobility and interferences. If an application grows, the network should be flexible enough to include other nodes anytime without impacting network performance. A WSN middleware should support mechanisms for fault tolerance and sensor nodes self-maintenance. In order to attend these requirements, **Topology Control** and **Fault Tolerance** mechanisms are required.

— **Dynamic network organization:** Unlike traditional networks, sensor networks must deal with resources that are dynamic, such as energy, bandwidth, and processing power. An important issue is to support applications in the efficient design of routing protocols and providing ad hoc network resource discovery, because knowledge of the networks is essential for it to operate properly.

— **Application knowledge:** An autonomic middleware for WSN must include mechanisms for injecting application knowledge of WSN infrastructure. This allows mapping the application requirements with the network parameters, and adjusts the process of network monitoring.

— **Focused on data:** WSN applications generally are not interested in node identity, but the data it produces, especially when the same types of nodes are deployed to produce the same type of data. A WSN middleware should support the centrality of data, providing mechanisms for routing and centralized query inside the network. Mechanisms for **Sensing and Data Delivery** are appropriate.

— **Quality of service (QoS):** Traditional networks only move data from one place to another, however, nodes in WSN work collaboratively to move data, monitor and control an environment. For this type of networks, data confidence determines that an event that should be detected was in fact detected.

3   Reference Architecture for Self-adaptive Management of WSN

This Section details the proposed approach. First is presented the architectural styles and design patterns used in the reference architecture designing process and after that the components of the architecture are detailed. We consider the interactions among the different activities of control loops realized by the MAPE-K components.

3.1   Architectural Styles and Design Patterns

Software architectures is almost never limited to a single architectural style, is often a combination of architectural styles that make up the complete software. To built our reference architecture we used combinations of the following architectural styles.

— **Layer Architectural Style:** Focuses on the grouping of related functionality within an application into distinct layers that is stacked vertically on top each other. The main benefits are abstraction, isolation, manageability, performance, reusability and testability. Our reference architecture contains three 3 layers (Figure 1a): Sensor MAPE-K Layer (SML), Network MAPE-K Layer (NML) and Goal Management Layer (GML). SML concerns the autonomic management inside sensor devices; NML concerns the autonomic management in the whole network and GML aims to set adaptation policies used by underlying layers in order to perform adaptations. Also, this layer allows to get the current network status. At this level of abstraction the NML acts as the autonomic a manager and the SML acts as a managed resource. The communication between GML and NML is based on SOA services, and the communication between NML and SML uses the Message Bus Architectural Style. Here, the communication is based on messages that use known schemas.

— **Component-based and Service-Oriented Architectural Style.** Component architectural style focuses on the decomposition of the design into individual functional
or logical components that expose well-defined communication interfaces containing methods, events, and properties. The main benefits of this approach are: easy of
deployment, reduced cost, easy to development, reusable and mitigation of technical complexity. Service-oriented architectural style enables application functionality to be provided as a set of service. At the component level we applied the
pattern proposed by [8] that describes the structure of service components for using
in self-adaptive systems. The interfaces are (see Figure 1b): Input, used to receive
information; Output, used to send information; Sensor, that makes the component
able to achieve information from the external; Effector, that makes the component
be able to manage the external; Emitter, used to emit status information to an external manager.

— **Decorator Pattern.** For the general implementation of the components we adopted
the design pattern Decorator that allows behavior to be added to an individual object, either statically or dynamically, without affecting the behavior of other objects
from the same class. This pattern, depicted in Figure 1c, is based on three types of
entities: (i) Interfaces that define services provided by components, (ii) Abstract
classes with the definition of basic methods, services and references to other components, and (iii) Implementation classes that define the specific required behavior.

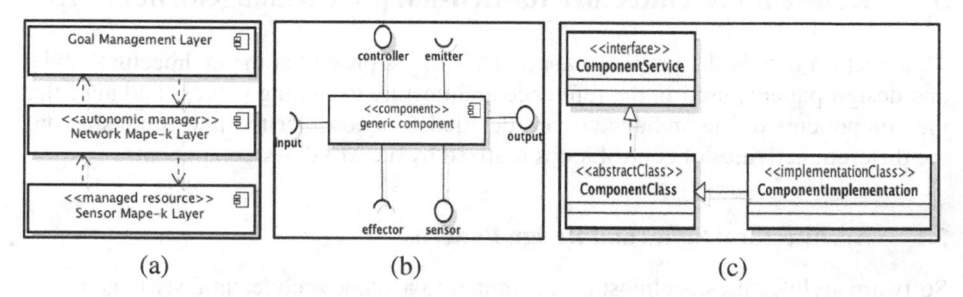

Fig. 1. (a) Layers of Reference Architecture (b) Structure of service components (c) General
implementation of components

3.2   Reference Architecture Components

Our reference architecture assumes a network as a set of heterogeneous nodes (node
manager and managed nodes) and sink nodes. The sink node acts as the gateway con-
necting WSN nodes and external networks and applications. Node manager acts as
autonomic managers of managed nodes; this type of nodes manages a group of nodes
organized in clusters. Node managers are cluster heads of clusters. On the other hand,
Managed nodes receive adaptation messages from Node managers.

The overall system is controlled by a hierarchical control structure where complete
MAPE-K loops are present at all architecture layers of the hierarchy. MAPE-K loops
at different levels interact with each other by exchanging information. The MAPE-K
loop at a given level may pass to the level above information it has collected, possibly
filtered or aggregated, together with information about locally planned actions, and
may issue to the level below directives about adaptation plans that should be refined

into corresponding actions. Our proposed architecture depicted in Figure 2, contains three levels of layers following the architectural style presented in Section 3.1.

The SML allows adapting a node configuration according to nodes context information and adaptation policies. At this point, our reference architecture considers as context information: battery level of sensor nodes, data delivery model/send rate of sensing data, state of nodes (active/inactive/idle), ID of nodes, type of node (node manager/managed node) function (routing/sensing/storing), power of signal, localization. Node managers may create new configurations for managed nodes localized inside the cluster. Each node manager is responsible for managing its own cluster. In order to determine all adaptation actions needed to reconfigure managed nodes of a cluster, a node manager receives continuously context information from its managed nodes and a MAPE-K process is performed to verify the need of an adaptation, if needed, a node configuration message is created. A node configuration message contains information able to modify the topology of the cluster (activating and deactivating managed nodes), to adjust tasks performed by cluster members (such as, data delivery model) and node functions (routing, sensing storing).

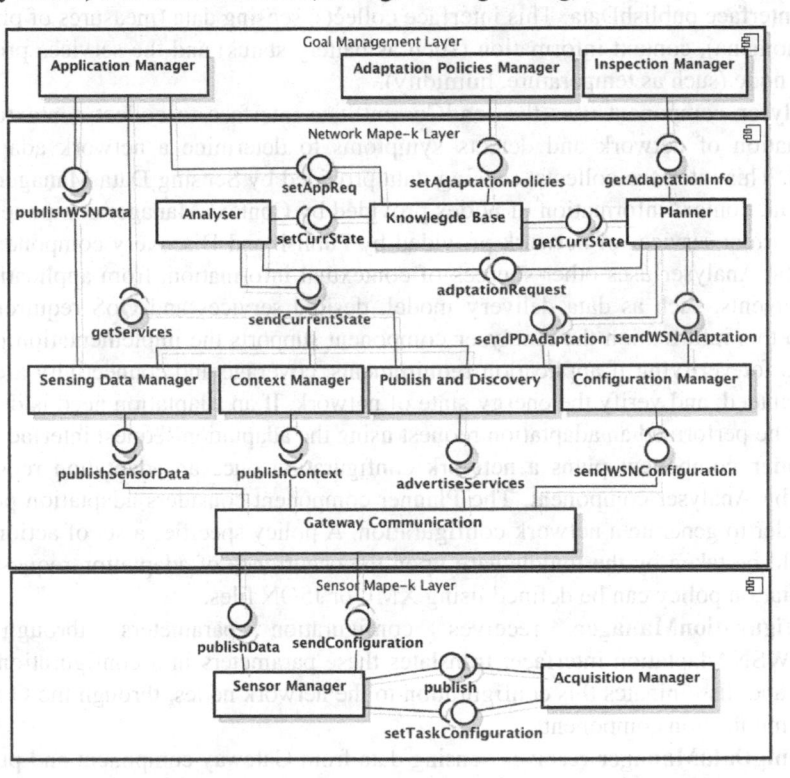

Fig. 2. Reference architecture for self-adaptive management of WSN

In addition, this layer is able to receive a cluster configuration message sent by NML. This message contains a set of task to be executed by sensor nodes and the adaptation policies used by the underlying layer in order to support adaptation decisions. SML consists in two service components: SensorManager and AcquisitionManager. All components of our architecture follow the pattern for autonomic computing components proposed by [8], presented in Section 3.1.

- **SensorManager** component manages the nodes behavior and determines all adaptation actions needed to reconfigure: (i) a cluster, if the node is configured as a manager, (ii) itself, if the node is configured as a managed node. This component is responsible for executing the MAPE-K process.
- **AcquisitionManager** component collects measures of physical phenomena monitored by sensors and executes the data delivery. If an adaptation request defines changes in the data delivery model, this component will be notified through the interface called setTaskConfiguration.

The NML performs adaptation actions to the network configuration. Thus, the contextual information used for this activity is provided by whole network. This layer contains service components that consists in:

- **GatewayCommunication**: This component provides to Analyser component, contextual information collected through the SML. This information is collected using the interface publishData. This interface collects: sensing data (measures of physical phenomena), context information (such as battery status) and the services provided by a node (such as temperature, humidity).
- **Analyser** component uses the sendCurrentState interface to collect contextual information of network and detects symptoms to determine a network adaptation need. This interface collects: sensing data provided by Sensing Data Manager component, context information of nodes provided by Context Manager component and the current services of network provided by Publish and Discovery component. Also, the Analyser uses other sources of contextual information, from application requirements, such as data delivery model, desired services and QoS requirements. With this information the Analyser component supports the implementation of methods for verifying if application requirements, coverage and connectivity are been guaranteed, and verify the energy state of network. If an adaptation need is detected must be performed an adaptation request using the adaptationRequest interface.
- **Planner** component plans a network configuration once an adaptation request is sent by Analyser component. The Planner component considers adaptation policies in order to generate a network configuration. A policy specifies a set of actions that should be taken by the middleware upon the occurrence of adaptation requests. An adaptation policy can be defined using XML or JSON files.
- **ConfigurationManager** receives configuration parameters through the sendWSNAdaptation interface, translates these parameters in a configuration message and disseminates this configuration to the network nodes, through the Gateway Communication component.
- **SensingDataManager** receives sensing data from Gateway component and publishes these data to application monitor component. Also, this component publishes the sensing data to Analyser component in order to analyze the context of the network.
- **ContextManager** receives sensor context information from Gateway Monitor and publishes this information to Analyser component.

- **PublishandDiscovery**, receives an advertise of service from Gateway Monitor, provided by sensor nodes. This data is published to Application Monitor and Analyser component.
- **KnowlodgeBase** store all context information and support the MAPE-K process.

The proposed reference architecture is based on self-adaptation principles and in order to perform this autonomic behavior a minimal human intervention is required. The components that allow human interaction to define the policies and configurations of network adaptation mechanisms are in the GML and its components are ApplicationManager, AdaptationPoliciesManger and Inspection Manager.

- **ApplicationManager** component is used to create applications, present to the end-user network provided services and monitoring sensing data.
- **AdaptationPoliciesManager** is used to define adaptation policies. This component uses the setAdaptationPolicies interface to offer these policies to the Network MAPE-K layer.
- **Inspection Manager** is used to inspect adaptation information of middleware that is accessible to external environment.

4   Case Study

In this section we defined a case study in order to instantiate a concrete architecture derived from our reference architecture. The concrete architecture consists in the definition of a specific WSN middleware to perform self-adaptation of network configuration in order to preserve energy consumption of the network. Energy management was the main adaptation requirement of this concrete middleware whereas WSN nodes have limited computing resources, thus energy saving is a key issue in these networks in order to prolong their operational lifetime. For such, this energy-aware middleware must guarantee: (i) application requirements (ii) the network has sufficient residual energy to attend all running applications, (iii) each sensor node becomes active whether it has residual energy to guarantee its work until the end of task allocated to it, and (iv) the network must be fully connected in terms of radio communication. Table 1 shows a mapping between the reference architecture layers and the case study requirements and depicts activities that must be executed in every feedback cycle. The NML and the GML of the concrete architecture were implemented in Java programming language. The SML was implemented in NesC (network embedded systems C) programming language, an extension of C programming language [9]. This layer was deployed in MicaZ sensor platform, which runs on TinyOS operating system.

Figure 3 shows the NML class diagram. Each component was implemented following the general structure of components (Decorator pattern). It is important to note that these abstract classes are connected to other service interfaces. This approach allows to clarify the component relationship and to define the behavior of components. Thus, we can see a clear and complete separation among mechanisms that handle adaptation issues of the reference architecture and the specificity of the instantiated middleware. In this case, seven implementation classes (gray classes) extend our reference architecture (white classes) in order to create the specific energy-aware middleware detailed in this case study: GatewayImpl, AnalyserImpl, PlannerImpl, ConfigurationImpl and

GatewayExecutorImpl. SML, implemented on MicaZ/TinyOS platform, publish context messages with residual energy information to the GatewayMonitor class, in order to process context message and select a list of best nodes.

Table 1. Specific actions of every concrete architecture layer

MAPE-K Components	SML	NML
Monitor tasks	-To monitor residual energy of nodes	-To monitor data delivery rate and residual energy -To monitor state of nodes
Analyzer tasks	-Residual energy must last by the allocated task time.	-Residual energy must last by runtime application time. -Network fully connected, coverage redundancy
Planner tasks	-When an undesirable energy level is detected: send an alert message, reduce data delivery interval.	-When an undesirable energy level is detected: reduce the percentage of active nodes, remove node redundancy. -When an undesirable state linked to QoS is detected: increase the percentage of active nodes, increase node redundancy.
Executor tasks	-Update the data delivery interval -Node only with router/sensing functionalities, Turn off the node.	-Translate the adaptation plan in a readable format by the MicaZ/TinyOS platform, and disseminate the new network configuration.

Thus, the GatewayImpl class contains specific methods to communicate the SML with the NML, receive these TinyOS context messages and translate them in Java objects. AnalyzerImpl and PlannerImpl class contains methods to manage the requirements of the concrete middleware, detailed in Table 1, and adjust choose which nodes are able, in terms of energy, to publish services and attend application requirements.

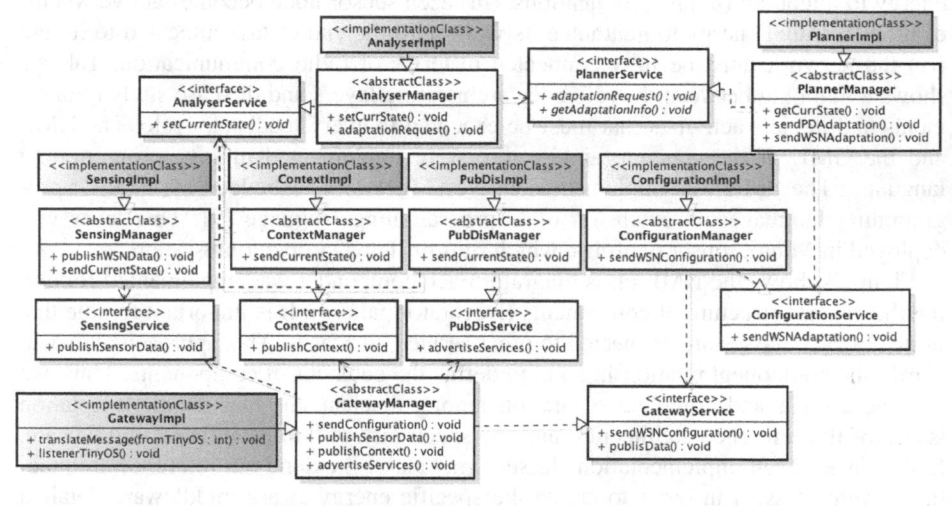

Fig. 3. Network MAPE-K Layer Instance

5   Final Remarks and Related Work

In this paper was proposed a reference architecture for self-adaptive service-oriented WSN in order to facilitate the building of middlewares capable of dynamically adapting to varying execution context. This reference architecture follows an autonomic computing model for making decisions aiming to attend self-adaptive WSN requirements.

Our reference architecture consists in two levels of autonomic management, one level of management inside sensor devices and the second level of management considers whole network. Both of them are based in the autonomic computing model MAPE-K. A case study was described to instantiate our proposed reference architecture in a specific energy-aware middleware, and showed how it supports designers of WSN middleware. In the current literature we found four different paradigms that allow building middleware systems for self-adaptive WSNs, namely component-based [10], service-oriented [11], multi-agent [12] and Software Product Line [13]. Our reference architecture adopts a component-based and service-oriented approach specific for self-adaptive WSNs.

Acknowledgments. This work is partially supported by FAPERJ, CNPq and CAPES.

References

1. Salehie, M., Tahvildari, L.: Self-adaptive software: Landscape and research challenges. ACM Trans. Auton. Adapt. Syst. 4(2), 1–42 (2009)
2. IBM: An Architectural blueprint for autonomic computing, Autonomic Computing (2005)
3. Brun, Y., et al.: Engineering Self-Adaptive Systems through Feedback Loops. In: Cheng, B.H.C., de Lemos, R., Giese, H., Inverardi, P., Magee, J. (eds.) Self-Adaptive Systems. LNCS, vol. 5525, pp. 48–70. Springer, Heidelberg (2009)
4. Wang, M., Cao, J., Li, J., et al.: Middleware for wireless sensor networks: A survey. Journal of Computer Science and Technology 23(3), 305–326 (2008)
5. Angelov, S., Grefen, P., Greefhorst, D.: A framework for analysis and design of software reference architectures. Information and Software Technology 54(4), 417–431 (2012)
6. Nakagawa, E.Y., Oquendo, F., Becker, M.: RAModel: A reference model of reference architectures. In: ECSA/WICSA 2012, Helsinki, Finland, pp. 297–301 (2012)
7. Delicato, F.C., Pires, P.F., Rezende, J., Pirmez, L.: Service Oriented Middleware for Wireless Sensor Networks. In: Editor (Ed.)^(Eds.): Book Service Oriented Middleware for Wireless Sensor Networks (2004)
8. Puviani, M., Cabri, G., Zambonelli, F.: A taxonomy of architectural patterns for self-adaptive systems. In: Proceedings of the International C* Conference on Computer Science and Software Engineering (C3S2E 2013), pp. 77–85. ACM, New York (2013)
9. nesC: A Programming Language for Deeply Networked Systems, http://nescc.sourceforge.net/ (last access: April 2014)

10. Conan, D., Rouvoy, R., Seinturier, L.: Scalable processing of context information with COSMOS. In: Indulska, J., Raymond, K. (eds.) DAIS 2007. LNCS, vol. 4531, pp. 210–224. Springer, Heidelberg (2007)
11. Ruiz, L.B., Nogueira, J.M.S., Loureiro, A.A.F.: MANNA: A Management Architecture for Wireless Sensor Network. IEEE Commun Mag. 41(2), 116–125 (2003)
12. Fok, C.-L., Roman, G.-C., Lu, C.: Agilla: A mobile agent middleware for self-adaptive wireless sensor networks. TAAS 4(3) (2009)
13. Gamez, N., Fuentes, L., Araguez, M.: Autonomic computing driven by feature models and architecture in FamiWare. Springer (2011)

Monitoring of Quality of Service in Dynamically Adaptive Systems

Sihem Loukil[1], Slim Kallel[1], Ismael Bouassida Rodriguez[2,3],
and Mohamed Jmaiel[1]

[1] ReDCAD Laboratory, University of Sfax, Tunisia
[2] CNRS, LAAS, 7 avenue du colonel Roche, F-31400 Toulouse, France
[3] Univ de Toulouse, LAAS, F-31400 Toulouse, France
sihem.loukil@redcad.org

Abstract. Dynamic reconfiguration has been widely recognized as an effective approach to deal with the increasing complexity of dynamically adaptive systems. One of the main challenges in such systems is to provide guarantees about the required runtime quality of service (QoS) attributes, such as performance, reliability, etc. Therefore, it is of paramount importance to make these systems able to monitor the QoS parameters that allow to evaluate such QoS attributes, analyze these parameters in order to detect QoS changes and therefore trigger reconfiguration actions. In this paper, we propose an approach that allows monitoring the QoS parameters of a dynamically adaptive system in order to detect QoS degradation. The proposed approach is based on the Aspect-Oriented Software Development (AOSD) paradigm which allows to keep the monitoring code separated from the business logic code.

1 Introduction

Dynamically Adaptive Systems that can automatically adapt to changes in their environments are increasingly requested [1]. To further increase its usability and reliability, such system needs to keep a certain Quality of Service (QoS) level during its execution. Therefore, it should be able to monitor some quantifiable parameters that allow to evaluate its QoS attributes. Such monitoring allows detecting degradation in the QoS of the system and therefore adapt its structure and/or behavior autonomously in response to this degradation.

As dynamically adaptive systems change behavior and structure at runtime, the monitoring of the QoS of such system poses some challenges. First, these systems need to continuously monitor QoS parameters in order to detect QoS degradation. These parameters are collected from different interacting entities that may be distributed which may require several QoS monitors displayed at different levels. Second, the level of the QoS specification is relatively low which requires access to source code to specify or modify QoS parameters such as data rate, error rate, etc. Thus, it is desirable to specify QoS parameters at a higher level of abstraction and then automatically map these specifications to source

A. Bouchachia (Ed.): ICAIS 2014, LNAI 8779, pp. 121–130, 2014.
© Springer International Publishing Switzerland 2014

code while providing sufficient flexibility. Third, the QoS concern need to be considered in several parts of the system. Mixing such concerns with business logic concerns increases the complexity of the system and makes both its development and maintenance more difficult [2].

In our previous work [3,4], we presented an approach which mainly consists in conceiving a whole development process of dynamically adaptive systems ranging from modeling to code generation. This approach allows to specify component-based systems and ensure their reconfiguration at runtime. It allows to handle both the anticipated and unanticipated reconfigurations at design time. This approach is based on the combination of the Architecture Analysis and Design Language (AADL) [5] and its aspect oriented extension AO4AADL [6,7].

In this paper, we present how our approach can be applied to monitor the QoS of a dynamically adaptive system. For this purpose, we first define and classify QoS parameters that can be monitored at runtime. The proposed classification is based on the architectural vision of distributed component-based systems. More specifically, this classification is tied to distributed component-based systems specified using AADL concepts. Second, we detail how our approach allows specifying QoS parameters at a high level of abstraction using the AOSD paradigm. In fact, several aspects are defined in our work in order to monitor QoS parameters at runtime. These aspects are specified at architectural level using the AO4AADL language. These AO4AADL aspects will be the input of an AspectJ generator, developed in our previous work [6,7], in order to generate aspects in AspectJ [8]. These aspects will be automatically weaved with the functional code of the system to obtain the final code to be executed. Third, we present how these high level QoS specifications are automatically transformed to executable code that allows the system to continuously monitor QoS parameters at runtime in order to detect QoS degradation.

The remainder of this paper is structured as follows: In Section 2, we present our proposed QoS classification for distributed component-based systems. Section 3 presents the proposed approach to ensure the monitoring of QoS parameters. An illustrative example is introduced in Section 4. Section 5 presents some research studies related to our work. Finally, Section 6 concludes the paper and gives some directions for future work.

2   Quality of Service: Parameters and Classification

We propose a classification of the QoS parameters in order to make easier the evaluation of the QoS attributes of a software system. This classification is inspired from the one proposed by the standard ISO/IEC 9126 [9]. This standard proposes to classify the QoS attributes into two categories : (1) internal quality attributes which are properties of subsystems and components, and (2) external ones that are visible on the system level. Inspired from this classification, we propose to classify the QoS parameters based on the architectural vision of a distributed component-based system specified using AADL concepts.

From an architectural perspective, the software architecture of a distributed component-based system (*system* in AADL) is composed of a set of communicating composite components (*processes* in AADL). Similarly, each composite component is composed of a set of interconnected indivisible components (*threads* in AADL). The communication between components is ensured via a set of connections (*connection* in AADL). Our idea consists in classifying QoS parameters according to the level at which such parameter can be monitored. An indivisible component and a composite component in AADL have the same architectural structure. For this reason, we consider that QoS parameters that can be monitored at indivisible component level and at composite component level are the same. We distinguish three levels of QoS monitoring according to the structure of distributed component-based systems : **indivisible component/composite component level, architecture level** and **communication level**.

The adopted generic QoS attributes that can be measured and evaluated at runtime for a distributed component based system are :

- *Performance* is an indication of the responsiveness of a system. It can be measured in terms of throughput, latency and processing time.
- *Reliability* is the ability of a system to remain operational over time. It can be measured through the loss rate of transmitted messages.
- *Load Balancing* is the distribution of workloads across system components. It can be measured as the distribution of the components on the system.

3   Overview of the Proposed Approach

In this section, we present a general overview of our proposed approach towards specifying and monitoring QoS parameters in order to detect QoS degradations.

Our approach involves a main component namely a QoS manager. This later is defined at two levels : at the composite component level (process level) to be able to manage QoS parameters of its interacting AADL subcomponents (threads), and at the architecture level to manage the QoS parameters of the interacting AADL composite components (processes) that form the whole system architecture. At both levels, the QoS manager is in change of monitoring QoS parameters, analyzing collected data and perform reconfiguration actions when QoS degradations are detected. Therefore, the activity of the QoS manager is divided into three main modules.

- A QoS monitor module : This module is composed of a set of *monitoring aspects* responsible for monitoring and collecting QoS parameters. Gathered QoS parameters are stored into a QoS database for further retrieval.
- A QoS analyzer module : Towards inspecting the collected information and track down QoS degradation. This module sends notifications to the reconfiguration module when QoS degradation is detected in order to trigger appropriate reconfiguration actions.
- A reconfiguration module : Defines a list of reconfiguration actions that can be applied to the system when QoS degradations are detected. These reconfigurations are encapsulated into a set of *reconfiguration aspects*.

The proposed QoS manager is then able to handle a closed feedback loop (MAPE) with four phases : Monitoring, Analysis, Planning and Execution. In this paper, we focus on the first phase of the MAPE loop. For this purpose, we detail in the following how the QoS parameters are specified at architectural level using AO4AADL aspects. We present also some examples of the generated AspectJ code from such AO4AADL specifications. These AspectJ aspects will ensure the monitoring of the QoS parameters at runtime.

3.1   QoS Monitoring

Monitoring the QoS of a dynamically adaptive system aims to observe its constituting components to collect data about QoS parameters. This monitoring is performed through a set of AspectJ aspects that are automatically generated from a high level QoS specification using the AO4AADL language. In fact, our proposed QoS monitor module is composed of a set of architectural monitoring aspects specified in AO4AADL. These aspects are intended to intercept the architectural elements through which QoS parameters can be captured.

As mentioned previously, the QoS parameters can be monitored at three levels. For each level, we define the considered QoS parameters and we give some examples of the structure of the AO4AADL aspects used to specify such QoS parameters. Such aspect is composed of two parts : pointcut and advice. The pointcut defines the architectural element to intercept in order to get the value of the corresponding QoS parameter. The advice defines the information value to save in the QoS database. We present also some examples of the generated AspectJ code from AO4AADL specifications to ensure the monitoring of QoS parameters at runtime.

QoS Parameters Monitored at Indivisible/Composite Component Level

Throughput is the number of sent messages through a set of output ports of a given indivisible or composite component within a time interval. Formula 1 is used to calculate this information.

$$Throughput_c = \sum Throughput_{outport_i} \tag{1}$$

- i=\{1..p\}, p ≤ n and n = the number of output ports of the component.
- $Throughput_{outport_i}$ is the number of sent messages through an output port of the component within a given time interval.

The monitoring of the throughput is achieved through one AO4AADL aspect whose structure is given in Listing 1.1. The pointcut (lines 2–3) of such an aspect intercepts the set of output ports of the given component to be monitored. The advice (lines 7–13) captures the number of sent messages through this set of output ports. Once the time interval of monitoring is elapsed, this advice sends the captured number of sent messages to the QoS database.

```
1  aspect Monitoring_Throughput_<Identifier> {
2    pointcut Throughput_<Identifier>(): execution(outport(<Out_port_identifier_1>(..)))
3                   || ... ||execution (outport(<Out_port_identifier_n>(..)));
4      variables{counter : Integer_Type; t : Time_Type;}
5      initially{counter = 0; t=System.currentTimeMillis()+period;}
6
7    advice after(): Throughput_<Identifier> (){
8          if(System.currentTimeMillis()<t){counter:=counter+1;}
9          else if(System.currentTimeMillis()=t){
10               counter:=counter+1;
11               send_Value!(counter);
12               counter=0;
13               t=System.currentTimeMillis()+period;}}}
```

Listing 1.1. Monitoring the throughput of a component

Listing 1.2 presents the generated AspectJ code from Listing 1.1. The interception of the execution of the output port is transformed to the interception of the method *sendOutput()* of the *PortsRouter* class (lines 3–4). This class carries out the correct routing of messages through ports. Moreover, the subprogram *send_Value* is transformed to a simple execution of the method *send_ValueImpl()* of a generated *SubPrograms* class (line 14).

```
1  aspect Monitoring_Throughput_<Identifier> {
2    pointcut Throughput_<Identifier>():
3          execution(* PortsRouter.sendOutput(<Out_port_identifier_1>(..)))
4          || ... ||execution (* PortsRouter.sendOutput(<Out_port_identifier_n>(..)));
5
6    public static final GeneratedTypes.IntegerType COUNTER = new GeneratedTypes.IntegerType(0);
7    public static final GeneratedTypes.TimeType T =
8                          new GeneratedTypes.TimeType(System.currentTimeMillis()+period);
9
10   void after(): Throughput_<Identifier> (){
11         if(System.currentTimeMillis()<T){COUNTER = COUNTER+1;}
12         else if(System.currentTimeMillis()==T){
13              COUNTER = COUNTER+1;
14              SubPrograms.send_ValueImpl(COUNTER);
15              COUNTER=0;
16              T=System.currentTimeMillis()+period;}}}
```

Listing 1.2. Generated AspectJ code from Listing 1.1

Loss rate of messages defines, within a time interval, the percentage of unprocessed messages compared with the number of received messages by a given component. This information can be measured only for components characterized as follows: To each input port that receives a message corresponds an output port that sends a result. To compute this information, we use formula 2.

$$Loss_c = 1 - \frac{\sum Throughput_{outport_i}}{\sum Input_{inport_i}} \tag{2}$$

- $i=\{1..p\}$, $p \leq n$ and n = the number of output ports of the component.
- $Input_{inport_i}$ is the number of received messages through an input port of the component within a given time interval.

To monitor the loss rate of messages within an indivisible/composite component, two architectural aspects are needed. The first aspect is intended to capture the throughput of the considered component. The second aspect captures the number of received messages through the set of input ports of the component.

Processing time measures the elapsed time to execute an operation within a given component. It is measured using the following formula:

$$Time_{Proc_{op}} = Time_{EndExec_{op}} - Time_{StartExec_{op}} \tag{3}$$

- $Time_{EndExec_{op}}$ is the end time of execution of the operation.
- $Time_{StartExec_{op}}$ is the start time of execution of the operation.

One architectural aspect is needed to monitor the processing time. This aspect intercepts the execution of the subprogram that corresponds to the operation to be monitored. Two types of advices are defined in this aspect : a before advice which will capture the start time of the execution and an after advice that will capture the end time of execution.

QoS Parameters Monitored at Architecture Level

Distribution measures the dispersion rate of a specified component type C_i on the set of composite components of the system. This information is related to the architectural style of the system. It is monitored at architecture level since its computation requires knowledge of the total number of components deployed throughout the system. It is measured for each composite component using formula 4:

$$Distribution_{node} = \frac{Node_{components(C_i)}}{System_{components(C_i)}} \tag{4}$$

- $Node_{components(C_i)}$ is the number of components of type C_i deployed in a given composite component.
- $System_{components(C_i)}$ is the number of components of the same type C_i deployed in the whole system.

The monitoring of the distribution parameter is performed through a set of aspects. One aspect is attached to every composite component that may contain components of type C_i. The structure of the corresponding AO4AADL aspect is given in Listing 1.3. The number of components of type C_i deployed on one composite component can change due to reconfiguration actions that can affect the system during its execution. To be able to capture the new number of components of type C_i within one composite component, the aspect should intercept the reconfiguration actions related to the addition, removal and migration of components (lines 2–4). Therefore, after each invocation of one of these reconfiguration actions, the aspect transmits the new number of components of type C_i to the QoS database module (lines 8–12).

```
1  aspect Monitoring_Distribution {
2    pointcut Distribution(): execution(subprogram(addThread(ComponentType,..)))
3      || execution(subprogram(removeThread(ComponentType,..)))
4      || execution(subprogram(migrateThread(ComponentType,..)));
5      variables {counter:Integer_Type;}
6      initially {counter=0};
7
8    advice after(): Distribution (){
9        if (this="addThread") {counter:=counter+1;}
10       else if((this="removeThread") or (this="migrateThread")) {counter:=counter-1;}
11       send_Value!(counter);
12   }
13 }
```

Listing 1.3. Monitoring the distribution on a composite component

Distribution can refer also to the dispersion rate of a specified composite component type N_i on the system. This information is monitored on a cluster of composite components. The formula used to monitor such parameter is similar to formula 4 except that here we are interested in composite components instead of indivisible components. To monitor such paramter, an aspect is attached to each composite component of the cluster. Such aspect intercepts the reconfiguration action related to the connection and disconnection of composite components of type N_i and transmits the new number of these components to the QoS database.

QoS Parameters Monitored at Communication Level

Loss rate of messages measures, within a time interval, the percentage of lost messages through a connection. This parameter is computed using formula 5.

$$Loss_{conn} = \frac{Received_{msg}}{Sent_{msg}} \tag{5}$$

- *Received_msg* is the number of received messages through the destination port of the connection.
- *Sent_msg* is the number of sent messages through the source port of the connection.

Two architectural aspects should be specified to monitor such QoS parameter. One aspect is used to monitor the throughput of the source output port of the connection. The other aspect is intended to monitor the number of received messages through the destination input port of the connection.

Latency represents the elapsed time to transfer a message through a given connection. Formula 6 is used to compute this parameter.

$$Latency_{conn} = Time_{Receipt_{msg}} - Time_{Sending_{msg}} \tag{6}$$

- $T_{Receipt_{msg}}$ is the receipt time of the message on the destination port.
- $T_{Sending_{msg}}$ is the sending time of the message through the source port.

The monitoring of this QoS parameter needs the specification of two architectural aspects as mentioned in the previous QoS parameter. The only difference here lies in the advice part. In fact, the first aspect in this case is intended to capture the sending time of the message through the source output port of the connection and the second one is responsible of capturing the receipt time of this message on the destination input port of the connection.

All gathered QoS parameters from the monitoring module are stored in a QoS database for later use by the analysis module in order to be able to detect QoS degradations. This QoS database allows keeping a trace of all the captured QoS parameters for further retrieval when needed.

4   Illustrative Example

To demonstrate the benefits of our approach, we introduce the Flood Prediction System (FPS) [10] as an illustrative example. This system presents a set of nodes that communicate and cooperate to carry out flood predictions. Three types of components are considered : sensor nodes, computation nodes and office nodes.

Sensor nodes sense and collect the data relevant for calculations such as pressure, rainfall, and temperature. Sensed data are periodically transmitted to the corresponding computational node. Computation nodes connect the sensor nodes, examine the data correctness and maintains a record of all draw values. Some calibrations are performed on the draw data. Later, a prediction operation is invoked to execute some static measurements in order to provide prediction on river flow. This prediction is transmitted to the office node. The Office Node verifies the results with the available online information, predicts for the entire region, issues alerts and initiates evacuation procedures.

In the following, we will detail the usefulness of monitoring the considered QoS parameters using aspects.

Processing Time. To ensure more system reliability, the processing time of data within computation nodes should not be out of a certain time interval. Results provided so quickly or so late are not reliable for prediction measurements performed at the office node level. Therefore, the processing time of subprograms responsible for data checking, calibration and prediction should be monitored. Listing 1.4 presents the AO4AADL aspect to monitor such QoS parameter.

```
1  aspect Monitoring_ProcTime_CompNode {
2    pointcut ProcTime_CompNode(): execution(subprogram(Data_Checking(..)))
3                        || execution(subprogram(Calibration(..)))
4                        ||execution(subprogram(Prediction(..)));
5
6    advice before(): ProcTime_CompNode(){send_Time!(System.currentTimeMillis());}
7    advice after(): ProcTime_CompNode(){send_Time!(System.currentTimeMillis());}}
```

Listing 1.4. Monitoring the processing time

Distribution. Due to several reconfiguration actions or to nodes failure, the distribution of sensor nodes may be unfair. For example, let's suppose that we dispose of three computation nodes. The first one is connected to six sensor nodes

(2 sensor nodes of each type), the second one is connected to three sensor nodes (one sensor node of each type), however, no sensor node is connected to the third one. To ensure a fair distribution of sensor nodes along the river, three sensor nodes (one of each type) which are connected to the first computation node should be disconnected from this later and connected to the third computation node. Listing 1.5 presents the structure of the AO4AADL aspect responsible for monitoring the distribution. This aspect is attached to every computation node of the system and intercepts the addition and removal of connections between a sensor node and a computation node.

```
1   aspect Monitoring_Distribution_Cluster {
2     pointcut Distribution_Cluster():
3     execution(subprogram(ConnectNodes(SensorNode, ComputationNode)))
4       || execution(subprogram(ConnectNodes(SensorNode, ComputationNode)))
5       || execution(subprogram(DisconnectNodes(SensorNode, ComputationNode)))
6       || execution(subprogram(DisconnectNodes(SensorNode, ComputationNode)));
7
8     variables {counter:Integer_Type;}
9     initially {counter=0};
10
11    advice after(): Distribution_Cluster (){
12        if (this="ConnectNodes") {counter:=counter+1;}
13        else if(this="DisconnectNodes"){counter:=counter-1;}
14        send_Value!(counter);}}
```

Listing 1.5. Monitoring the distribution on a cluster of nodes

5   Related Work

Authors in [11] propose an approach for monitoring the QoS of web services. This approach relies on monitoring tools such as Jpcap for latency measurement. It is based on aspect-oriented programming and requires implementation details. Therefore, this approach stills implementation dependent, as the language of coding aspect is dependent on the selected programming language. Our approach is different since it allows the monitoring of QoS parameters through specifying architectural aspects at a high level of abstraction (architectural level) independently from the programming language.

Authors in [12] present an approach to Cloud service monitoring based on Aspect-Oriented Programming. This approach monitors QoS parameters using AspectJ aspects. Similarly to [11], aspects are hard coded and the approach is dependent on the selected programming language.

The work presented in [13] proposes an aspect-oriented QoS specification method based on the combination of UML and RTL. The main objective of this approach is to specify the QoS parameters separately from the system concerns and facilitate their monitoring. Similarly to our approach, this work allows to specify the QoS parameters at a high level of abstraction. However, no details are mentioned about the code generation of these aspects.

6   Conclusion and Future Work

In this paper, we have proposed an approach for monitoring QoS attributes in dynamically adaptive systems. For this purpose, we proposed a QoS parameters classification taking into account the level at which a QoS parameter can be monitored in the case of a distributed component-based system specified using AADL concepts. We presented later how our approach ensures the monitoring of the QoS parameters using the AOSD paradigm. First, these QoS parameters are specified into AO4AADL. Then, they are automatically translated into AspectJ code to ensure the monitoring of these parameters at runtime.

As future work, we aim to focus on the analysis and reconfiguration phases. We plan to apply our approach to specific domains such as event-based systems.

References

1. Salehie, M., Tahvildari, L.: Self-adaptive software: Landscape and research challenges. ACM Transactions on Autonomous and Adaptive Systems 4, 1–42 (2009)
2. Dowling, J., Cahill, V.: The K-component architecture meta-model for self-adaptive software. In: Matsuoka, S., Cahill, V. (eds.) Reflection 2001. LNCS, vol. 2192, pp. 81–88. Springer, Heidelberg (2001)
3. Loukil, S., Kallel, S., Jmaiel, M.: Managing architectural reconfiguration at runtime. International Journal of Web Portals 5, 55–71 (2013)
4. Loukil, S., Kallel, S., Jmaiel, M.: Verifying runtime architectural reconfiguration of dynamically adaptive systems, pp. 169–176 (2013)
5. SAE: Architecture Analysis & Design Language (2004)
6. Loukil, S., Kallel, S., Zalila, B., Jmaiel, M.: Toward an Aspect Oriented ADL for Embedded Systems. In: Babar, M.A., Gorton, I. (eds.) ECSA 2010. LNCS, vol. 6285, pp. 489–492. Springer, Heidelberg (2010)
7. Loukil, S., Kallel, S., Zalila, B., Jmaiel, M.: Ao4aadl: Aspect oriented extension for aadl. Central European Journal of Computer Science 3, 43–68 (2013)
8. Kiczales, G., Hilsdale, E., Hugunin, J., Kersten, M., Palm, J., Griswold, W.G.: An overview of aspectJ. In: Lindskov Knudsen, J. (ed.) ECOOP 2001. LNCS, vol. 2072, pp. 327–353. Springer, Heidelberg (2001)
9. Organization, I.: ISO/IEC 9126: Information Technology - Software Product Evaluation - Quality Characteristics and Guidelines for Their Use (1991)
10. Hughes, D., Greenwood, P., Coulson, G., Blair, G.: Gridstix: Supporting flood prediction using embedded hardware and next generation grid middleware. In: Proceedings of the 2006 International Symposium on World of Wireless, Mobile and Multimedia Networks, pp. 621–626 (2006)
11. Rosenberg, F., Platzer, C., Dustdar, S.: Bootstrapping performance and dependability attributes of web services. In: Proceedings of the IEEE International Conference on Web Services (ICWS 2006), pp. 205–212 (2006)
12. Mdhaffar, A., Halima, R.B., Juhnke, E., Jmaiel, M., Freisleben, B.: Aop4csm: An aspect-oriented programming approach for cloud service monitoring. In: Proceedings of the 11th International Conference on Computer and Information Technology, pp. 363–370 (2011)
13. Zhang, L.: Aspect-oriented qos modeling for cyber-physical systems. Journal of Software 7, 1083–1093 (2012)

Future Prospects of Human Interaction with Artificial Autonomous Systems

Andrzej M.J. Skulimowski[1,2]

[1] AGH University of Science and Technology, Chair of Automatic Control
and Biomedical Engineering, Decision Science Laboratory, 30-050 Krakow
[2] International Centre for Decision Sciences and Forecasting,
Progress & Business Foundation, 30-048 Kraków, Poland
ams@agh.edu.pl

Abstract. The growing complexity of intelligent systems and technologies raises questions concerning their interaction with human intelligence. The loss of an ability to control artificial intelligent and autonomous decision systems (AADS) due to their high level of sophistication exceeding human analytic capabilities may be referred to as one aspect of 'singularity'. The latter term is often used to describe potential threats to the mankind coming from the development of AADS that may outperform human intelligence in its most relevant aspects. This paper presents some results of a recent foresight project SCETIST which shed a new light on the above 'singularity' dilemma. The project aimed at building the scenarios and trends of selected advanced information technologies. Based on a classification of AI enabling technologies, two basic scenarios concerning the development of AADS have been built. The first one points out that the newly emerging global expert systems (GES) coupled with the Brain-Computer Interfaces (BCI) will allow the human societies to explore in full all data streams and knowledge repositories available. The global knowledge from all sources will be further processed by GES so that rational human decisions will not be outperformed by those made by AADS. In the second scenario, the AADS enabling technologies will develop faster than BCI and GES, so that autonomous decision systems can dominate. The third scenario, ranked as least probable, indicates a possibility of slowing down the development of ICT and AI, so that the singularity problem is deferred. The time horizon of the above scenarios was 2030. Finally, we will present the recommendations arising from SCETIST from the point of view of shaping the R&D policies.

Keywords: Artificial Autonomous Systems, AI Foresight, IT Scenarios, Global Expert Systems, Brain-Computer Interfaces, Anticipatory Networks.

1   Introduction

Following earlier results on the emergence of global expert systems [14], this paper tackles a more general problem related to the perspectives of human interactions with the artificial intelligent and autonomous decision systems (AADS). We will also

A. Bouchachia (Ed.): ICAIS 2014, LNAI 8779, pp. 131–141, 2014.

present the recommendations concerning the preferred paths of development of AI-related technologies and the role of AI researchers in shaping the holistic knowledge development system of the future.

The results presented in this paper have been obtained during the recent foresight project SCETIST (Scenarios and Development Trends of Selected Information Society Technologies [16]). Its goals included the elaboration of recommendations to R&D and IT policy makers as well as pointing out the prospective IT development and research directions to software companies, individual researchers and research teams. The time horizon of foresight was 2025, with an analysis of consequences up to 2030, while the project scope included the following areas:

(1) the economic and social aspects of Information Society development,
(2) e-commerce, e-government, and e-business,
(3) decision support systems and recommenders,
(4) diagnostic and embedded expert systems,
(5) computer vision,
(6) robotics and autonomous intelligent systems,
(7) neurocognitive systems,
(8) molecular computing,
(9) quantum computing.

The areas (3), (4), (6), and (7) are of particular relevance to the subject of this paper. The SCETIST findings in these areas may provide new background for an analysis of singularity-related issues within the project forecasting period, i.e. by 2025. The latter term, coined in the context of machine intelligence by Vinge [19] and popularized by Kurzweil [9] is often used to describe potential threats to the mankind coming from the development of AADS that may outperform human intelligence in all its aspects.

The other areas investigated in SCETIST are too specific to provide general hints concerning the AI science development directions, but they may contribute to show the AI application potential in science, such medicine and astronomy (5), physics and cryptography (9), biology and pharmacology (8) etc. The corresponding results are presented in a series of papers cited in [16].

Building scenarios and computing development trends was based on manifold information sources and analytic methods, including

- patent and bibliometric analysis,
- an expert Delphi,
- system dynamics of social and macroeconomic variables describing main Information Society development drivers [13],
- anticipatory networks built by experts.

For AI technology foresight purposes the computer-assisted Delphi questionnaire research turned out most useful as the knowledge acquisition tool. The analysis of expert responses was combined with the information retrieval strategy from the open web and from the major bibliographic databases. Different procedures to fuse quantitative and qualitative knowledge and to combine forecasts as well as to generate recommendations have been elaborated. One of the main problems that arise when analysing Delphi research outputs is the diversified trustworthiness of individual respondents who may possess different qualifications, expertise, and access to information and modelling tools. In addition, experts' responses may be burdened by a tendency to present views that coincide with individual gains rather than provide an objective picture. This problem has been especially relevant in SCETIST [16], where the research covered large multi- and interdisciplinary areas. It has been difficult to find an expert sufficiently competent in all areas under study. This is why a weighting factor system was used so that the Delphi respondents might indicate their varying degrees of trustworthiness in specific or all the areas covered by the survey. Thus the credibility of each expert has been modelled by a vector whose coordinates corresponded to the subject areas in the Delphi questionnaires listed above. The results shown in the next subsections already consider the differentiated trust and credibility of responses by applying a weighted combination of individual responses wherever appropriate.

This paper is organized as follows: in the next section we will outline the development trends and perspectives of decision support systems and expert systems as relevant AI application areas. We will present the results of Delphi on these topics performed in 2013. A particular attention will be paid to the global expert systems in the context of ever-growing information flows, so called 'big data'. We will point out a need for new knowledge fusion methods [13], including the anticipatory networks [15], Hogarth's [7] approaches to combine qualitative recommendations and forecast combination methods preserving different optimality criteria [4]. Then, in section 3 we will discuss the opportunities, challenges and threats arising from the development of brain computer interfaces BCI and their deployment to fast access to global information streams and repositories, its storing and processing. We will present the trend showing that the AI tools and approaches will eventually merge, to an extent defined in different future scenarios. The recommendations and hints to R&D policy makers, advanced software companies and individual AI researchers as well as the research teams will be discussed in the conclusion section.

2   Future Decision Support and Expert Systems as Research Tools

Following [14], by a global expert system (GES) we will mean all knowledge and information sources, such as sensors, databases, repositories, experts and processing units, regardless of whether they are human, artificial, or hybrid, provided that all they are mutually connected and endowed with a holistic information management system. The latter should possess the usual expert system functionalities from the point of view of each node marked as 'user'. There may exist a specific user hierarchy in each GES. Moreover, a GES must be fully interoperational for its nodes and permanently able to transfer knowledge on demand of every user.

The emergence of GES results from the evolutionary capability increase of global information exchange networks powered by growing data transmission rates, a persistent trend to store various information on the websites and make it accessible to the others, as well as by the availability of efficient search engines and autonomous webcrawlers. In the next section we will argue that GES may play an important role to solve the human-computer convergence problem. This claim is backed by the following four general development trends related to GES that have been identified within the research project [16]:

- a growing level of integration and interoperability of heterogeneous information sources,
- a growing level of interconnection of knowledge units via Internet and otherwise,
- an increase in the average amount of information and sophistication of information processing within individual units, and
- a common growth of the information amount available on the web.

These are supplemented by qualitative trends regarding the degree of refinement of the information stored and processed in each unit according to the well-known scheme: information→knowledge→wisdom. The latter term may be defined as a highly processed and refined knowledge base capable of responding to complex queries. Other trends touch upon the structure of this information. For instance, the percentage of all data stored on the web and indexed by the Google search engine rose from 1% in January 2007 to 6% in January 2010 and exceeded 10% in January 2012. At the same time, the estimated amount of information available on the web rose to 800 exabytes (10^{18} B) in 2012 and 1,3 zettabytes (10^{21} B) in 2013. According to IDC Research (www.idc.com) it is expected to rise to 40 zettabytes in 2020 while a recent Delphi survey [16] yields an expected value of 300 zettabytes in 2025. The number of web sites exceeded 560 million in 2012 [20]. The forecasts of its further rise until 2025 and beyond diverge considerably depending on whether the exclusively machine-operated and used (M2M) sites in the Internet-of-Things are considered or not. Estimations vary between 3 and 50 billion sites in 2020. When the tools offered by search engines become increasingly sophisticated, this system of interconnected web sites may become a real GES endowed additionally with a variety of analytic methods.

Another inspiration for the research of human-AADS relations comes from studies on collective intelligence [17],[18], specifically from creating wisdom by extensive knowledge elicitation and exchange. The expert Delphi may serve as an example of such a process. AADS as well as human experts may create queries and reply to them within an anytime process [3], monotonic with respect to the number of intelligent agents involved and information sources taken into account. The knowledge thus gathered is verified, fused, refined, and merged with knowledge from other sources, aiming at fulfilling the above rough definition of wisdom. Any kind of information source in a GES is dealt with in a uniform way, irrespective of whether it is human or artificial. It is characterised solely by the (query→ reply) transformation and its further assessment.

Trust and credibility management [6,8] turns out to be the first main issue that can hinder or allow the use of heterogeneous knowledge repositories and their interconnected systems as a GES. A basic principle related to trust management, discussed e.g. in [14], is the distinction between trust in an individual knowledge source and the credibility of information received from it. Detecting that a source of information provides false responses with a high probability results in assigning a low trust coefficient to this source. However, the information received therefrom can be useful when assigned a negative weight within an information fusion procedure [4],[7].

In [14] we have formulated the hypothesis that due to the high and ever-growing level of interconnection of knowledge sources, sensors, processing units, knowledge bases and repositories, a specific new type of intelligence may emerge, which under certain assumptions can outperform the intelligence and creativity of any of its individual elements. As soon as AADS and human users are parts of the same GES, it is mandatory that no artificial unit has a higher priority information access than certain human user. This principle, together with other information access hierarchies, may lead to complicated knowledge and software architectures of GES. In addition, the design of GES must ensure that each query is replied at a specified level of trust.

Another relevant issue is the complexity of queries processed by a GES. As usual, the more complex the query, the more complicated is the data retrieval strategy. The latter should take into account the expected information contents at each source, its credibility, data retrieval time and price, if applicable. In addition, GES functioning is based on a snowball principle, i.e. a unit that generated a query activates other knowledge units in the following way: if the information sought cannot be provided by a knowledge unit K_i, or if it can be provided only in part, K_i passes the updated query to further knowledge units, which may recursively activate 3rd order knowledge providers. Thus, each activated unit K_i:

a)   provides the information specified in a query q to this knowledge unit K_j which generated and sent this query,

b)   if the query q could not be fully responded, K_i transforms it and passes to further knowledge units, solving an appropriate retrieval strategy optimization problem,

c)   fuses the information received from activated units and sends it back to K_i,

d)   passes the deactivation signal received from K_i to all activated units.

The overall information retrieval strategy should avoid repeated activation of the same knowledge unit when replying to the same query. It should also ensure getting maximum information in minimum time, use a minimum number of time of all activated units, and be an anytime incremental procedure. A multicriteria optimization problem that yields a strategy of this kind has been considered in [11]. Such strategy can be designed as a *creative decision process* [12].

3   Future Augmented Human Intelligence Based on BCI

Despite of obvious advantages, there arise also new problems to be encountered in relation to future automated expert-level information processing tools. These identified in [16] in the first order of importance are:

- The need for trust and credibility assessment of the information yielded by automated processes will grow at least so fast as the total amount of the information available. Credibility checking and trust calculation may require a commensurate amount of time as the data processing and will be harder to automate, however.

- As it is already evidenced in the social media and the agency news, the open information space will more and more become a playground of disinformation actions of different nature: commercial, political, ideological etc. These phenomena will affect the information acquisition procedures for research purposes.

The knowledge processing scheme applying the credibility and trust of experts interacting in a structured way and other knowledge units selected from a plethora of potentially useful information sources was presented in [14].

Another problem related to the impact of AI technologies on the future is the dilemma of whether there does exist a social capability of accommodating any kind of machine intelligence and use it for the good of mankind. One alternative is to accept highly-developed capabilities of artificial systems in an increasing number of intellectual areas of activity and gradually empower such systems (Skulimowski et al. [16]), i.e. intentionally endow them with a higher degree of freewill, according to the hierarchical freewill definition given in [12]. One aspect of empowering has been discussed above, where an emerging GES may supply results which cannot be comprehended by its users, but which nevertheless cannot be neglected without causing severe losses to the recipients of the response.

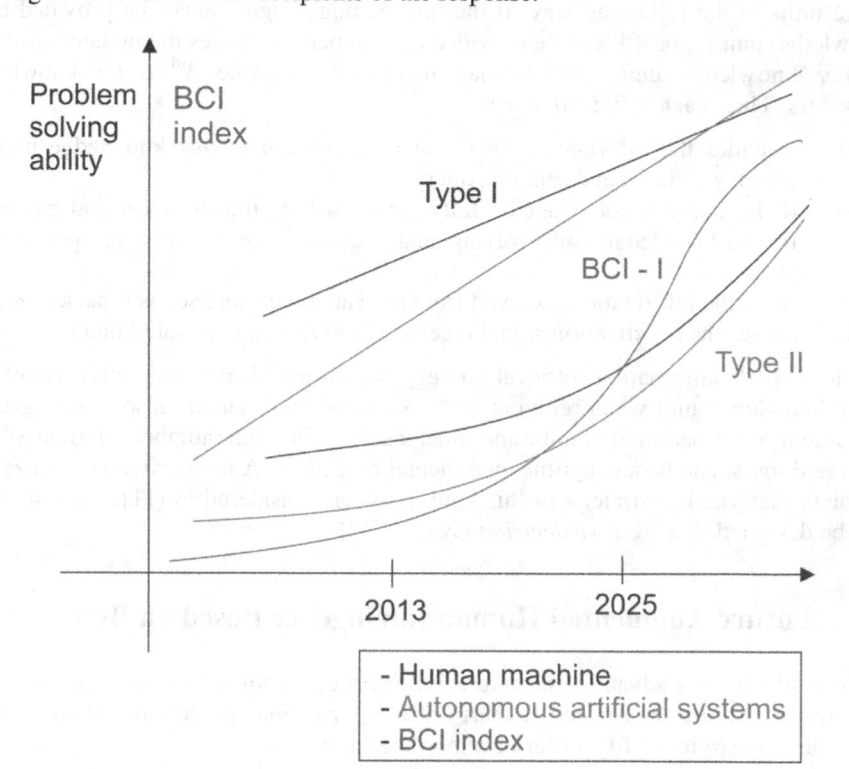

Fig. 1. An illustration of two types of technology development scenarios: type I is a potential technology that is not susceptible to being merged with humans by BCI, in contradistinction to type II technologies that are capable of enhancing human performance. The vertical axis shows the technology capability indices for type I, type II technologies and the BCI capability index on an ordinal scale.

It turns out that a partial response to this challenging problem can be provided by analysing future development trends of neurocognitive Brain-Computer Interfaces (BCI). In terms of the foresight terminology, BCI development may serve as a driver in evolution models of intelligent autonomous systems, both, mobile and virtual.

Fig. 1 shows two scenarios of autonomous system development: in the scenario concerning technologies of type 1, the development of BCI technology is only weakly correlated with the capability of absorbing new intelligent technologies in human-machine systems. The other ways of coupling humans and artificial systems do not prevent the AADS, when considered as stand-alone systems, from outperforming humans in terms of any useful performance index that can be represented on the vertical axis. This is the scenario which is considered a threat to mankind [1].

In the second scenario, BCI technology, and human-machine interfaces in general, allow technology providers to offer an efficient coupling between humans and artificial systems, irrespective of how 'intelligent' they are, in a reasonable time, which is reversely proportional to the development of BCI technology described by the BCI Capability Index (BCI-CI). This scenario prevents, in general, the dangers related to the pessimistic vision of a future with machine-replacing human in most fascinating creative activities.

It should be stressed that BCI is not a unique technology and it may be based on different communication principles [2]. Therefore BCI-CI, for simplicity's sake denoted below by $b(t)$, aggregates technical and biological indicators for alternative technologies. Its anticipated value for k different BCIs can be represented as

$$b(t)=max\{\psi_1(x_{1,1},..x_{1,n(1)},t),..., \psi_k(x_{k,1},..x_{1,n(k)},t)), \tag{1}$$

where $x_{i,1},..x_{i,n(i)}$ are technological, biological, and economical parameters of the i-th BCI technology at time t and ψ_i is an aggregating function characteristic for the i-th technology and such that if $n(i)=n(j)$ then $\psi_i =\psi_j$.

An important question to ask is whether all technologies are of type II. Having analysed different drivers, which may lead to either of the opposite responses, we have found that BCI-related technologies are a salient technological driver. Another driver is the ability to build hierarchical ontologies, allegories [5] and constructive procedures in an automated way, so that complex notions created by future automated expert systems can be explained to humans. This is in fact a remedy to the above mentioned issue. Whether such approaches exist is subject to further research.

The above scenarios have been derived from expert replies to Delphi and panel discussions organized within the project SCETIST [16]. Over 60% of experts supported the optimistic perspective, while almost 30% (28%) could not agree with the perspective of catching-up the machine intelligence by humans augmented by the BCI. However, roughly 1/8 of experts (12%) supposed that the above dilemma will become meaningless. Among the reasons mentioned by the experts are: a slow-down of the IT development caused by economic crises, the altered directions of technological evolution towards biotechnology and sustainable energy, a lack of drivers to use AADS in manufacturing, or international conventions that prohibit further development and deployment of AADS for military purposes.

The compensation of the growing empowerment of autonomous artificial systems by the ability to control them directly with the BCI and use their capabilities by merging them with the brains assumes a continual empowerment synchronised with the development of BCI. This optimistic picture may be disturbed by uncontrolled trends and events. The foresight project [16] identified the following threats:

- A growing share of approximate computing methods used in science, engineering and technology may cause a superposition of errors to produce unintended phenomena in autonomous systems, such as identification of goals that do not conform to the higher-level objectives defined by human supervisors.
- A growing number of decision-making processes in autonomous or semi-autonomous systems that should be supervised by humans but cannot due to the lack of such capacities. This process forces higher-level empowerment.

The first observation is related to the facts that the convergence and other analytical properties of most heuristic algorithms, which are becoming more and more popular in science, such as most evolutionary algorithms, is not known.

Some of these methods use ad hoc coefficients, specifically most of the multicriteria decision making algorithms, the other simulate decision processes in nature, assuming implicitly their sub-optimality. The scenario of the threat generated by the approximate methods is somehow similar to the year 2K problem, yet it may become more severe. It can be presented as follows:

An autonomous systems optimises a general objective that should be translated into particular goals. The achievement of the latter will invoke certain real-life actions

$\rightarrow$ the system calculated goals using natural computing methods,
$\rightarrow$ the specific goals are biased by errors,
$\rightarrow$ the action planning is performed using approximate heuristic methods,
$\rightarrow$ the errors cumulate, the actions undertaken by the autonomous agents are far from being desirable.

When such methods are used to support relevant decisions such as the prioritization of research projects, resource assignment to different activities, system reliability estimation etc., they may cause severe strategic consequences to the decision makers affected.

Another important new feature that will appear in decision support, artificial decision-making, and expert systems is their (digital) creativity. This will have at least a twofold meaning and use: it can be artificial creativity (delegating complicated search strategy selection tasks to autonomous agents) as well as creativity of users aided by intelligent agents. Furthermore, it can be expected that the opinion dynamics and their distribution within the same group of experts can be forecasted using the state-space model and Kalman filtering as proposed in [13].

Further tools may eventually lead to identify knowledge sources on the web to complete missing or incomplete data, using the recursive k-th to $(k+1)$-information source level transition scheme presented in [14]. The combination of the *ex-ante* error analysis with the usual *ex-post* approaches could convert the semi-supervised trust learning scheme to a supervised scheme as soon as the verification of foresight results is possible. A further discussion on the application of a similar approach to refine expert information processed during a foresight project is given in [16].

4 Conclusions

We have outlined the foresight research on two emerging AI trends, related to the development of expert systems and BCI, pointing out their potential role in overcoming hypothetic future machine intelligence supremacy that is sometimes referred to as the 'singularity' phenomenon. During the next decade well-known knowledge elicitation and processing tools based on crowdsourcing, Delphi surveys, autonomous webcrawlers, group model building systems [18] will evolve to yield almost-universal and almost-autonomous Global Expert Systems. Beyond facilitating individual web user's work, the new tools will allow the networked organizations to improve the efficiency and quality of business intelligence. They will also increase the efficiency of research on complex systems, merging biological, physical, and socio-economic evolution models [13]. The GES will also make it possible to optimize the choice of human experts to taking part in particular tasks. Users' records of activity and their *ex-post* evaluation will be stored in a GES knowledge base and retrieved when necessary to derive their trust and competence assessments. Expected trustworthiness of the team and the quality of the work output can be used as the performance criteria and optimized during the team formation [17]. The combined, human-machine resource management systems based on GES will also be capable of investigating the possibility of replacing human labour by the activities of AADS. The average team composition (human/non-human) for a sample of standard tasks that require human creativity, taken into account as a function of time, can thus serve as a quantitative indicator describing the process of replacing human creativity by the artificial one.

The deployment of BCI as an interface to GES will facilitate the implementation of creative decision-making processes designed by human users of GES according to the creativity notion proposed in [12]. Therefore, one can expect that future BCI will be capable of filtering the incoming information to reduce the data stream to the factors that can be perceived and processed by, perhaps augmented, human brain. On the other hand, as – by principle – the behaviour of all its human users will be recorded by a GES, the phenomena accompanying human creative activity will be analysed, optimised, and implemented by GES. Thus, the performance and autonomy of the knowledge acquisition processes in GES will grow within an adaptive learning process. This process will be stable if the knowledge transfer in the opposite direction is assured as well, i.e. if the any improvement of a human decision made by a GES is communicated to the decision-maker.

An important feature that will be required from the global search and information fusion algorithms used in future GES will be their interoperability to assure an efficient and reliable access to heterogeneous sources of information, such as experts, expert systems, web databases, books and articles etc. This will also impose further requirements on the web communication and information storage standards. A parallel trend in software engineering of GES tools will consist in supplying intelligent procedures to cope with data and access protocols heterogeneity.

The GES will be also endowed with the functionalities allowing users to manage trust, confidence, and credibility of information retrieved or exchanged. Even those information sources that are directly unattainable by a knowledge unit can be assigned credibility vectors and trust coefficients, using the Kalman filter and other uncertainty handling techniques. Queries related to the future can be modelled and replied to using backcasting [10] automated within an anticipatory network framework [15], and supplemented by traditional extrapolation-based forecasting methods.

Acknowledgement. The results presented in this paper are based on expert Delphi and panel discussions organized during the research project "Scenarios and Development Trends of Selected Information Society Technologies until 2025" financed by the ERDF within the Innovative Economy Operational Program 2006-2013, Contract No. WND-POIG.01.01.01-00-021/09.

References

1. Bostrom, N.: When machines outsmart humans. Futures 35, 759–764 (2003)
2. Brunner, P., Bianchi, L., Guger, C., Cincotti, F., Schalk, G.: Current trends in hardware and software for brain–computer interfaces (BCIs). J. Neural Eng. 8, 025001, 7p. (2011), http://iopscience.iop.org/1741-2552/8/2/025001
3. Dean, T.L., Boddy, M.: An analysis of time-dependent planning. In: Proceedings of the Seventh National Conference on Artificial Intelligence AAAI 1998, St. Paul, MN, pp. 49–54 (1988)
4. Elliott, G., Timmermann, A.: Optimal forecast combinations under general loss functions and forecast error distributions. Journal of Econometrics 122, 47–79 (2004)
5. Freyd, P., Scedrov, A.: Categories, Allegories, vol. 39. Mathematical Library, North-Holland (1990)
6. Gligor, V., Wing, J.M.: Towards a Theory of Trust in Networks of Humans and Computers. In: Christianson, B., Crispo, B., Malcolm, J., Stajano, F. (eds.) Security Protocols 2011. LNCS, vol. 7114, pp. 223–242. Springer, Heidelberg (2011)
7. Hogarth, R.: A note on aggregating opinions. Organizational Behavior and Human Performance 21, 40–46 (1978)
8. Jøsang, A.: A Logic for Uncertain Probabilities. Int. J. Uncertainty, Fuzziness Knowl.-Based Syst. 9(3), 279–311 (2001)
9. Kurzweil, R.: The Singularity is Near: When Humans Transcend Biology, p. 652. Viking, New York (2005)
10. Quist, J., Vergragt, P.: Past and future of backcasting: The shift to stakeholder participation and a proposal for a methodological framework. Futures 38(9), 1027–1045 (2006)
11. Skulimowski, A.M.J.: Optimal strategies for quantitative data retrieval in distributed database systems. In: Proceedings of the Second International Conference on Intelligent Systems Engineering, Hamburg, September 5-9, pp. 389–394. IEE Conference Publication No. 395, IEE, London (1994)
12. Skulimowski, A.M.J.: Freedom of Choice and Creativity in Multicriteria Decision Making. In: Theeramunkong, T., Kunifuji, S., Sornlertlamvanich, V., Nattee, C. (eds.) KICSS 2010. LNCS, vol. 6746, pp. 190–203. Springer, Heidelberg (2011)
13. Skulimowski, A.M.J.: Discovering Complex System Dynamics with Intelligent Data Retrieval Tools. In: Zhang, Y., Zhou, Z.-H., Zhang, C., Li, Y. (eds.) IScIDE 2011. LNCS, vol. 7202, pp. 614–626. Springer, Heidelberg (2012)

14. Skulimowski, A.M.J.: Universal intelligence, creativity, and trust in emerging global expert systems. In: Rutkowski, L., Korytkowski, M., Scherer, R., Tadeusiewicz, R., Zadeh, L.A., Zurada, J.M. (eds.) ICAISC 2013, Part II. LNCS, vol. 7895, pp. 582–592. Springer, Heidelberg (2013)
15. Skulimowski, A.M.J.: Anticipatory Network Models of Multicriteria Decision-Making Processes. Int. J. Systems Sci. 45(1), 39–59 (2014), doi:10.1080/00207721.2012.670308
16. Skulimowski, A.M.J. (ed.): Scenarios and Development Trends of Selected Information Society Technologies until 2025. Final Report, Progress & Business Publishers, Kraków, Progress & Business Foundation (2013), http://www.ict.foresight.pl
17. Tapscott, D., Williams, A.D.: Wikinomics: How Mass Collaboration Changes Everything, 3rd edn. Portfolio Trade (2010)
18. Tovey, M. (ed.): Collective Intelligence: Creating a Prosperous World at Peace. Earth Intelligence Network, Oakton (2008)
19. Vinge, V.: The Coming Technological Singularity: How to Survive in the Post-Human Era. In: Landis, G.A. (ed.) Vision-21: Interdisciplinary Science and Engineering in the Era of Cyberspace, NASA Publication CP-10129, pp. 11–22 (1993)
20. http://en.wikipedia.org/wiki/Exabyte (accessed July 15, 2014)

Empirical Identification of Non-stationary Dynamics in Time Series of Recordings

Emili Balaguer-Ballester[2], Alejandro Tabas-Diaz[1], and Marcin Budka[1]

[1] Faculty of Science and Technology, Talbot Campus, Poole,
Dorset, BH12 5BB Bournemouth University, UK
[2] Bernstein Center for Computational Neuroscience Heidelberg-Mannheim,
University of Heidelberg
eb-ballester@bournemouth.ac.uk

Abstract. Non-stationarity time series are very common in physical, biological and in real-world systems in general, ranging from geophysics, econometrics or electroencephalography to logistics. Identifying, detecting and adapting learning algorithms to non-stationary environments is a fundamental task in many data mining scenarios; however it is often a major challenge for current methodologies. Data analysis in the context of time-varying statistical moments is a very active research direction in machine learning and in computational statistics; but theoretical insights into latent causes of non-stationarity in empirical data are very scarce. In this study, we evaluate the capacity of the *trajectory classification error* statistic in order to detect a significant variation in the underlying dynamics of data collected in multiple stages. We analysed qualitatively the conditions leading to observable changes in non-stationary data generated by Duffing nonlinear oscillators; which are ubiquitous models of complex classification problems. Analyses are further benchmarked in a dataset consisting of atmospheric pollutants time series.

Keywords: Non-stationarity, non-autonomous dynamics, phase space reconstruction, high dimensional spaces, Duffing oscillator, trial-to-trial variability.

1 Introduction

Non-stationarity dynamics is ubiquitous in physical and biological systems, ranging from geophysics or econometrics (e.g., [12] and references therein) to electroencephalography [20].

Data analysis in the context of time-varying statistical moments is a very active research direction in machine learning and computational statistics. In particular, it has been central to change detection approaches [5] and in the development of algorithms to achieve competitive predictions in dynamic environments [6]. Non-stationary settings are pervasive in areas such as streaming data mining, on-line dimensionality reduction or meta-learning to name a few (e.g., [6,18]). Recently, some algorithms focused on identifying invariant subspaces in multivariate data; the goal was to restrict the models to such stationary regions of the space [20]; where model predictions are more robust. A common assumption in such approaches is that stationarity is preserved in segments of the time series where underlying generative distributions are constant. Thus,

A. Bouchachia (Ed.): ICAIS 2014, LNAI 8779, pp. 142–151, 2014.

the source of non-stationarity is typically a drift on the statistical moments of time-varying likelihoods $P(\mathbf{x}|C; t)$ (and/or priors) generating d-dimensional input patterns x of class C [18].

In this work, we propose a complementary angle for the analysis of non-stationary empirical data based on dynamical systems theory. The focus here is on investigating the conditions in which observed drifts are caused by changes in the parameters of a subjacent, non-autonomous deterministic tend and not only by stochastic fluctuations. As a canonical description of complex two-class classification problems we used the simplest nonlinear dynamical system exhibiting two attractors which can subtly modify their position over time, the Duffing oscillator [8,21]. This system is widespread model used in many physics and engineering areas such as nonlinear electrical circuits, optics, sound vibration, quantum field theory or for the study of chaotic oscillations (see for instance [10]). Thus, it has been extensively analysed for decades [21]; however, despite its simplicity, exact solutions remain unknown and were only found in certain conditions [10]. Here we will empirically reconstruct the two-attractor dynamics of the Duffing dynamical system in high dimensional state spaces [3,9]. Then we will show how a very simple statistic, the *trajectory classification error* is an instantaneous signature of a significant variation in the underlying dynamics.

This nonlinear system will be used as a metaphor of a more general framework. For instance, it may serve to explain the source of variability observed in atmospheric pollution time series. More precisely, it will be used to analyse the putative non-stationary behavior of time series of tropospheric ozone [11].

2 Analyses

This section presents an intuitive view of the bistable system used in the study (the Duffing family). This system will serve as a canonical model for understanding arbitrarily complex two-class problems from a nonlinear dynamical systems angle. Moreover, this approach will enable us to define a simple empirical index of *coherent* behavior of trajectories with respect to the class-boundaries; which allow us to identify changes in parameters of the underlying dynamics.

2.1 Canonical Model of Two-Class Problems

One of the simplest yet ubiquitous ordinary dynamical system capable of a wide range of attracting dynamics is the Duffing family of oscillators; consisting of first order and cubic nonlinearities (the perturbation term) and an external periodic force:

$$\ddot{x}(t) + \delta\dot{x}(t) - \beta x(t) + \alpha x^3(t) = \Omega \cdot \cos(wt), \tag{1}$$

where α, β and $\delta \in \Re$ are the parameters of the model. This dissipative system enable us to generate complex datasets as will be shown in short. For a range of parameter values ($\delta \geq 8\beta$; $\beta, \alpha > 0$; $\Omega = 0$) the system has a very simple behavior, a saddle at $x = 0$ and two sinks at the symmetric equilibrium points $x_1 = -\sqrt{\frac{\beta}{\alpha}}, x_2 = \sqrt{\frac{\beta}{\alpha}}$ (Figure 1a).

Trivially, the linearized system matrix

$$\begin{pmatrix} 0 & 1 \\ \beta - 3x^2 & -\delta \end{pmatrix} \tag{2}$$

has eigenvalues $-\frac{\delta}{2} \pm \frac{\sqrt{\delta^2+4\beta}}{2}$ for $x = 0$ and $-\frac{\delta}{2} \pm \frac{\sqrt{\delta^2-8\beta}}{2}$ for $x_{1,2}$ (see for instance [21]).

A nonlinear two-class classification problem is then naturally defined: Figure 1a shows the basin of attraction of the two sinks; constructed by generating thousands of random initial conditions from static, two-dimensional gaussian distributions centered at the fixed points (standard deviation=3), and then sustained to the flow induced in Equation 1 with $\alpha = 0.25, \beta = -0.6, \delta = 0.5, \Omega = 0$. Basins of attraction are concentric structures induced by the perturbation term $-\alpha x^3(t)$; blue and red colours indicate wether trajectories will end up on each one of the sinks i.e., they will belong either to class C_1 (red, left sink) or to class C_2 (blue, right, sink).

This system, as many other nonlinear dynamical systems radically modifies its dynamics as a function of β, δ, Ω. For instance, a chaotic attractor emerges for a range of Ω values (Figure 1b, top right) or limit cycles suddenly appear via Pitchfork bifurcations (Figure 1b, bottom right) [10]. However, and crucially, this scenario has not interest here because it leads to abrupt variations in class-association probabilities $P(\mathbf{x}|C_1;t), P(\mathbf{x}|C_2;t)$; where $\mathbf{x} = (x, \dot{x})$. Therefore, class-specific statistical moments strongly differ after the bifurcation and the change detection is a trivial task for most of current change identification methods (Figure 1b, e.g., [18,13,22]). In brief, detection of those bifurcations is typically not a challenging task for existing approaches and thus will not be the focus of this study.

2.2 Non-stationary Perturbations

The main focus in this work is to infer subtle variations in the underlying system dynamics which are not significantly represented in statistical moments. Towards this goal, an arbitrary small linear perturbation, i.e., $\alpha(t_0) \to \alpha(t_1) = \alpha(t_0) + \Delta\alpha$ is induced, while distribution originating the initial conditions is held fixed as well as β, δ, Ω. In this example (Figure 1c) the alpha parameter is linearly increased by less than 0.01 percent. As the fixed points get closer to each other (the α parameter increases), no statistical differences are observed. However, trajectories crossing the neighborhood of the center fixed point $(0, 0)$ may switch the attractor and thus will be misclassified after a subtle drift on the α parameter (Figure 1c, red trajectory which becomes blue after this small variation). Therefore, from this simple example, we envisage that an arbitrary accurate classifier at $t = t_0$, will still fail to predict the true class of such trajectories at $t = t_1$. Remarkably, this change is very subtle and will not be detected by any statistical analysis based only in the posterior probabilities $P(C_1|\mathbf{x};t), P(C_2|\mathbf{x};t)$ (Figure 1c). Posteriors were estimated by tiling the phase space in equal rectangular bins; the limits of the gird are defined by the maximum and minimum values of $x, \dot{x}$ axes (using 200 random initial conditions, only ten are plotted in Figure 1c for clarity). The histogram of classes is then normalized, yielding to posteriors estimates.

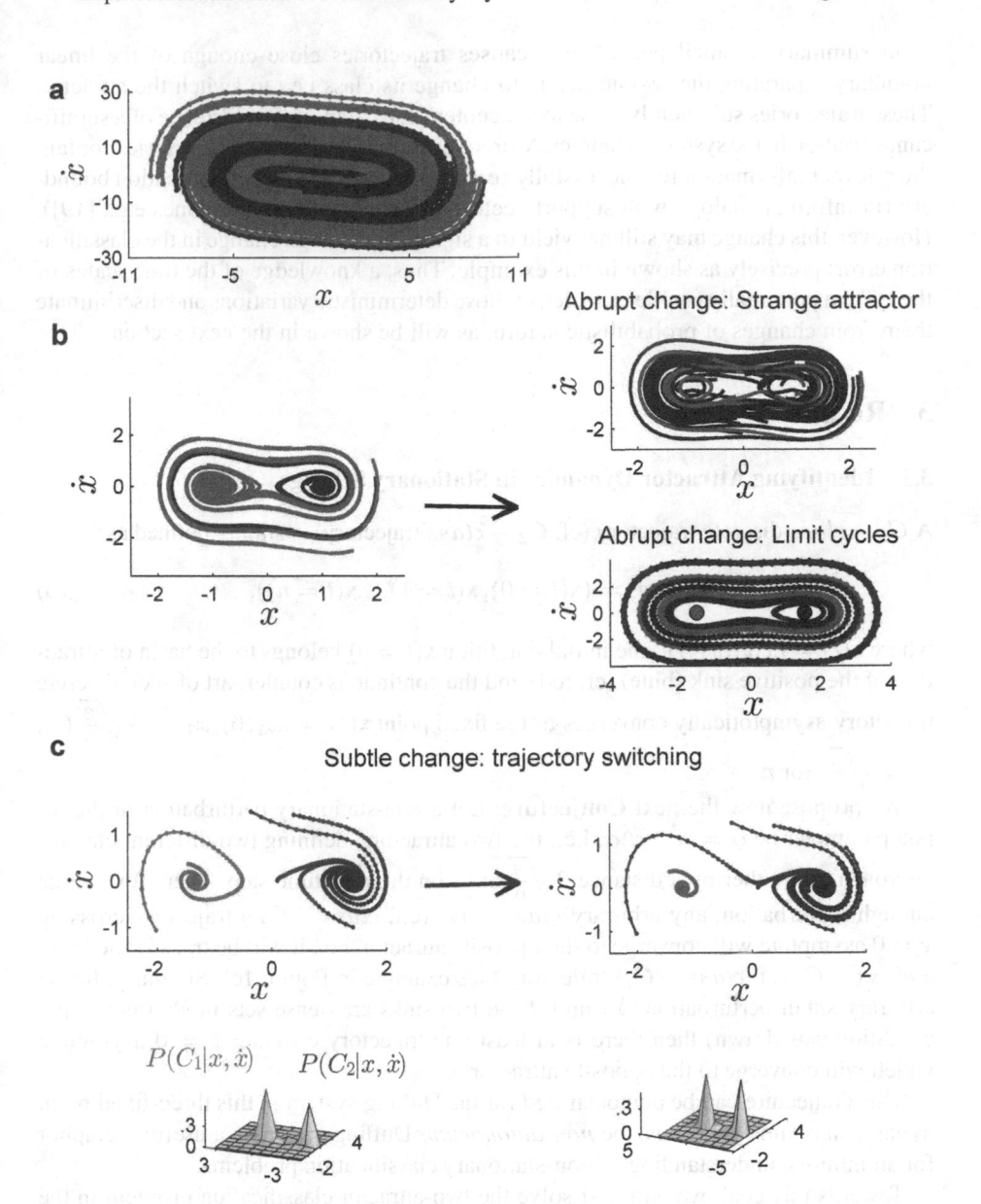

Fig. 1. Duffing non-linear oscillator. a) Basin of attraction (red trajectories correspond to the left sink, blue trajectories converge to the right sink). b) Parameter change (β, δ, ω) leading to a chaotic attractor and a limit cycle. c) Subtle parameter change $\Delta\alpha$ leading to a small drift in sinks' positions (Equation 1), causing, in this example, that a single trajectory switches the attractor. Note that posterior probabilities $P(C_1|x, \dot{x}; t), P(C_2|x, \dot{x}; t)$ do not change significantly (Ranksum test, $p > 0.05$). Posterior probabilities were computed in a larger simulation setting, see text.

In summary, a small perturbation causes trajectories close enough of the linear boundary separating the two attractors to change its class i.e., to switch the attractor. These trajectories sufficiently close to the center $(0,0)$ alert of the existence of a significant variation in the system dynamics. Moreover, these misclassified trajectories contain the relevant information for successfully re-computing an optimal classification boundary (in informal analogy with support vectors of delta margin hyperplanes e.g., [19]). However, this change may still not yield to a significant enough change in the classification error; precisely as shown in this example. Thus, a knowledge of the time scales of the system potentially enable us to detect those deterministic variations and discriminate them from changes of probabilistic nature, as will be shown in the next section.

3   Results

3.1   Identifying Attractor Dynamics in Stationary Settings

A $C_1 - class$ discrete trajectory (cf. $C_2 - class$ trajectory) is simply defined as

$$T(t = n) = (\mathbf{x}(t = 0), \mathbf{x}(t = 1), ...\mathbf{x}(t = n)), \tag{3}$$

where $\mathbf{x}(t) = (x(t), \dot{x}(t))$, the initial condition $\mathbf{x}(t = 0)$ belongs to the basin of attraction of the positive sink (blue) (cf. red) and the continuous counterpart of such discrete trajectory asymptotically converges to the fixed point $\mathbf{x}(t) = (x_1, 0); x_1 = -\sqrt{\frac{\beta}{\alpha}}$ (cf. $x_2 = \sqrt{\frac{\beta}{\alpha}}$) for $n \to \infty$.

We propose now the next **Conjecture**: Let a non-stationary perturbation in the alpha parameter be $\tilde{\alpha} = \alpha + \Delta\alpha$, i.e., the two attractors, defining two different classes, approach each other by a distance $2\sqrt{\frac{\beta}{\tilde{\alpha}}}$ units on the next time step. Then, for a large enough perturbation, any arbitrary $class - C_1$ (c.f. $class - C_2$) trajectory crossing $x = 0$ asymptote will converge to the opposite attractor, i.e., it will be transformed into a $class - C_2$ (cf. $class - C_1$) trajectory (see example in Figure 1c). Similarly, for an arbitrary small perturbation $\Delta\alpha$ and if the two sinks are dense sets in $\Re^2$ (any initial condition was drawn) then there is at least one trajectory crossing $x = 0$ asymptote which will converge to the opposite attractor□.

This conjecture can be demonstrated for the Duffing system in this three-fixed point dynamical regime [1]. Thus, the *non-autonomous* Duffing system is a useful metaphor for an intuitive understanding of non-stationary classification problems.

Towards this goal, we will first solve the two-attractor classification problem in the non-autonomous case by expanding the phase space such that basins of attraction are separable. A polynomial expansion of a phase space is also valid to reconstruct attractor dynamics (for instance [17,3]), thus we will use an expansion of dimension $\frac{p+2!}{p!2}$; which includes all high-order interactions of the phase space variables up to a $p^{th} order$; which is a well-know reproducing-kernel Hilbert space [19]. The dot product of two feature vectors is the well-known inhomogeneous polynomial kernel (see for instance [3,19])

$$k(t, t') = \Phi\Phi^T = (1 + \mathbf{x}(t)\mathbf{x}(t'))^p - 1. \tag{4}$$

This classifier was then 40-fold cross-validated using 6 blocks of 10^5 patterns $(1,000$ trajectories of 100 patterns each). Optimal regularisation values for a range of polynomial orders $(p\epsilon[1,10])$ were previously obtained on an independent dataset of the same size, not shown here. In this simulation, a $class - C_1$ trajectory is defined empirically as a set of $n = 100$ patterns with a random initial condition $\mathbf{x}(t = 0)$ in which $\|\mathbf{x}(t = n) - \mathbf{x}_1\| < \|\mathbf{x}(t = n) - \mathbf{x}_2\|$, were $\mathbf{x}_1, \mathbf{x}_2$ are the two fixed points.

As expected, the lower normalized classification error (1.2%, Figure 2a, rightmost blue symbol) corresponds to a 3rd-order expansion because this is precisely the nonlinear order of the perturbation term in Equation 1 (full analysis across expansion orders omitted for space, see for instance [3]). Thus, a expanded space of third order effectively capture the underlying class-pattern associations for this two-attractor dynamical regime.

3.2 Inferring Subtle Variations in Attractor Dynamics

In a second phase, a small perturbation $\frac{\Delta\alpha}{\alpha} = 0.001$ was introduced for simulating a multi-stage data acquisition setting. The optimally discriminant subspace is computed for the first trial (Figure 2a, rightmost marker corresponding to a distance between attractors = 3.08) and held fixed. Thus, the classification error smoothly increases on the next trials, such that, critically, there are no statistical differences in the classification error from a block to the next (two-tailed t-tests, $p > 0.209$). In other words, the change is so subtle that the deterministic drift is masked by the random initial conditions, consequently no significant change in distribution moments cannot be statistically detected.

From the perspective of classification algorithms, updating the estimated class-boundaries is only compelling when the classification error increases significantly with respect to the first trial. In this simulation, this variation occurs at trial number 6 ($p = 0.012$; Figure 2a); but it is not reflected in an increase of the error on trial number 6 with respect to the previous one ($p = 0.291$). In summary trial-to-trial classification error comparisons fail to identify such critical event.

Trajectory classification statistics, in contrast, enable to detect such critical change on a trial-by-trial basis. As expected by the Conjecture stated above, when attractors approach each other, at least an entire trajectory changes its basin of attraction. As a result, the fraction of *misclassified* trajectories abruptly increases at trial number 6 with respect to the previous trial and reaches significance ($p = 0.050$); identifying the effective lost of generalization capability of the classifier. Importantly the classification error is unable to detect such change on a trial-by-trial basis.

The reason of this result is intuitively straightforward: Consider an autonomous dynamical system

$$\dot{\mathbf{x}}(t) = \nabla(\mathbf{x}(t), \alpha), \tag{5}$$

where $\mathbf{x}$ is a d-dimensional phase space and ∇ is a nonlinear differential operator parameterized by $d \times p$ coefficients (α), such that the system has at least two attractors of any kind. This equation, equipped with i.i.d initial random conditions, defines a natural mapping into a classification problem and generates our observable dataset D of size $n \times l$ patterns (n discrete trajectories of length l).

Let us consider an identical dataset $\tilde{D} \equiv D$ but in which all patterns have been i.i.d drawn form the static joint probability distribution. In this context, $c(\mathbf{x}(t))$ is a classifier such that the true error $e(\alpha)$ given that the pattern $\mathbf{x}$ belongs to class C_i is

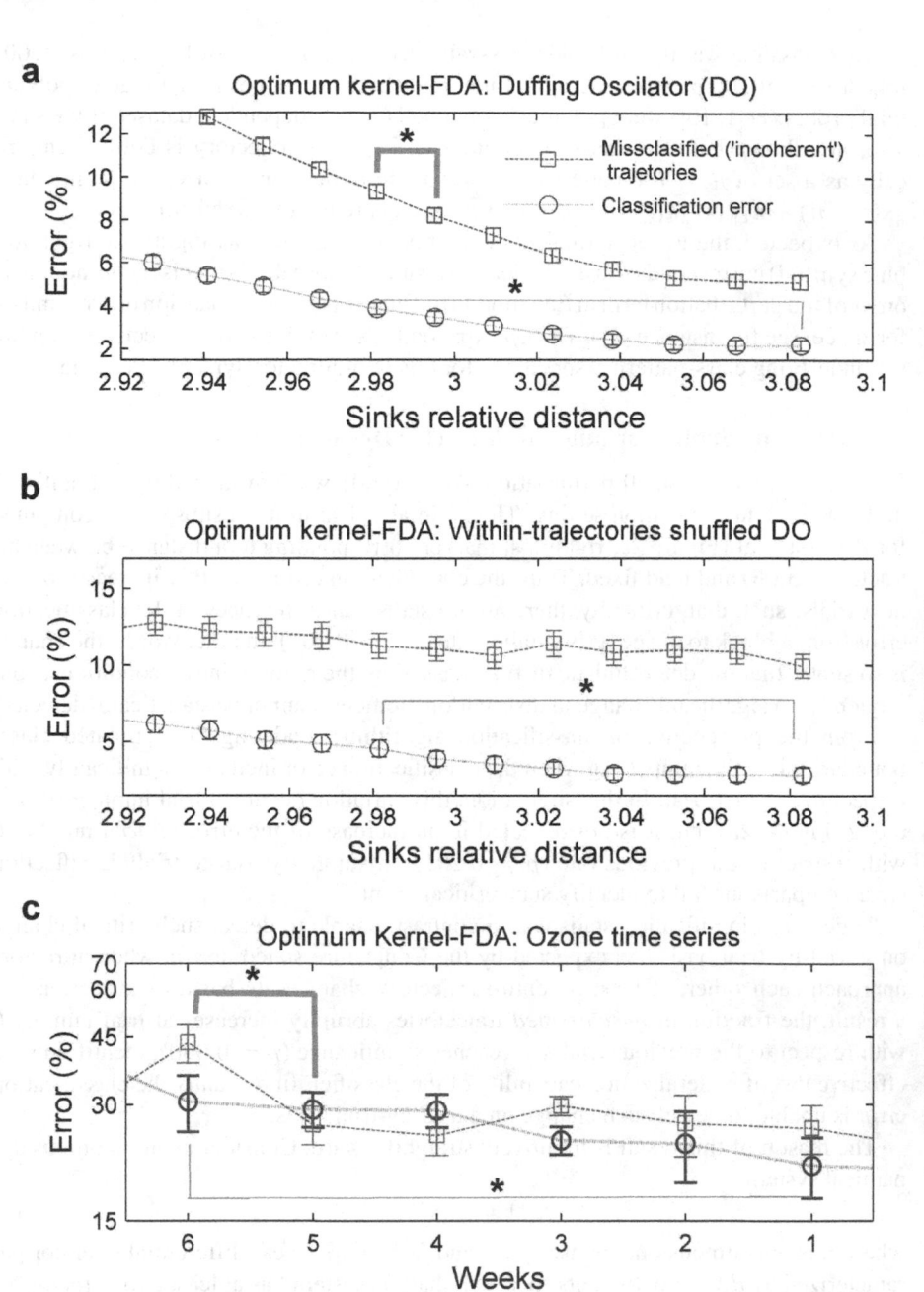

Fig. 2. Temporal drift in a *non-autonomous* Duffing oscillator and analysis in real data. A regularized kernel-fisher discriminant (KFD) with a polynomial kernel of 3rd order was used (parameters were optimized by 40-fold cross-validation in a separate dataset). KFD was computed for the first trial and then the discriminant solution was applied to subsequent trials. a) Errors for subtle drifts on the perturbation parameter. b) Data shuffled within each trajectory. c) Tropospheric ozone hourly concentrations [11]. * $p < 0.05$.

$$e(\alpha) = P(c(\mathbf{x}) \neq C_i, \alpha). \tag{6}$$

It is assumed that the classified is optimized such that this error is minimum. Equivalently, the *trajectory classification error* is simply defined as

$$e_T(\alpha) = P(c(T(t)) \neq C_i, \alpha), \tag{7}$$

$\forall t > M$ for any arbitrarily large M. The trajectory class $c(T(t))$ is defined as $c(T(t)) \equiv c(\mathbf{x}(t = 0), ..., c(\mathbf{x}(t))$ and $c(T(t)) \neq C_i$ means that $c(\mathbf{x}(t) \neq C_i \forall t > M$, where the correct class of $\mathbf{x}(t)$ is $C_i = c(\mathbf{x}(t))$. In other words, a trajectory is well-classified when all its last vectors are correctly classified, see for instance [3,1].

Then, an arbitrarily small perturbation in at least one of the model parameters α will have a different effect depending on the underlying source of the observed dataset. If D was generated by a dynamical system, at least one trajectory of length l will potentially converge to a different attractor because their last $\tilde{l}$ vectors will be misclassified. In this scenario, the increase in the empirical trajectory classification error ($\triangle e_T$, aka *trajectory incoherence* index, [1]) is, trivially, larger than the increase in the raw classification error ($\equiv \triangle e$), i.e.,

$$\triangle e_T \equiv e_T(\alpha + \triangle \alpha) \geq \frac{1}{n} = \frac{l}{n \cdot l} \geq \frac{\tilde{l}}{n \cdot l} \equiv \triangle e; \tag{8}$$

i.e., $\triangle e_T \geq \triangle e$, the increase in the classification error. This is precisely the scenario shown in Figure 2b.

However, this is only the case if the system is driven by deterministic dynamics. In Figure 2b vectors $\mathbf{x}(t)$ within each trajectories have been shuffled while class-associations are maintained. Thus, $\triangle e$ is not altered, but the temporal flow within trajectories is corrupted. In this setting, the bound in Equation 8 cannot be established in general, because there is no guarantee that trajectories get attracted to the opposite sink; thus, it is expected that $\triangle e_T$ will not significantly increase. This is precisely the scenario shown in Figure 2b, indicating that there is no a multi-stable deterministic dynamics underlying data generation.

To conclude, we used this approach for analysing the non-stationary behavior in a well-known periodic time series, where limit cycles gently drift their position over time. The dataset consists of hourly concentrations of tropospheric ozone and other atmospheric variables. Ozone time series are strongly periodic on a daily basis, but they are subtly modulated by a seasonal trend [11,2] (for details on data collection etc. see [11]). Ozone concentrations were classified into three categories; and a regularized kernel discriminant was used to map atmospheric variables to these three classes (like in the dynamical systems model, regularization penalty and 3rd-order polynomial order of the kernel discriminant were optimized by cross validation on a separate dataset).

The discriminant solution was then computed for the first week of data and applied to the following weeks (Figure 2c). Classification error and trajectory divergence increase following a similar pattern, but the fraction of misclassified trajectories increases abruptly in the last week (6) precisely when the classification error exceeds the confidence level with respect to trial 1, like in the Duffing model. This suggests that the observed seasonal variability is driven by a deterministic trend, as would be expected from previous studies (for instance [11]).

4 Discussion and Conclusions

In this work, we aimed to identify when a data set, observed at different times (for instance, on a series of experimental trials), undergone deterministic changes in its parameters' dynamics. In short, the trajectory classification error is a trivial to compute statistics, sensitive to smooth non-stationary variations of deterministic nature in multi-attracting systems; and particularly advantageous when statistical moments do not significantly vary from trial to trial (Figures 2a, 2c). Classical tests of non-stationarity based in fourier analysis and more recently in in wavelets [7,15,16] require a larger sample than the simple statistic developed here, limiting their scope.

Moreover , if data was i.i.d generated by time-varying distributions -as it is typically the assumption in data analyses- both trajectory and pattern classification behave similarly (Figure 2b). This indicates that deterministic data generators are not the sources of observed patters. The analyses performed in time series of hourly ozone concentrations are consistent with the results obtained in the dynamical system model and in previous studies (Figure 2c).

To discern latent deterministic components is essential in a number of data analyses settings. For instance, the nature of trial-to-trial variability source often observed in neurophysiological recording modalities has been debated in many works (for instance [14]). Recently, it has been proposed that trial-to trial variability in neural recordings is not mainly due stochastic internal fluctuations in brain activity as traditionally assumed; but the result of deterministic processes involving challenging computations for sensory systems [4]. The identification of the origin of trial-to-trial variability in neural recordings has been addressed in detail in our recent study ([1]).

To conclude, this work has implications for adaptive learning. A practical interest in contemporary machine learning for non-stationary environments is to quickly detect when a classifier needs to be updated in conditions where the memory buffer of the model is limited [18,6]. In such settings, provided the time scales of the problem are approximately known, trajectory classification error would be more sensitive to drifts of deterministic nature than other classification statistics. Thus, this approach is potentially useful in streaming data mining analyses.

Acknowledgments. The research leading to these results has received partial funding from the European Union 7th Framework Programme (FP7/2007-2013) under grant agreement 251617. ATD has been funded by The Graduate School, Bournemouth University.

References

1. Balaguer-Ballester, E., Tabas-Diaz, A., Budka, M.: Can we identify non-stationary dynamics of trial-to-trial variability? PLoS ONE 9, e95648 (2014)
2. Balaguer-Ballester, E., Camps-Valls, G., Carrasco-Rodriguez, J.L., Soria-Olivas, E., del Valle-Tascon, S.: Effective one-day ahead prediction of hourly surface ozone concentrations in Eastern Spain using linear models and neural networks. Ecological Modelling 156, 27–41 (2002)

3. Balaguer-Ballester, E., Lapish, C., Seamans, J., Durstewitz, D.: Attracting dynamics of frontal cortex ensembles during memory guided decision making. PLoS Computational Biology 7, e1002057 (2011)
4. Beck, J.M., Ma, W.J., Pitkow, X., Latham, P.E., Pouget, A.: Not noisy, just wrong: The role of suboptimal inference in behavioral variability. Neuron 74, 33–39 (2012)
5. Blythe, D.A.J., von Bunau, P., Meinecke, F.C., Robert-Muller, K.: Feature extraction for change-point detection using stationary subspace analysis. IEEE Trans. Neural Networks 23, 631–643 (2012)
6. Bouchachia, A.: Incremental learning with multi-level adaptation. Neurocomputing 74, 1785–1799 (2011)
7. Chen, J.S., Hu, N.J.: A frequency domain test for detecting nonstationary time series. Computational Statistics and Data Analysis (in press, 2014)
8. Du, J., Cui, M.: Solving the forced duffing equation with integral boundary conditions in the reproducing kernel space. International Journal of Computer Mathematics 87, 2088–2100 (2010)
9. Durstewitz, D., Balaguer-Ballester, E.: Statistical approaches for reconstructing neuro-cognitive dynamics from high-dimensional neural recordings. Neuroforum 1, 89–98 (2010)
10. Feng, Z., Chen, G., Hsu, S.: A qualitative study of the damped duffing equation and applications. American Institute of Mathematical Sciences 6, 1097–1112 (2006)
11. Gomez-Sanchis, J., Martin-Guerrero, J.O., Soria-Olivas, E., Vila-Frances, J., Carrasco, J.L., del Valle-Tascon, S.: Neural networks for analysing the relevance of input variables in the prediction of tropospheric ozone concentration. Atmospheric Environment 40, 6173–6180 (2006)
12. Haraa, S., Kawaharaa, Y., Washioa, T., von Bnau, P., Tokunagac, T., Yumotod, K.: Separation of stationary and non-stationary sources with a generalized eigenvalue problem. Neural Networks 33, 7–20 (2012)
13. Kuncheva, L.I., Rodriguez, J.J.: Interval feature extraction for classification of event-related potentials (erp) in eeg data analysis. Progress in Artificial Intelligence 2, 65–72 (2012)
14. Masquelier, T.: Neural variability, or lack thereof. Frontiers in Comput. Neurosci. 7, 1–7 (2013)
15. Nason, G.: A test for second-order stationarity and approximate confidence intervals for localized autocovariances for locally stationary time series. J. R. Statist. Soc. B 75, 879–904 (2013)
16. Priestley, M.B., Subba, T.: A test for non-stationarity of time-series. J. R. Statist. Soc. B 31, 140–149 (1969)
17. Sauer, T., Yorke, J., Casdagli, M.: Embedology. J. Stat. Phys. 65, 579–616 (1992)
18. Sayed-Mouchaweh, M., Lughofer, E. (eds.): Learning in Non-Stationary Environments. Springer (2012)
19. Scholkopf, B., Smola, A.J.: Learning with kernels. MIT Press (2002)
20. von Bunau, P., Meinecke, F.C., Kiraly, F.J., Robert-Muller, K.: Finding stationary subspaces in multivariate time series. Phys. Rev. Lett. 103, 214101 (2009)
21. Wiggins, S.: Introduction to applied nonlinear dynamical systems and chaos. Springer (2013)
22. Zliobaite, I., Bifet, A., Pfahringer, B., Holmes, G.: Active learning with drifting streaming data. IEEE Transactions on Neural Networks and Learning Systems (2013) (in press)

Physical Time Series Prediction Using Dynamic Neural Network Inspired by the Immune Algorithm

Abir Jaafar Hussain, Haya Al-Askar, and Dhiya Al-Jumeily

Applied Computing Research Group, Liverpool John Moores University,
Byroom Street, Liverpool, L3 3AF, UK
{a.hussain,d.aljumeily}@ljmu.ac.uk, H.Alaskar@2011.ljmu.ac.uk

Abstract. Time series analysis is a fundamental subject that has been addressed widely in different fields. It has been exploited and used in different scientific fields for example, natural, biomedical, economic and industrial data as well as financial time series. In this paper, we consider the application of a novel neural network architecture inspired by the immune algorithm and the recurrent links for the prediction of Lorenz and earthquake time series by exploiting the inherent temporal capabilities of the recurrent neural model. The performance of this network is benchmarked against "traditional", rate-encoded, neural networks; a Multi-Layer Perceptron network, a Jordan and an Elman neural network as well as the self organized neural network inspired by the immune algorithm. The results indicate that the inherent temporal characteristics of the recurrent links network make it extremely well suited to the processing of time series based data.

Keywords: Recurrent neural network, self organised neural network, and physical time series prediction.

1 Introduction

A time series is a collection of observations of a particular problem measured during a period of time. In theory, it is known as a sequence of variables ordered in time. Mathematically, for any given system, a time series can be referred to as $x(t)$ or $\{x(t),t \in T\}$, and it contains two variables; the first one is the time variables (t) while the second one is the observation variables $x(t)$, where x can be a value that varies continuously with t, such as the temperature, solar and earthquake time series, etc.

In reality, there are many motivations for conducting time series analysis and modelling. It has recently gained much attention from scientists and researchers, whose interest has led to different types of time series for different applications and for different fields. In industrial applications, time series can be used to monitor industrial processes [1-2]. Time series analysis also has important applications in economics. The main motivation of analysing financial time series is to gain the ability to identify and understand the internal structure that creates the data in time series. In other words, as Herrera [3] asserted, it attempts to explore the underlying properties of sequences of observations taken from a system under examination. In addition, it helps find the

A. Bouchachia (Ed.): ICAIS 2014, LNAI 8779, pp. 152–161, 2014.

optimal model to fit the time series data and apply this model to predict the future observations of data based on past data series [4]. For example, financial market prediction is performed by the computations of the next value of trade sales each month [5].

Two main features characterise time series data: the stationary and non-stationary concepts. It is very important to identify these two concepts before starting the process of time series analysis. This will help to find the best mathematical model to deal with this type of data. The simplest way to observe stationary and non-stationary data is the plotting of the observations. The concept of stationary in time series means that the probability distribution between data does not change when shifted in time. Hence, the statistical properties (e.g. mean, variance and autocorrelation) of the data are stable with respect to time, such as climate oscillations [6].

In mathematics, stationary can be defined as follows, when the distribution of $(xt_1, \ldots, xt_n)$ is the same as the distribution of $(xt_{1+k}, \ldots, xt_{n+k})$ where $t_1, \ldots, t_n$ is refers to time step, and k is an integer [7]. The behaviour of any intervals in this series is similar to one another, even if the segments have been taken from the beginnings of the time series or the ends. Therefore, this type of time series is very easy to model.

Non-stationary characterises another type of time series. It means that parameters of the information (e.g. mean and variance) of the data always change over time. Therefore, behaviours of the signals are changing from one interval to the next. Most real-world time series are non-stationary, such as physical series data or biomedical signals. Non-stationary time series are difficult to deal with. However, some models require the application of a pre-processed method in order to smooth out the noise and reduce the trend of the non-stationary data. Therefore, they can be transferred from non-stationary to stationary.

There are a number of studies which have investigated the ability to use different techniques to improve the generalisation ability of feed-forward neural networks and to automatically select the best number of hidden units and their weights. One of these techniques was proposed by Widyanto et al. [8]. They designed a self-organised hidden layer inspired by immune algorithm (SONIA). SONIA contains an immune algorithm in the self-organised hidden layer. The main aim of this network is to improve the recognition and the generalisation propriety of the MLP neural network. SONIA was used to predict temperature-based food quality; it showed 18% improvement in correct recognition in comparison to the MLP network [8]. However, SONIA is a feed-forward neural network, which means that it can solve static problems but cannot remember past behaviours. Therefore, in this paper neural network architecture is presented which is called recurrent Self-organized Multilayer neural network inspired by Immune Algorithm (DSMIA). The proposed network combines the properties of the self organized map inspired by the immune algorithm and the recurrent networks. In this paper, the proposed network will be used for physical time series prediction, which includes the Lorenz attractor and the earthquake time series. The aim is to improve the generalization capability of the neural network for time series forecasting by using recurrent links structure.

The remainder of this paper is organized as follows. Section 2 describes Self-organized Multilayer network inspired by the Immune Algorithm (SONIA). In section 3, the proposed Dynamic Self-organized Multilayer neural network which is inspired by Immune Algorithm is presented while section 4 describes the data that has been used and the simulation results in this paper. Finally, the conclusions of this paper and future directions are discussed in Section 5.

2   Self-organised Multilayer Network Inspired by Immune Algorithm (SONIA)

A Self-Organised Network inspired by the Immune algorithm (SONIA) [8] is a single hidden layer neural network, which uses a self-organization hidden layer inspired by the immune and back-propagation algorithms for the training of the output layer. The immune algorithm is simulated as the nature immune system, which is based on the relationship between its components, which involve antigens and cells (Recognition Ball). Thus, the immune system can allow its components to change and learn patterns by changing the strength of connections between individual components. The inspiration of the immune system in the self-organized neural network will provide hidden unit creation in backpropagation neural networks (BP-NN). The SONIA network was proposed to improve the generalization and recognition capability of the back-propagation neural network [8].

The input units are called antigens and hidden units are called recognition balls (RB). RBs in the immune system are used to create hidden units. The relation between the antigen and the RB is based on the definition of local pattern relationships between input vectors and hidden nodes. These relationships help SONIA to easily recognize and define the input data's local characteristics, which increases the networks ability to recognize patterns. The mutation process, which is biologically, a B cell, can be created and mutated to produce a diverse set of antibodies in order to remove and fight viruses that attack the body. In SONIA, the mutated hidden nodes are designed to deal with unknown data, which is the test data, to develop the generalization ability of the network.

3   Dynamic Self-organised Multilayer Network Inspired by the Immune Algorithm (DSMIA)

The Dynamic Self-organised Multilayer network Inspired by the Immune Algorithm (DSMIA) is proposed to capture some of the complex patterns found in the natural time series [14]. The structure of the DSMIA network is shown in Fig. 1. The DSMIA network has three layers: the input, the self-organising hidden layers, and the output layer with feedback connections from the output layer to the input layer. The input layer holds copies of the current inputs as well as the previous output produced by the network. This provides the network with memory. As such, the previous behaviour of the network is used as an input affecting current behaviour. Similar to the Jordan recurrent network [9], the output of the network is fed back to the input through the context units.

Suppose that N is the number of external inputs $x(n)$ to the network, and $y_k(n-1)$ is the output of the network from the previous time step $(n-1)$ and let O represents the number of outputs. In the proposed *DSMIA*, the overall input to the network will be the component of $x(n)$ and $y_k(n-1)$ and the number of inputs to the network is $N+O$ defined as U where

$$U(n) = \begin{cases} x_i(n) & i = 1,....N \\ y_i(n-1) & i = 1,....,O \end{cases} \quad (1)$$

The output of the hidden layer is computed as

$$v_{hj}(n) = \alpha \sqrt{\sum_{i=1}^{N}(w_{hj} - x_{hj}(n))^2} \quad (2)$$

$$z_{hj}(n) = \beta \sqrt{\sum_{k=1}^{O}(wz_{hjk} - y_k(n-1))^2} \quad (3)$$

$$D_{hj}(n) = v_{hj}(n) + z_{hj}(n) \quad (4)$$

$$x_{hj}(n) = f_{ht}(D_{hj}(n)) \quad (5)$$

$$\hat{y}_k = f_{ot}\left(\sum_{j=1}^{N_H} W_{ojk} \, x_{Hj} + B_{ok}\right) \quad (6)$$

Where f_{ht}, f_{ot} are nonlinear activation functions, N is the number of external inputs, O is the number of output units. w_{ojk} is the weight corresponds to the external input while wz_{hjk} is the weight corresponding to the previous output, and n is the current time step, while α, β are selected parameters with $0 < \alpha$ and $0 < \beta$.

The first layer of the DSMIA is a self-organised hidden layer trained similar to the recursive self-organized map RecSOM [15]. In this case, the training rule for updating the weights is based on the same technique for updating the weights of the self-organized network inspired by the immune algorithm (SONIA) network [8]. The change in this network is that the weights of the context nodes wz_{hjk} are also updated in the same way as the weights of the external inputs w_{hj}. This is done by first finding D, which is the distance between the input units and the centroid of the jth hidden units:

$$D_{hj}(n) = \alpha \sqrt{\sum_{i=1}^{N}(w_{hji} - x_{hj}(n))^2} + \beta \sqrt{\sum_{k=1}^{O}(wz_{hjk} - y_k(n-1))^2} \quad (7)$$

From $D_{hj}(n)$, the position of the closest match will be determined as :

$$c(n) = argmin(D_{hj}(n)) \quad (8)$$

If the shortest distance D_c is less than the stimulation level value, $s_1 \in (0, 1)$, then the weight from the external input vector and the context vector are updated as follows:

$$W_{hji}(n+1) = W_{hji}(n) + \gamma D_c(n) \quad (9)$$

$$Wz_{hji}(n+1) = Wz_{hjk}(n) + \gamma D_c(n) \quad (10)$$

Where Wz_{hji} is the weight of the previous output and W_{hji} is the weight for the external inputs, and γ is the learning rate which is updated during the epochs.

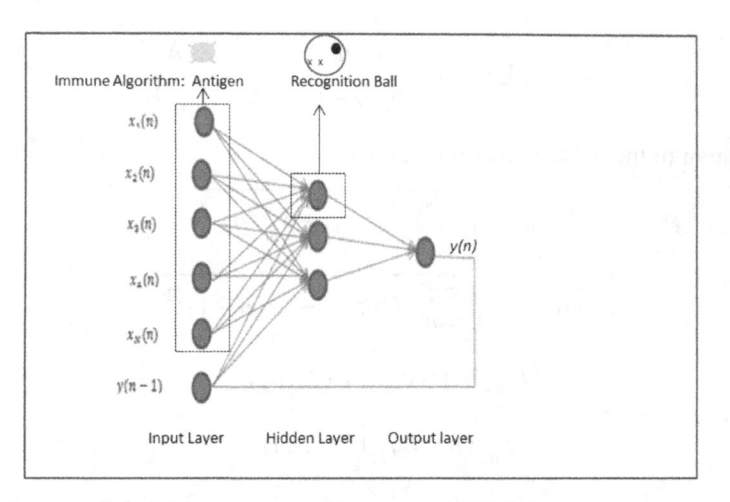

Fig. 1. The structure of the proposed DSMIA network

4   Time Series Prediction Using the Dynamic Self-organised Multilayer Network Inspired by the Immune Algorithm

4.1   Time Series Used in the Experiments

Two time series have been used for our experiments, namely the Lorenz attractor and the earthquake time series.

The Lorenz attractor is a set of three deterministic equations introduced by Lorenz [16], a meteorologist working on weather models, when he was studying the non-repeatability of the weather patterns. The equations approximate the two-dimensional flow of a fluid heated along the bottom. The Lorenz attractor can be obtained by simultaneously solving the following equations:

$$\begin{cases} dX / dt = \sigma(-X + Y), \\ dY / dt = -XZ + \tau X - Y, \\ dZ / dt = XY - bZ, \end{cases} \tag{11}$$

The earthquake signal is one of the most difficult types of signals that are very difficult to predict. The correlogram of the earthquake time series indicates that the autocorrelation coefficient drops to zero for large values of the lag. As a result, we can conclude that the time-series is a non-stationary signal.

4.2   Experimental Designs

The performance of the proposed network was benchmarked with the performance of the multilayer perceptrons (MLP), the Self organized self organized inspired by the Immune algorithm (SONIA), the Jordan [12] and the Elman [13] neural networks.

Table 1. Performance Metrics and their Calculations

Metrics	NMSE	SNR
Calculations	$NMSE = \dfrac{1}{\sigma^2 n} \sum\limits_{i=1}^{n} \left(y_i - \hat{y}_i\right)$ $\sigma^2 = \dfrac{1}{n-1} \sum\limits_{i=1}^{n} (y_i - \bar{y})^2$ $\bar{y} = \sum\limits_{i=1}^{n} y_i$	$SNR = 10 * \log_{10} \left(sigma\right)$ $sigma = \dfrac{m^2 * n}{SSE}$ $SSE = \sum\limits_{i=1}^{n} (y_i - \hat{y}_i)^2$ $m = max(y)$

The prediction performance of our networks was evaluated using the normalised mean square of the error (NMSE) and the signal to noise ratio (SNR) matrices as shown in Table 1. The NMSE is an estimator of the overall deviations between target and predicted values. The lower NMSE values show that the prediction signals closely follow the trend of the actual target. The SNR is a measurement used to compare the amount of information on a desired signal to the amount of background noise. The highest ratio of SNR means the signal levels are higher than the noise level.

All the input variables were scaled in order to avoid computational problems and to meet algorithm requirements. A few reasons for using data scaling is to reduce range difference in the data and to process outliers, which consist of sample values that occur outside the normal (expected) range. Furthermore, the data are scaled to accommodate the limits of the network's transfer function. Manipulation of the data using this process produces a new bounded dataset. The calculation for the standard minimum and maximum normalization method is as follows:

$$x' = (max_2 - min_2) \times \left(\frac{x - min_1}{max_1 - min_1} \right) + min_2 \tag{12}$$

where x' refers to the normalized value, x refers to the observation value (original value), min_1 and max_1 are the respective minimum and maximum values of all observations, and min_2 and max_2 refer to the desired minimum and maximum of the new scaled series. The input-output variables were normalized between the interval [0.2, 0.8]. The choice of this interval is to avoid difficulty in getting network outputs too close to the two endpoints of sigmoid transfer function.

The data sets used in this work were segregated in time order. In other words earlier period of data are used for training, and the data of the later period are used for testing. The main purpose of sorting them into this order is to discover the underlying structure or trend of the mechanism generating the data, that is to understand the relationship exist between the past, present and future data.

4.3   Simulation Results

The simulation results for the prediction of the Lorenz attractor and the sunspot time series using the proposed DSMIA will be presented.

Two sets of experiments were performed, in the first set of experiments the physical signals are passed directly to the network as nonstationary data while in the second set of experiments the signals are transformed into stationary signals using the following equation:

$$R(t) = \frac{S(t)}{S(t-1)} - 1 \tag{12}$$

where $S(t)$ is the input signal and $R(t)$ is the one step relative increase value at time t. This transformation has been shown to achieve better results [17]. The one step relative increase value is used since $R(t)$ has a relative constant range of values, while the original data $S(t)$ vary so much which make it very difficult to use a valid model for a long period of time [18]. Another advantage of using this transformation is that the distribution of the transformed data will become more symmetrical and will follow more closely to a normal distribution.

The amount of input units must be selected carefully. Therefore, neural network inputs for this type of data are represented as lagged values and the output values are corresponding to the future value. The input layer will hold the time series data points of N days, and the output layer will produce the prediction values for next days "$(N + 1)^{th}$" day. Using too many past periods as input will lead to much difficulty in training the Artificial Neural Network (ANN), whereas too few periods may not be enough to train the ANN. In this research work, the number of inputs is set to five, as recommended by a number of studies [4, 10].

Table 2. Five steps ahead prediction for the Lorenz attractor and the earthquake using non-stationary signals

Networks	Lorenz attractor NMSE	Lorenz attractor SNR	Earthquake signal NMSE	Earthquake Signal SNR
MLP	0.4349	21.4001	0.9757	21.8492
Elman	0.9027	18.6730	2.1076	19.8572
Jordan	0.4040	21.7200	5.1569	19.1289
SONIA	0.504945	17.68	1.168576	21.070
DSMIA	0.4889	20.9099	1.0692	21.4520

In terms of selecting the number and size of the hidden layers in the ANN and other neural parameters such as learning rate and momentum, it has been recommended that trial and error is needed to determine the optimal structure of the neural network. The best way to evaluate the performance of the ANN learning is to split the raw data not only into training and test sets, but also a separate validation set. Therefore, the time series was divided into three parts, the first 50% of the data are used for the training set; the second 25% for the validation set, used to estimate the neural network parameters, and the third 25% is selected for testing the performance of the network. The testing period is kept for final performance evaluation and comparison. This has been done in order to evaluate the accuracy of the model for understanding the past, present and future data sets. The initial weights are selected between [-0.5, 0.5]. The momentum term and the learning rate parameters are selected experimentally. The best values for these parameters are based on the training data set.

Table 3. Five steps ahead prediction for the Lorenz attractor and the earthquake using the stationary signals

Networks	Lorenz attractor NMSE	Lorenz attractor SNR	Earthquake signal NMSE	Earthquake Signal SNR
MLP	1.00863	32.29	1.00853	37.36
Elman	1.3022	31.2338	1.131196	36.87
Jordan	4.4221999	28.44	1.0319327	37.263
SONIA	1.008816	32.30	1.276895	36.36
DSMIA	0.999675	32.34	1.0080	37.3633

Table 2 shows the average results of 30 simulations obtained on unseen data from the neural networks when the physical signals are passed directly to the network without any transformation and Table 3 displays the average results of 30 simulations obtained on unseen data from the neural networks when the data are transformed into stationary as in equation 11.

Table 4. Number of hidden nodes in the DSMIA and the SONIA networks for five step ahead stationary signals using the best simulation results

	Nonstationary prediction		Stationary prediction	
	SONIA	DSMIA	SONIA	DSMIA
Lorenz	6	5	4	2
Earthquake	17	4	8	7

As it can be shown from Tables 2 and 3, the transformation of the signals from nonstationary to stationary has significantly improved the results for all the neural network architectures. For the nonstationay prediction, the proposed DSMIA showed better results than the SONIA network for both the Lorenz and the earthquake signals using the NMSE and the SNR measures. This is clearly indicating that the recurrent links has provided the network with memory and hence better prediction. For the stationary prediction, the proposed network shows slightly improved results than all the benchmarked networks.

To further analysis the significant of the results, we have conducted a paired t-test [11] on the best simulation results to determine if there is any significant difference among the proposed DSMIA and the other neural network architectures based on the absolute value of the error. The calculated t-value showed that the proposed technique outperforms the other ANNs with $\alpha = 5\%$ significance level for a one tailed test.

Table 4 shows the number of hidden nodes utilized for the prediction of the Lorenz attractor and the earthquake signals on the best out of sample simulation results between the proposed and the SONIA networks. The results indicated that the proposed network required less number of hidden units. In addition, these results indicated that when the data are transformed in stationary less number of hidden units were required for both the DSMIA and the SONIA network.

5   Conclusion

In this paper a novel neural network architecture based on a self organied network inspired by immune algorithm is proposed for the prediction of physical time series. Two physical time series were utilised in these experiments, the Lorenz attractor and the earthquake signals. The signals were transformed into stationary signal and the results for 5 step ahead prediction were shown. The simulation results indicated that using recurrent links can slightly improve the results due to the temporal aspect of the time series.

One of the major limitations of the proposed network is computational performance. Hence, another direction of research must be taken which investigates the best choice of network architecture and this includes the number of hidden units and the use of higher order terms in the input units. The utilising of high order terms in the neural network can provide reduced computational time and reduced number of input units in the ANN. This may improve the performance of the proposed network. In addition, improving the efficiency of the prediction methods and procedures can be done by combining the Elman and Jordan architectures in the proposed network. This combination can enhance the network performance. Future direction will include the use of fuzzy logic in the structure of the proposed dynamic self-organised neural network to improve the classifier performance. Another problem that has been encountered is the selection of the best values for the learning rate and momentum parameters that are used in the neural networks. This is a challenging problem as there is a need to carefully test many variables manually using trial and error method. One direction for future improvement to overcome this problem is to use some type of genetic algorithm to automatically identify suitable neural network parameters.

References

1. Roverso, D.: Multivariate temporal classification by windowed wavelet decomposition and recurrent neural networks. In: Proceedings of the 3rd ANS International Topical Meeting on Nuclear Plant Instrumentation, Washington, DC, USA, Control and Human-Machine Interface Technologies, pp. 527–538 (2000)
2. Mirea, L., Marcu, T.: System identification using Functional-Link Neural Networks with dynamic structure. In: 15th Triennial World Congress, Barcelona, Spain (2002)
3. Herrera, J.L.: Time Series Prediction Using Inductive Reasoning Techniques. Instituto de Organizacion y Control de Sistemas Industriales (1999)
4. Ghazali, R., Hussain, A., Nawi, N., Mohamad, B.: Non-stationary and stationary prediction of financial time series using dynamic ridge polynomial neural network. Neurocomputing 72(10-12), 2359–2367 (2009)

5. Yümlü, S., Gürgen, F.S., Okay, N.: A comparison of global, recurrent and smoothed-piecewise neural models for Istanbul stock exchange (ISE) prediction. Pattern Recognition Letters 26(13), 2093–2103 (2005)
6. Mengistu, S.G., Quick, C.G., Creed, I.F.: Nutrient export from catchments on forested landscapes reveals complex nonstationary and stationary climate signals. Water Resources Research 49(6), 3863–3880 (2013), http://doi.wiley.com/10.1002/wrcr.20302 (accessed October 2013)
7. Aamodt, R.: Using Artificial Neural Networks to Forecast Financial Time Series. Unpublished Master's thesis. Norwegian University of Science and Technology (2010)
8. Widyanto, M.R., Nobuhara, H., Kawamoto, K., Hirota, K., Kusumoputro, B.: Improving recognition and generalization capability of back-propagation NN using a self-organized network inspired by immune algorithm (SONIA). Applied Soft Computing 6(1), 72–84 (2005)
9. Jordan, M.I.: Attractor dynamics and parallelism in a connectionist sequential machine. In: Artificial Neural Networks, pp. 112–127. IEEE Press, Piscataway (1990)
10. Mahdi, A.A., Hussain, A.J., Al-Jumeily, D.: The Prediction of Non-Stationary Physical Time Series Using the Application of Regularization Technique in Self-organised Multilayer Perceptrons Inspired by the Immune Algorithm. 2010 Developments in E-systems Engineering, pp. 213–218 (2010), http://ieeexplore.ieee.org/lpdocs/epic03/wrapper.htm?arnumber=5633838 (accessed February 11, 2014)
11. Montgomery, D.C., Runger, G.C.: Applied Statistics and Probability for Engineers. Wiley, New York (1999)
12. Jordan, M.I.: Attractor dynamics and parallelism in a connectionist sequential machine. In: Artificial Neural Networks, pp. 112–127. IEEE Press, Piscataway (1990)
13. Elman, L.J.: Finding Structure in Time. Cognitive Science 14, 179–211 (1990)
14. Al-Jumeily, D., Hussain, A., Alaskar, H.: Recurrent Neural Networks Inspired by Artificial Immune Algorithm for Time Series Prediction. In: International Joint Conference on Neural Networks, Dallas, USA, August 3-9 (2013) ISBN: 978-1- 4673-6128-6
15. Voegtlin, T.: Context quantization and contextual self-organizing maps. In: Proc. Int. Joint Conf. on Neural Networks, vol. 5, pp. 20–25 (2000)
16. Lorenz, E.N.: The statistical prediction of solutions of dynamics equations. In: Proceedings International Symposium on Numerical Weather Prediction, pp. 629–635. Meteorological Society Japan (1962)
17. Dunis, C.L., Williams, M.: Modelling and trading the EUR/USD exchange rate: Do neural network models perform better? Derivatives Use, Trading and Regulation 8(3), 211–239 (2002)
18. Hellstrom, T., Holmstrom, K.: Predicting the Stock Market. Technical Report IMa-TOM-1997-07, Center of Mathematical Modeling, Department of Mathematics and Physis, Mälardalen University, Västeras, Sweden (August 1998)

Collaborative Wind Power Forecast

Vânia Almeida[1] and João Gama[1,2]

[1] LIAAD - INESC TEC, University of Porto, Porto, Portugal
vania.g.almeida@inescporto.pt
[2] Faculty of Economics, University of Porto, Portugal
jgama@fep.up.pt

Abstract. There are several new emerging environments, generating data spatially spread and interrelated. These applications reinforce the importance of the development of analytical systems capable to sense the environment and receive data from different locations. In this study we explore collaborative methodologies in a real-world problem: wind power prediction. Wind power is considered one of the most rapidly growing sources of electricity generation all over the world. The problem consists of monitoring a network of wind farms that collaborate by sharing information in a very short-term forecasting problem. We use an auto-regressive integrated moving average (ARIMA) model. The Symbolic Aggregate Approximation (SAX) is used in the selection of the set of neighbours. We propose two collaborative methods. The first one, based on a centralized management, exchange data-points between nodes. In the second approach, correlated wind farms share their own ARIMA models. In the experimental work we use 1 year data from 16 wind farms. The goal is to predict the energy produced at each farm every hour in the next 6 hours. We compare the proposed methods against ARIMA models trained with data of each one of the farms and with the persistence model at each farm. We observe a small but consistent reduction of the root mean square error (RMSE) of the predictions.

Keywords: Wind Power, Time Series Analysis, Collaborative Forecast, Correlation, Arima.

1 Introduction

Emerging environments generate data spatially spread and interrelated. These applications reinforce the importance of the development of analysis systems capable to sense the environment and receive data from different locations [1]. The capability to integrate the overall set of information available can be meaningful and can be used in the development of proper adaptive data analysis algorithms.

Wind power is considered one of the most rapidly growing sources of electricity generation all over the world [2]. The main problems remain on the modelling of the wind turbine output [3] and on the development of accurate wind power forecast methodologies, capable to deal with the uncertain and variability of this resource. The suitability of a forecasting model is determined by the forecasting

A. Bouchachia (Ed.): ICAIS 2014, LNAI 8779, pp. 162–171, 2014.

horizon which is the time ahead for which the forecast is made [4], being mainly separated into very short-term (30min-6hrs), short term (up to 72hrs ahead) and long term forecasting (several days ahead) [2,5]. Statistical methods are commonly used for short-term wind forecast, taking as input the past values from the forecast variable. The most popular models are auto-regressive moving average (ARMA) models and their variants, *e.g.*, Auto-Regressive Integrated Moving Average (ARIMA), seasonal- and fractional-ARIMA and ARIMA with exogenous input (ARMAX or ARX). The development of prediction tools is not a new subject, and there is a considerable number of important contributions on this topic [6,7].

Motif discovery commonly used to reveal trends, relationships, and anomalies can provide some guidance on the analysis of correlations between wind farms. This subject was studied by Kamath and Fan (2012) [8] using the Symbolic Aggregation Algorithm (SAX) [9]. In this work, it was discussed the role of motifs in scheduling operations.

The evolution of weather fronts over an extended area generates dependencies between power generations at different locations that can be useful to improve forecast methodologies. It was demonstrated that the combination of Numerical Weather Predictions (NWP) from different stations leads to the error decrease [10]. Berdugo et al. [11] described a collaborative short term forecasting methodology for photovoltaic problem. The results indicate the improvement of the forecast error when collaboration among sites is employed, comparatively to standard reference methods. A similar methodology for short-term wind speed prediction using both temporal and spatial characteristics also demonstrated the relevance of the spatio-temporal prediction tasks [12]. The forecasting task for geo-referenced time series also demonstrates the effectiveness of spatial and temporal ARIMA modelling with respect to univariate time series [13].

Although ARIMA is broadly used in time series analysis, there are few few studies considering the spatially correlation among data from different locations. This paper proposes a collaborative approach where wind-farms share data. We start by identifying correlations, trends, and patterns between farms, and exploit these correlations for optimizing predictions. The main contribution is the development of a collaborative wind power forecast approach, considering the interrelation among neighbour farms. The preliminary selection of potentially correlated farms consisted on the search for motifs using the SAX.

The organization of the paper is as follows. In Section 2 the collaborative forecast methodology is described. Experimental validation on real wind power dataset is presented in Section 3. The final section concludes the paper, including foreseen future work.

2   Collaborative Forecast for Network Data

A collaborative prediction approach applied to wind power forecast is proposed. However, this approach is no dependent on this particular application and can be seen as a general approach to other real world domains that have similar forecasting problems with the same type of network data. The application to sensor network problems lead us to consider the computational power a problem, even being aware that for this specific application be a less important requirement.

The goal consists of monitor a network of N synchronized sites (wind farms), numbered $i=1,2,...,N$. Each site has a set (NG_i) of correlated neighbour sites that collaborate to optimally fit the wind power forecast, at a 6-hours ahead horizon. The expected output is to minimize the forecast error of a site i, sharing relevant information but using minimum communication costs.

2.1   Finding Motifs

The preliminary selection of the potentially correlated neighbours to include in collaborative wind power model was performed searching for recurring motifs in historical data. A subsequence that repeats at least once is a motif. For the evaluation of the relationship between two subsequences, a distance measure must be used, as well as a match threshold. It is important to consider that a re-occurrence of the subsequence needs not to be exact for it to be considered as a motif. To map into a lower dimensional space, the SAX algorithm proposed by Lin *et al.* [14] was adopted.

The relation of patterns for different wind farms with different installed capabilities is a difficult task. So, before to apply SAX, data was scaled to maximum installed capacity, assuring the minimization of the distance between subsequences. This task is essential for the definition of the similarity threshold value.

2.2   Computation from Correlation Matrices

The computation of spatial and temporal correlation plays an important role in distributed environments [15], being possible to determine the strength of the influence of the distributed data. Along this work, different types of networks (and thus correlation measures) describing interactions between nodes are considered. The Pearson correlation is used in centralized management, while distributed approaches use the dot-product analysis.

Pearson correlation measures the linear correlation (dependence) between two variables x and y, giving a value between $+1$ and -1 inclusive, where 1 is total positive correlation, 0 is no correlation, and -1 is total negative correlation.

The dot product is also considered as a correlation metric, allowing to measure how closely two feature vectors are related. It is defined as the cosine of the angle of a paired data represented as vectors, $x.y = |x|\,|y|\,cos(\theta)$. For each single site, we compute the inner product between consecutive subsequences of fixed length (6-hours in this case). Both methods require the determination of a minimum threshold for the correlation coefficient.

2.3   Persistence

The persistence is a common used baseline prediction model. It considers that the wind power in the next time step is the same as occurred in the present time.

A known generalization was used, considering the prevision at time instant t for a look-ahead time $t+k$ ($\hat{p}_{t+k|t}$) the average value of the last n observations ($n = 6$ hours in this case), being defined as follows:

$$\hat{p}_{t+k|t} = \frac{1}{n} \sum_{i=0}^{n-1} p_{t-i}$$

2.4   ARIMA Modelling

The ARIMA modelling approach was introduced by Box and Jenkins (1976) [16] to analyse stationary univariate time series, taking as input the past values from the forecast variable. Along this work all models were implementation in R using the *forecast* package.

Three models were implemented, a ARIMA reference model (RefARIMA) comprised the train for the historical observations of each one of the farms, using the *auto.arima* function, and two collaborative models. The collaborative models were denominated CentARIMA and DistARIMA. CentARIMA is a model based on centralized management that employs exchange of the values of time series between nodes. The another one, DistARIMA, takes into account the limited computational power associated to the sensor network topologies. In this case, the correlated wind farms share their own ARIMA models.

Centralized Approach. The first idea to solve the forecast problem consisted on the combination of correlated subsequences from the network data. The Pearson correlation is used to search for correlated sequences, considering the NG set. A threshold *thd* is defined to considerate a correlation (*thd* > 0.7). Wind power production at a given site i is a weighted linear combination of past production values at a set of neighbour sites. The *auto.arima* model is performed for the weighted time series (w_i) at each site. From the analysis of the correlation value, it is clear that a high correlation value could arise from data at different amplitude scales. The prediction values need to be adjusted to the correct baseline level. The adjustment consists in the removal of the difference observed between the past 6-values (mean value) and the first prediction value. This algorithm is described in Alg. 1.

Distributed Approach. For each wind farm, the past 2 subsequences of length k are used to compute the dot product. If the dot value is higher that the established threshold (*thd* > 0.97), the predicted values are computed normally, using the *auto.arima* function. Otherwise, being the dot product value lower than the acceptable, the correlated set of wind farms share their own ARIMA models. The final prediction is the weighted sum at each hour of the predicted values obtained for the N considered models. This methodology intends to avoid higher prediction errors that may occur when the actual situation is not correlated with the past, using information from the other farms that experienced similar conditions previously. This procedure is described in Alg. 2.

Algorithm 1. CentARIMA: Centralized ARIMA.

---

input : S_i: Stream of wind power values for farm i
NG_i: Set of correlated neighbour sites
k: Length of sequences used in correlation
j: Identification of past values
n: Number of observations used to ARIMA train
thd: Correlation threshold
output: 6-hours ahead wind power forecast
begin
    foreach *farm i* **do**
        foreach $t \in S_i$ **do**
            $s_i \leftarrow$ Set of sequences $(< x_i(t-k-j), ..., x_i(t-j) >)$ from NG_i
            Compute Pearson correlation A for the sequences in s_i
            if *correlation > thd* **then**
                $A_{i,j} \leftarrow 1$
                $count_c \leftarrow count_c +1$
            else
                $A_{i,j} \leftarrow 0$
            $w_i(\text{t}) \leftarrow \frac{1}{count_c} \sum_{j \in s_i} x_i(t-j).A_{i,j}$
            if $t > n$ **then**
                Fit *auto.arima* for $< w_i(t-n), ..., w_i(t) >$
                $\hat{x}_i(t+1), ..., \hat{x}_i(t+6) \leftarrow$ predicted data
                $\hat{x}'_i(t+1), ..., \hat{x}'_i(t+6) \leftarrow$ adjust predictions to amplitude scale

---

3 Experimental Setup

3.1 Data

For the experiments, we took data from 16 wind farms, distributed at different geographical sites. Data from one year of power production at a hourly-step are available. The set of neighbour farms was chosen based on the number of pairs and motifs occurrence at different lengths, using the SAX representation. The maximum time horizon was set up to 720 hrs (30 days).

3.2 Error Measure

The accuracy of the models is measured by the root mean squared error (RMSE), expressed as a percentage between $\hat{x}_t$ (the forecast at time t) and x_t (the observed value). The analysis was performed in a hour-ahead step until to 6-hours (eq. below).

$$RMSE = \sqrt{\frac{1}{6} \sum_{t=1}^{6} (\hat{x}_t - x_t)^2}$$

Algorithm 2. DistARIMA: Distributed ARIMA.

---

input : S_i: Stream of wind power values for farm i
k: Length of correlated sequences
n: Number of observations used to ARIMA train
NG_i: Set of correlated neighbour sites
N: Length of NG set
thd: Correlation threshold
output: 6-hours ahead wind power forecast
begin

    foreach *farm i* **do**

        foreach $t \in S_i$ **do**

            Collect last 2 consecutive sensed data sequences of length k:
            $(x_1, ..., x_k$ and $y_1, ..., y_k)$
            Compute DOT$=< x_1, ..., x_k > . < y_1, ..., y_k >$
            if $DOT > thd$ **then**
                Run *auto.arima* function for the last n observations
                $(\hat{x}_{t+1}, ..., \hat{x}_{t+6}) \leftarrow$ predicted data
            else
                Receive ARIMA model parameters from the NG_i set
                Fit N ARIMA models for the last n observations
                $(\frac{1}{N}\sum_{i \in NG_i} \hat{x}_i(t+1), ..., \frac{1}{N}\sum_{i \in NG_i} \hat{x}_i(t+6)) \leftarrow$ predicted data

---

3.3   Evaluation of the Predicted Methods

The evaluation was performed for the entire dataset (1 year) in a hourly-step, being the first n observations required to initialize the models.

Centralized Model. The data analysis consisted on the training of an ARIMA model with 100 observations. The evaluation results are presented in Figure 1, using the RefARIMA with the same number of observations, as comparison. For all the farms, we observe lower prediction errors associated to the CentARIMA. The average decrease value is 0.56%. Using the Wilcoxon test, and considering a p-value< 0.01, the differences between models are significant for all the farms excluding the WF15 with $p = 0.37$.

We consider that the exchange of 100 observations for a large network is a number not acceptable in sensor networks. Several experiments for different data length were performed. Figure 2 shows that the historical data length is preponderant on the ARIMA model error. Large historical data length are associated to lower errors but implies more computation cycles and memory usage. The collaborative model, CentARIMA is more stable compared to the traditional univariate model RefARIMA. In this case, the number of historical observations has no prominent influence on the error value, up to less than 100 observations. On the other hand, the historical data length has a preponderant effect on the accuracy of RefARIMA that increases for the models using fewer historical data.

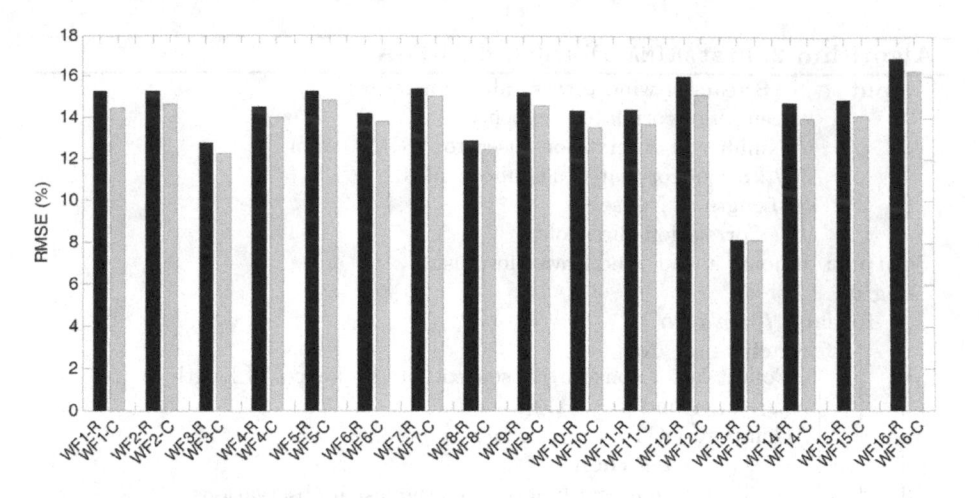

Fig. 1. RMSE values (8600 experiments) from RefARIMA (black bars) and CentARIMA (grey bars), trained with 100 observations for a horizon of 6-hours

It is possible to conclude that the collaborative model presents competitive advantages, if the historical data length is a requirement, without compromising the error value and avoiding computation cycles and memory usage.

Distributed Model. Some textbooks provide rules to minimum sample sizes for various time series models. In the case of ARIMA, 30 observations is often refereed as the minimum acceptable number. So, the DistARIMA model was implemented using 30 observations, being the results compared to the RefARIMA.

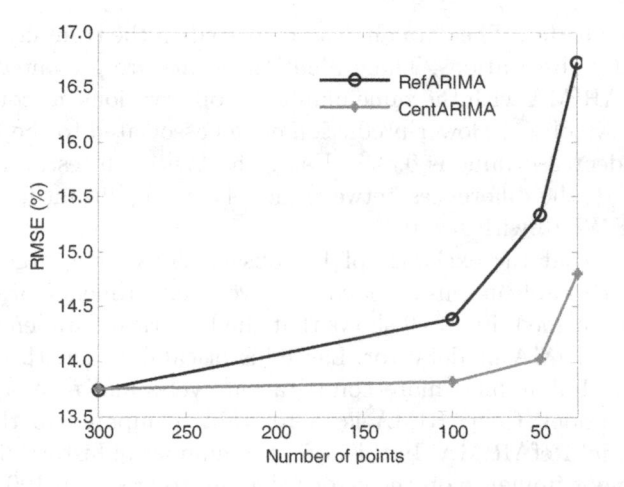

Fig. 2. RMSE error for different historical data length used on the ARIMA model train, at black the RefARIMA and at grey the CentARIMA simulations

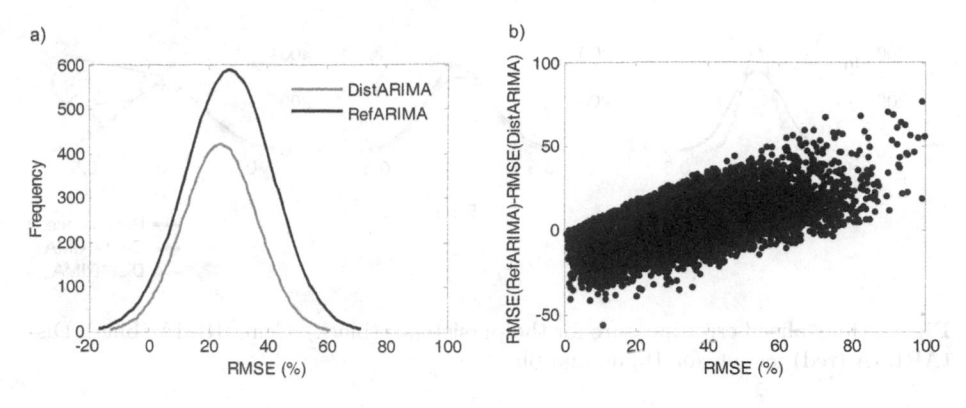

Fig. 3. a) RMSE values when *dot* < 0.97 for the RefARIMA (black) and DistARIMA (grey) models, being visible the lower error distribution for the DistARIMA. b) RMSE difference, being visible the improvement of the DistModel for higher RMSE values.

Results are presented in Figure 3, at the left panel is represented the RMSE error distribution for both models, and at the right the observed differences are plotted. It was observed an average decrease of 3.24% for the DistARIMA, considering the zones where dot product <0.97 (the predefined threshold). It is also visible at the right panel that the error associated to the DistARIMA decreases for zones where the absolute error is higher, such as expected. The Wilcoxon test was applied and results indicate significant differences between the models for all of the farms.

Comparison of the Models. The comparison included persistence and ARIMA models trained with 100 points. Firstly, the RMSE is compared at each hour ahead. The performance of three of the farms is presented in Figure 4. The relevance of the collaborative approaches is exposed, with lower error values comparatively to the persistence that only outperforms (average for all farms)

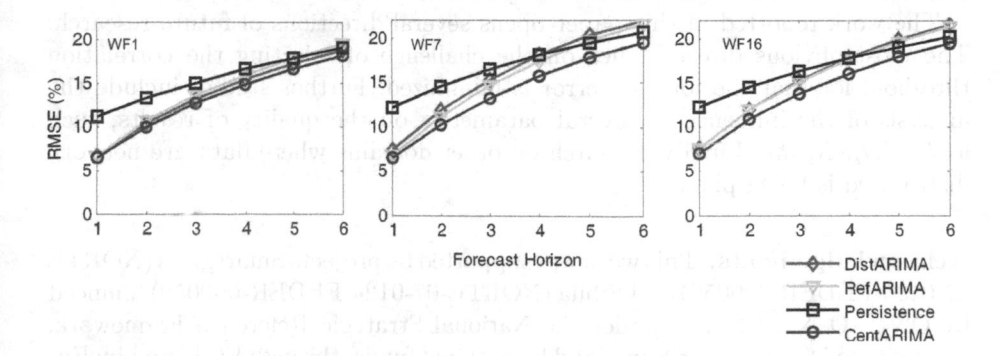

Fig. 4. Hour-ahead forecast for the persistence (black), RefARIMA (grey), CentARIMA (blue), DistARIMA (red) models for the WF1, WF7 and WF16

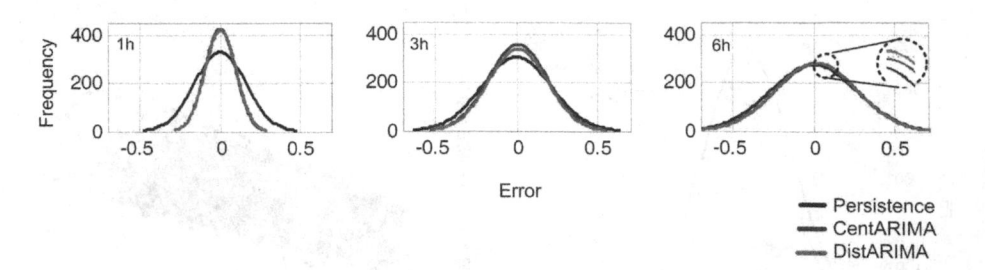

Fig. 5. Hour-ahead error measure for the persistence (black), CentARIMA (blue), DistARIMA (red) models for 1h, 3h and 6h

one of the collaborative models (DistARIMA) for forecast horizons between $4-6$ hours. Comparing the ARIMA models with persistence, the improvement of DistARIMA is not so good comparatively to CentARIMA (average improvement of 0.38% *vs.* 2.46%, respectively).

We also present the analysis of the error distribution. Figure 5 points-out that no bias is present, considering all the models. For the persistence model in $1 - hour$ horizon is visible a wider dispersion comparatively to the ARIMA models. However, the difference is attenuated for $6 - hour$ horizon. Although, these numbers may seem relatively small, they have an interesting impact on the production costs.

4   Conclusions and Future Work

This paper discusses the advantages of a collaborative approach in short term wind power forecast. Two scenarios were tested, a centralized approach sharing time series between nodes and a distributed version that exchanges only the model parameters between nodes. It was observed RMSE decrease by 2.46% for the centralized and 0.38% for the distributed approach comparatively to the persistence values. These values result from 8600 experiments. In overall, a small but consistent RMSE reduction of the predictions was observed.

The work reported in this paper opens several directions of future research. The most obvious direction lies on the challenge of selecting the correlation threshold for that the forecast error is minimized. Further studies include the analysis of the influence of several parameters on the quality of results, such as k, NG_i, N, thd. Finally, research on other domains where data are network distributed is being planned.

Acknowledgements. This work was supported by projects Smartgrids (NORTE-07-0124-FEDER-000056) and Sibila (NORTE-07-0124-FEDER-000059) financed by ON.2−O Novo Norte, under the National Strategic Reference Framework, through the Development Fund, and by national funds, through FCT, and by European Commission through the project MAESTRA (Grant number ICT-2013-612944). The authors also acknowledge the support of Prewind.

References

1. May, M., Saitta, L.: Introduction: The challenge of ubiquitous knowledge discovery. In: May, M., Saitta, L. (eds.) Ubiquitous Knowledge Discovery. LNCS (LNAI), vol. 6202, pp. 3–18. Springer, Heidelberg (2010)
2. Foley, A.M., Leahy, P.G., Marvuglia, A., McKeogh, E.J.: Current methods and advances in forecasting of wind power generation. Renewable Energy 37(1), 1–8 (2012)
3. de Jess Rubio, J.: Analytic neural network model of a wind turbine. Soft Computing, 1–9 (2014)
4. Soman, S.S., Zareipour, H., Malik, O., Mandal, P.: A review of wind power and wind speed forecasting methods with different time horizons. In: North American Power Symposium (NAPS), pp. 1–8 (September 2010)
5. Monteiro, C., Keko, H., Bessa, R., Miranda, V., Botterud, A., Wang, J., Conzelmann, G.: A quick guide to wind power forecating: state-of-the-art 2009. Technical report, Argonne National Laboratory (2009)
6. Wang, X., Guo, P., Huang, X.: A review of wind power forecasting models. Energy Procedia 12, 770–778 (2011); The Proceedings of International Conference on Smart Grid and Clean Energy Technologies (ICSGCE 2011)
7. Monteiro, C., Bessa, R., Miranda, V., Botterud, A., Wang, J., Conzelmann, G.: Wind power forecasting: State-of-the-art 2009, Technical report, Argonne National Laboratory (2009)
8. Kamath, C., Fan, Y.J.: Finding motifs in wind generation time series data. In: 2012 11th International Conference on Machine Learning and Applications (ICMLA), vol. 2, pp. 481–486 (December 2012)
9. Chiu, B., Keogh, E., Lonardi, S.: Probabilistic discovery of time series motifs, pp. 493–498 (2003)
10. Larson, K.A., Westrick, K.: Short-term wind forecasting using off-site observations. Wind Energy 9(1-2), 55–62 (2006)
11. Berdugo, V.G., Chaussin, C., Dubus, L., Hebrail, G., Leboucher, V.: Analog method for collaborative very-short-term forecasting of power generation from photovoltaic systems. In: Next Generation Data Mining Summit: Ubiquitous Knowledge Discovery for Energy Management in Smart Grids and Intelligent Machine-to-Machine (M2M) Telematics (2011)
12. Ohashi, O., Torgo, L.: In: ECAI (Raedt, L.D., Bessire, C., Dubois, D., Doherty, P., Frasconi, P., Heintz, F., Lucas, P.J.F. (eds.), pp. 975–980. IOS Press
13. Pravilovic, S., Appice, A.: The intelligent forecasting model of time series. Automation, Control and Intelligent Systems 1, 90–98 (2013)
14. Lin, J., Keogh, E., Lonardi, S., Chiu, B.: A symbolic representation of time series, with implications for streaming algorithms. In: Proceedings of the 8th ACM SIGMOD Workshop on Research Issues in Data Mining and Knowledge Discovery, pp. 2–11. ACM Press (2003)
15. Guestrin, C., Bodik, P., Thibaux, R., Paskin, M., Madden, S.: Distributed regression: an efficient framework for modeling sensor network data. In: Third International Symposium on Information Processing in Sensor Networks, IPSN 2004, pp. 1–10 (April 2004)
16. Box, G.E.P., Jenkins, G.: Time Series Analysis, Forecasting and Control. Holden-Day, Incorporated (1990)

QoS-Based Reputation Feedback Fusion under Unknown Correlation

Mohamad Mehdi[1], Nizar Bouguila[2], and Jamal Bentahar[2]

[1] Computer Science and Software Engineering Department, Concordia University,
QC, H3G 1M8, Canada
mo_mehdi@encs.concordia.ca
[2] Concordia Institute for Information Systems Engineering (CIISE),
Concordia University, Montreal, QC, H3G 1M8, Canada

Abstract. Due to the flood of web services that offer similar function-alities, service consumers are left with a challenging selection decision. A popular approach to assist them with the service selection task is based on the reputation of web services. However, the propagation of reputation feedback in an open and distributed system of web services yield correlated reputation estimates. The existing web service reputa-tion literature still lacks a system that handles the aggregation of repu-tation feedback under unknown correlation. To fill this gap, we employ two data fusion algorithms, the covariance intersection and ellipsoidal intersection, to aggregate QoS-based reputation feedback. Our exper-imental results endorse the advantageous capability and scalability of the proposed methods in aggregating reputation estimates, and show an enhanced performance when compared with the Kalman filter method.

1 Introduction and Related Work

The proliferation of distributed systems and service oriented architecture (SOA) has encouraged the emergence of deploying business applications in the form of web services. A web service is defined by the W3C consortium as "an abstract notion that must be implemented by a concrete agent." The agents acting on the behalf of these web services are deluging the web with similar functionalities, rendering the selection of agents a challenging task. We use the terms agent-based services, agents and web services interchangeably throughout this paper.

In QoS-based trust systems, the reputation of agents is equivalent to the es-timated value(s) of a single or multiple QoS metric(s) [4,11]. A popular method for aggregating reputation feedback is the summation method. However, the embraced simplicity of the this method opens the door for malevolent agents to maneuver it for their own benefits [6]. This could be achieved by deceitfully increasing their own reputation or decreasing the reputation of others. eBay is a popular commercial example of reputations systems that employ the summation method. In eBay buyers and sellers rate each others based on their transactions as positive, neutral, or negative. The overall reputation of a seller is mostly repre-sented by a feedback score that is computed by summing all the positive ratings

A. Bouchachia (Ed.): ICAIS 2014, LNAI 8779, pp. 172–181, 2014.

minus all the negative ones. Eigentrust, a reputation management framework in P2P networks, also adopted the summation method for feedback aggregation [10]. In Eigentrust, the truster weighs the trust feedbacks received from other peers by their corresponding trust scores. The aggregated trust score assigned to a trustee is then the sum of the product of the trust feedbacks and the trust scores of the feedbacks senders. PeerTrust, another P2P trust system, also employs the summation method with various trust metrics, taking into account the credibility of the feedbacks senders [17]. Alternatively, [16,5] introduced multiple operators to handle different scenarios of trust propagation in a network of interacting agents. For instance, the "Concatenation" operator is used when computing the trust of an agent A in agent C based on the trust of agent B in C discounted by the trust of A in B.

Driven by the uncertainty nature of trust, Bayesian reputation models, based on binary or multi-valued ratings, compute the reputation scores by statistically updating the Beta [3] or Dirichlet [7,11] probability density functions, respectively. When a new rating arrives after an interaction with a service, it is added to the previous ratings (a priori) to compute the new reputation score (a posteriori). The Bayesian approach of updating reputation scores also follows the summation concept. To overcome the vulnerability of the summation method, other studies exploited the Kalman filter capabilities to aggregate the reputation feedbacks [19,15]. These studies argued that the Kalman-based reputation aggregation repels malicious feedbacks by keeping track of the estimates' variances.

However, the above methods lack the capability of dealing with the unknown correlations between reputation feedback provided by different sources. Consider the following scenario: let X_{abc} and X_{adc} be the reputation estimates of agent a supplied by agents b and d to agent c, respectively. Suppose, c aggregates X_{abc} and X_{adc}, then supplies the result, X_{acb}, back to b. This scenario exposes the dependency between X_{acb} and X_{abc}. Therefore, there should be a method to combine X_{abc} and X_{acb} while taking into consideration their unknown correlation. To handle such cases, we extend the literature by the following main contributions:

- We present a QoS-based reputation model that considers the subjectivity of interacting agents in their QoS requirements. As such, two agents communicating with the same service might be interested in different QoS metrics. Our model suggests a customized aggregation of feedbacks based on the QoS requirements of the agent.
- We propose a feedback aggregation approach based on the covariance intersection (CI) and ellipsoidal intersection (EI) data fusion methods. The former aims to handle the aggregation of two reputation estimates in cases where the error's ellipse of one of the estimates is contained in the error's ellipse of the other. The latter aggregates the reputation estimates based on their exclusive information by introducing their mutual mean and covariance.

The rest of the paper is organized as follows. Section 1 introduces and reviews the literature of the web service reputation problem. In Section 2, we present a QoS-based reputation model and discuss the reputation aggregation problem. The Kalman filter reputation model is then described in Section 3, after which we overview the two fusion algorithms, CI and EI, in Sections 4 and 5, respectively. We present the experimental results in Section 6 and conclude the paper in Section 7 that highlights our future work.

2   QoS-Based Reputation

In this section, we propose a QoS-based reputation model that incorporates the subjectivity matter of interacting agents and maintains a consistent representation of reputation reports.

1. We model the reputation feedback as vectors of multiple QoS metrics and their corresponding values. As such, Each agent will consider the QoS metrics that fit its requirements. These metrics are either monotonically increasing or decreasing metrics [18]. Monotonically increasing and decreasing refer to QoS metrics whose values are positively and negatively correlated with the overall quality of a service, respectively. Popular QoS metrics include *response time, throughtput, availability, reliability,* and *cost.*
2. The reported values of the QoS metrics are then scaled to different ranges each of which is defined by two thresholds. These represent a lower and upper bounds on the values of these metrics, T_l and T_u, respectively. The scaling of these values allows each agent to define the ranges of values of the various QoS metrics it deals with. The scaling to the range $[T_l, T_u]$ is given by:

$$Q'_{m_i} = \begin{cases} Q_{m_i} & \text{if } i = 1 \ \& \ T_l < Q_{m_i} < T_u \\ T_l & \text{if } i = 1 \ \& \ Q_{m_i} < T_l \\ T_u & \text{if } i = 1 \ \& \ Q_{m_i} > T_u \\ \frac{(T_u - T_l)(Q_{m_i} - \min(Q_{m_i}))}{\max(Q_{m_i}) - \min(Q_{m_i})} + T_l & \text{otherwise,} \end{cases} \tag{1}$$

where Q_{m_i} is the value of the observed QoS metric m after the ith interaction. $\min(Q_{m_i})$ and $\max(Q_{m_i})$ are the minimum and maximum of the values of the QoS metric m up to the ith interaction.
3. Afterwards, the scaled values are normalized to the $[0, 1]$ range. The values of monotonically increasing metrics are normalized by $Q''_{m_i} = \frac{Q'_{m_i} - \min(Q'_{m_i})}{\max(Q'_{m_i}) - \min(Q'_{m_i})}$. The normalization of the scaled values of monotonically decreasing metrics is given by $Q''_{m_i} = 1 - \frac{Q'_{m_i} - \min(Q'_{m_i})}{\max(Q'_{m_i}) - \min(Q'_{m_i})}$.

This approach allows each agent to select and later aggregate the values of specific QoS metrics. Scaling and normalizing the values of the QoS metrics give the agents that receive reputation feedback the choice of aggregating the values of a selective set of QoS metrics. They also decrease the impact of malicious feedback by restricting the values to fit within specific ranges. These ranges could be based on prior direct interactions between the agent that requests the feedback and the evaluated agent.

In most probability-based trust systems, the reputation is communicated through the sufficient statistics of either the Beta or Dirichlet distributions [3,7].

However, applying the sufficient statistics undergoes the issue of redundant information when passing reputation among agents. The authors in [13] proposed the partitioning of information between *private* and *shared*. The former denotes information that has not been communicated to other agents. The latter represents information that could have been sent to or received from other agents. Despite being attractive, this solution requires each agent to keep track of two separate information. It also involves identity issues of sending and receiving agents.

To overcome these shortcomings, we propose an alternative solution to the aggregation of reputation feedback of web services. We exploit the CI and EI fusion methods commonly used for information fusion in distributed networks. We compare the results of these methods with those of the Kalman filter reputation models proposed in [15,20]. The next section is dedicated to overview the Kalman filter method for reputation aggregation.

3   Kalman Filter for Service Reputation

Kalman filter is considered a form of a Gaussian process model and a predictive filter based on recursive algorithms [1]. Given a noisy dynamic system with unknown states, the Kalman filter predicts the state using the dynamic model of the corresponding system. Afterwards, the prediction results are corrected and updated by considering a noisy measurement in what is called the observation model. For example, given a moving robot, the dynamic model can be employed to estimate the robot's position (the unknown state) at a certain time. This estimate is then updated using the measurements of the robot's position that are supplied by a camera (observation model). In the context of this paper, the unknown states represent the reputation scores of an agent's QoS metrics. The dynamic and observation models are given by:

- **Dynamic model:**
$$x_{t+1} = Fx_t + w_t,$$ (2)

  where x_t is the state vector at time t, $w_t \sim N(0, Q)$ is the Gaussian noise associated with the dynamic model at time t, and F is the state transition matrix.
- **Observation model:**
$$y_t = Hx_t + v_t,$$ (3)

  where y_t is the observation at time t, $v_t \sim N(0, R)$ is the Gaussian noise associated with the observation model at time t, and H is the observation transition matrix.

The Kalman filter iterates recursively over the following two steps to minimize the covariance of the estimation errors:

1. Prediction: This step computes the a priori estimates of the current state by ignoring the dynamic noise. The prediction equations are obtained by solving the dynamic model's differential equations, and are given by:

$$\hat{x}_{t+1} = F x_t \tag{4}$$

$$\hat{P}_{t+1} = F P_t F^T + Q, \tag{5}$$

where $\hat{P}_{t+1}$ is the covariance matrix of the predicted state.

2. Correction: This is where the a priori estimates are enhanced by adding the measurements observed at time t. The correction equations are the following:

$$x_{t+1} = \hat{x}_{t+1} + K(y_t - \hat{x}_{t+1}) \tag{6}$$

$$P_{t+1} = (I - KH)P_t, \tag{7}$$

where K, the Kalman gain matrix, is given by $K = P_t H^T (H P_t H^T + R)^{-1}$.

This model is suitable for the estimation problem of the reputation of web services and has been employed in multiple studies such as [20] and [19]. This is due to the dynamic nature of reputation and the possibility of modeling it by a linear function disturbed by a Gaussian noise.

4   Proposed Aggregation Methods

The main limitation of the Kalman filter is the independence assumption between the estimation error at time t and the measurement error at time $t + 1$ [2]. Let's consider the following scenario: $Ag4$ receives two feedback reports of $Ag1$'s reputation from both $Ag2$ and $Ag3$. Afterwards, $Ag2$ requests reputation feedback about $Ag1$. $Ag4$ then responds to $Ag2$'s request and sends the information it formerly received from the latter as it did not have additional experience with $Ag1$ since then. Using Kalman filter, when $Ag2$ combines this information with its own estimates of $Ag1$'s reputation, the covariance matrix is unjustifiably decreased. Suppose $Ag2$'s estimates of the availability AV and response time RT of $Ag1$ are given by the state vector $x_t = \{0.8504, 0.7154\}$ and the covariance matrix is given by: $P_t = \begin{pmatrix} 0.0367 & 0.0044 \\ 0.0044 & 0.0367 \end{pmatrix}$. Also, let the feedback sent by $Ag4$ be the observation vector $y_t = \{0.8504, 0.7154\}$. Moreover, let the following be the state transition and covariance matrices, and the observation transition and covariance matrices, respectively: $F = \begin{pmatrix} 1 & 0 \\ 0 & 1 \end{pmatrix}$, $w_t = \begin{pmatrix} 0.02 & 0 \\ 0 & 0.02 \end{pmatrix}$, $H = \begin{pmatrix} 1 & 0 \\ 0 & 1 \end{pmatrix}$, $v_t = \begin{pmatrix} 0.03 & 0 \\ 0 & 0.03 \end{pmatrix}$. The Kalman filter yields the same state estimates $x_{t+1} = \{0.8504, 0.7154\}$. However, the covariance matrix becomes $P_{t+1} = \begin{pmatrix} 0.0164 & 0.0009 \\ 0.0009 & 0.0164 \end{pmatrix}$. This means the uncertainty in the corrected estimates is reduced when it should have remained unchanged. The methods below are proposed to deal with such scenarios.

4.1   Covariance Intersection

The CI algorithm was developed to overcome the independence assumption of the Kalman filter and the under/overestimation of the covariance matrix. CI combines estimates (mostly Gaussian) from different sources when the error ellipse of one estimate includes the error ellipse of the other [9]. In a nutshell, CI creates a convex combination of the means and covariances of two estimates to provide consistent fused estimates with appropriate covariance matrices:

$$P_f^{-1} = wP_i^{-1} + (1-w)P_j^{-1} \tag{8}$$

$$\hat{p}_f = P_f(wP_i^{-1}\hat{p}_i + (1-w)P_j^{-1}\hat{p}_j) \tag{9}$$

where $\hat{p}_f$ and P_f are the fused mean and covariance of the unknown state and are based on the estimates $\hat{p}_i$ and $\hat{p}_j$ and their respective covariances P_i and P_j. $w \in [0,1]$ is a regulating parameter. The two equations of CI yield consistent estimates regardless of the cross-correlation errors among the combined estimates [12]. This is achieved by having P_f include the intersection of P_i and P_j. The CI algorithm also provides the uncertainty in the combined estimates through the new covariance matrix P_f. More details about the derivation of the CI equations are available from [9,8].

4.2   Ellipsoidal Intersection

Despite solving the consistency of the covariance matrix of fused estimates, CI still considered a combination of two local estimates without distinguishing between accurate and inaccurate estimates. The EI fusion method was proposed in [14] to handle the separation of the mutual information that might be included in the two local estimates. The update of the estimates is then only based on the exclusive information received to avoid incorrect and "over confident" estimates. The mutual information introduces two estimates, the mutual covariance and mutual mean. The mutual covariance is used to optimize the fused covariance by maximizing the effect of the mutual information, $P_f = (P_i^{-1} + P_j^{-1} - \Gamma^{-1})^{-1}$,

where P_i and P_j are the covariances of the state vector estimated by agents i and j. Γ is the mutual covariance and is defined as $\Gamma = S_i D_i^{0.5} S_j D_\Gamma S_j^{-1} D_i^{0.5} S_i^{-1}$, where S_i and D_i contain the eigenvectors and eigenvalues of the covariance matrix P_i, respectively, such that $P_i = S_i D_i S_i^{-1}$. S_j is a matrix that contains the eigenvectors of $D_i^{-0.5} S_i^{-1} D_j S_i D_i^{-0.5}$, and D_Γ is given by:

$$[D_\Gamma]_{qr} = \begin{cases} \max([D_\Gamma]_{qr}, 1) & \text{if } q = r, \\ 0 & \text{otherwise.} \end{cases} \tag{10}$$

The mutual mean aims at representing an estimate of the mean of the state vector based on mutual information between initial estimates $\hat{p}_i$ and $\hat{p}_j$, and is given by:

$$\gamma = (P_i^{-1} + P_j^{-1} - 2\Gamma^{-1} + 2\eta I)^{-1} \times \tag{11}$$
$$((P_j^{-1} - \Gamma^{-1} + \eta I)\hat{p}_i + (P_j^{-1} - \Gamma^{-1} + \eta I)\hat{p}_j),$$

where ηI is added to guarantee $P_i^{-1} - \Gamma^{-1}$ and $P_j^{-1} - \Gamma^{-1}$ are both positive definite. Let $H = P_i^{-1} + P_j^{-1} - 2\Gamma^{-1}$ and $\lambda_{0_+}(H)$ be the smallest eigenvalue of H, η is defined in [14] as:

$$\eta = \begin{cases} 0, & \text{if } \det(H) \neq 0 \\ c \ll \lambda_{0_+}(H), & \text{if } \det(H) = 0 \end{cases} \tag{12}$$

Γ and γ are then employed to optimize the fusion of both estimates $\hat{p}_i$ and $\hat{p}_j$:

$$x_f = (P_i^{-1} + P_j^{-1} - \Gamma^{-1})^{-1}(P_i^{-1}\hat{p}_i + P_j^{-1}\hat{p}_j - \Gamma^{-1}\gamma). \tag{13}$$

5   Experimental Evaluation

In this section, we evaluate the performance of CI and EI by running two simulations. The first implements the scenario discussed earlier in which we model the aggregation of $Ag4$'s reputation feedback sent by $Ag2$ and $Ag3$ to $Ag1$. The second simulation extends the same scenario to the case of 100 agents rather than 4. These simulations were executed with the following three estimators:

The first, KF, consists of a regular Kalman filter reputation model. In this estimator, $Ag1$ receives the reputation observations of $Ag4$ provided by $Ag2$ and $Ag3$ based on which a Kalman filter is employed to predict and correct the reputation estimation. This is similar to the models proposed in [15,20]. The second estimator, $KFCI$, encompasses two modules the first of which is a local Kalman filter (LKF) applied to obtain the reputation estimations of $Ag2$ and $Ag3$. The second module employs the CI algorithm to fuse the LKF estimation with each of the estimations sent by $Ag2$ and $Ag3$. The third estimator, $KFEI$, is similar to the second except CI is substituted by the EI in the second module.

The simulation setup consists of various parameters that are defined as follows. First, we assume a two dimensional reputation where each dimension represents one QoS metric, $R = \{QoS_1, QoS_2\}$. In real settings, the values of these metrics are scaled and normalized to the $[0, 1]$ range as discussed in the QoS-based Reputation Section. In this simulation, the dynamic model that represents the reputation of $Ag4$ is assumed to be a vector of two time varying linear functions, one for each of QoS_1 and QoS_2. We employ the functions used in the Kalman feedback model proposed in [20]: $R = \{\log_{100}(0.02 * t + n), \log_{100}(0.03 * t + n)\}$, where t is the time step and n is a random number between 15 and 30. We used n rather than a constant to reflect the fluctuating (increasing and decreasing) nature of QoS metrics. Thus, the model consists of two unknown states that will be estimated. It also requires observations of the values of the two states supplied by $Ag2$ and $Ag3$. The state and observation matrices are both set to 2×2 identity matrices.

The system covariance is set to 0.02 and the observations covariances are set to 0.01 and 0.03 for $Ag2$ and $Ag3$, respectively. Figures 3 and 4 show the aggregated reputation scores given by the three estimators for each of QoS_1 and QoS_2 at 100 time steps. As illustrated by these figures, the reputation estimates of *KFCI* and *KFEI* are much smoother and more accurate than those of *KF*. The accuracy aspect is confirmed by the mean square errors (MSE) of the three estimators displayed in the first two columns of Table 1.

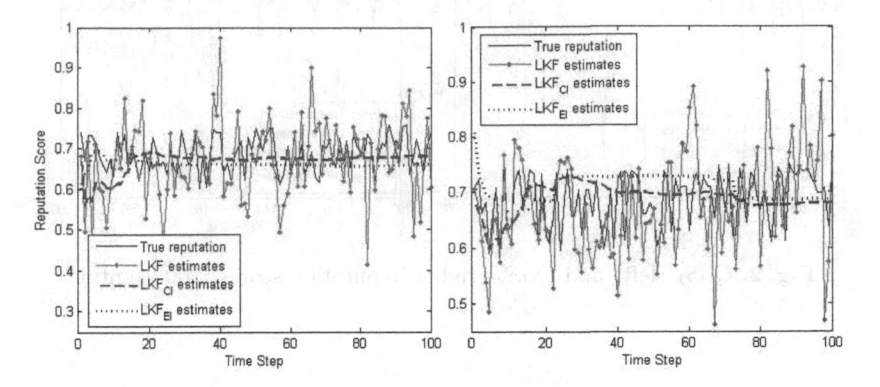

Fig. 1. QoS_1 (left) and QoS_2 (right) Reputation scores (4 agents)

Table 1. MSE of the three estimators with 4 and 100 agents

	4 agents		100 agents	
Estimator	QoS_1	QoS_2	QoS_1	QoS_2
KF	0.96	0.928	1.87	1.84
KFCI	0.525	0.526	1.17	1.5
KFEI	0.499	0.572	0.97	1.23

To demonstrate the scalability of our approach, we run the same experiment with 100 agents. In this simulation, 98 agents send reputation feedback of the 99th agent to the 100th that aggregates them using each of *KF*, *KFCI*, and *KFEI*. Furthermore, to evaluate the robustness of these estimators, we increase the number of feedback sessions to 300 and have the dynamic model of the 99th agent's reputation drop significantly half way through these sessions. The results of this simulation are displayed in Figures 4 and 5 and the last two columns of Table 1. For clarity purposes, we only show the estimations between the time steps 100 and 200. The smoothness of the *KFCI* and *KFEI* curves is noticeable in comparison with that of *KF*. These figures also show that *KFEI* detects the drop in the reputation scores faster than *KFCI* which is more conservative in changing the aggregated estimates. Table 1 (last 2 columns) shows that *KFEI* has the smallest MSE followed by *KFCI* and *KF*.

It is worthy to mention that the challenge of the CI algorithm is the selection of an appropriate w for Equations 8 and 9. We set w to $\frac{\text{Tr}(P_b)}{\text{Tr}(P_a)+\text{Tr}(P_b)}$ as proposed in [12]. As for the EI algorithm, one drawback is the extensive inversion of matrices involved in its equations. To avoid the inversion of singular matrices, we used an approximate inversion function which gave better results than those of the Kalman filter estimator.

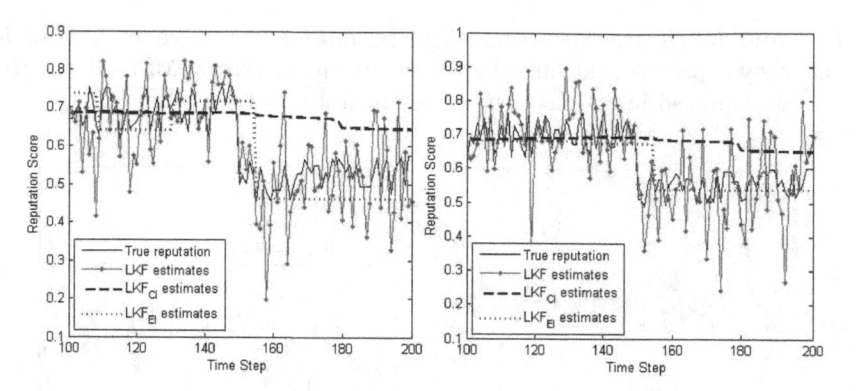

Fig. 2. QoS_1 (left) and QoS_2 (right) Reputation scores (100 agents)

6 Conclusion

We presented, in this paper, two methods for aggregating reputation feedback of web services in distributed systems; covariance intersection and ellipsoidal intersection. These methods handle the dependency between the information that propagates through networks of interacting agents. They also avoid inaccurately over confident estimates caused by redundant information. By considering the correlation between the feedback estimates of an agent, both methods provide consistent fused estimates at proximity from the agent's real reputation. Our experiments showed that these methods outperform the estimations of the traditional Kalman filter model. In our future work, we will extend our reputation aggregation approach to identify malicious feedback. We also extend it by employing extended Kalman filter to capture the probable non-linearity of the quality of service. Additionally, we will consider an alternative aggregation method by modeling reputation feedback as multivariate time series.

References

1. Bishop, C.M.: Pattern Recognition and Machine Learning (Information Science and Statistics). Springer-Verlag New York, Inc., Secaucus (2006)
2. Chen, L., Arambel, P.O., Mehra, R.K.: Estimation under unknown correlation: covariance intersection revisited. IEEE Transactions on Automatic Control 47(11), 1879–1882 (2002)
3. Commerce, B.E., Jøsang, A., Ismail, R.: The beta reputation system. In: Proceedings of the 15th Bled Electronic Commerce Conference (2002)
4. Hang, C.W., Singh, M.P.: Trustworthy service selection and composition. ACM Transactions on Autonomous and Adaptive Systems 6(1), 5:1–5:17 (2011)
5. Hang, C.W., Wang, Y., Singh, M.P.: Operators for propagating trust and their evaluation in social networks. In: Proceedings of the 8th International Conference on Autonomous Agents and Multiagent Systems, AAMAS 2009, Richland, SC, vol. 2, pp. 1025–1032 (2009)

6. Hoffman, K., Zage, D., Nita-Rotaru, C.: A survey of attack and defense techniques for reputation systems. ACM Comput. Surv. 42(1), 1:1–1:31 (2009)
7. Jøsang, A., Haller, J.: Dirichlet reputation systems. In: Proceedings of the Second International Conference on Availability, Reliability and Security, ARES 2007, pp. 112–119. IEEE Computer Society, Washington, DC (2007)
8. Julier, S.J., Uhlmann, J.K.: General Decentralized Data Fusion with Covariance Intersection. In: Handbook of Multisensor Data Fusion, ch. 12. CRC Press, Boca Raton (2001)
9. Julier, S.J., Uhlmann, J.K.: A non-divergent estimation algorithm in the presence of unknown correlations. In: Proceedings of the American Control Conference, pp. 2369–2373 (1997)
10. Kamvar, S.D., Schlosser, M.T., Garcia-Molina, H.: The eigentrust algorithm for reputation management in p2p networks. In: Proceedings of the 12th International Conference on World Wide Web, pp. 640–651. ACM, New York (2003)
11. Mehdi, M., Bouguila, N., Bentahar, J.: A qos-based trust approach for service selection and composition via bayesian networks. In: 2013 IEEE 20th International Conference on Web Services (ICWS), pp. 211–218 (2013)
12. Niehsen, W.: Information fusion based on fast covariance intersection filtering. In: Proceedings of the Fifth International Conference on Information Fusion, vol. 2, pp. 901–904 (2002)
13. Reece, S., Rogers, A., Roberts, S., Jennings, N.R.: Rumours and reputation: evaluating multi-dimensional trust within a decentralised reputation system. In: Proceedings of the 6th International Joint Conference on Autonomous Agents and Multiagent Systems, AAMAS 2007, pp. 165:1–165:8. ACM, New York (2007)
14. Sijs, J., Lazar, M., van der Bosch, P.: State fusion with unknown correlation: Ellipsoidal intersection. In: American Control Conference (ACC), pp. 3992–3997 (2010)
15. Wang, X., Liu, L., Su, J.: Rlm: A general model for trust representation and aggregation. IEEE Transactions on Service Computing 5(1), 131–143 (2012)
16. Wang, Y., Singh, M.P.: Trust representation and aggregation in a distributed agent system. In: Proceedings of the 21st National Conference on Artificial Intelligence, AAAI 2006, vol. 2, pp. 1425–1430. AAAI Press (2006)
17. Xiong, L., Liu, L.: Peertrust: Supporting reputation-based trust for peer-to-peer electronic communities. IEEE Transactions on Knowledge and Data Engineering 16, 843–857 (2004)
18. Xu, Z., Martin, P., Powley, W., Zulkernine, F.H.: Reputation-enhanced qos-based web services discovery. In: ICWS, pp. 249–256. IEEE Computer Society (2007)
19. Ye, B., Pervez, A., Ghavami, M., Nekovee, M.: A trust-based model for quality of web service. In: International Conference on Advanced Service Computing, Valencia, Spain, pp. 39–45 (2013)
20. Zhou, H., Wang, X., Su, J.: A general self-adaptive reputation system based on the kalman feedback. In: International Conference on Service Sciences, Los Alamitos, CA, USA, pp. 7–12 (2013)

Multi-resident Activity Recognition
Using Incremental Decision Trees

Markus Prossegger[1] and Abdelhamid Bouchachia[2]

[1] Carinthia University of Applied Sciences,
Department of Engineering and IT, Klagenfurt, Austria
m.prossegger@cuas.at
[2] Bournemouth University, Faculty of Science and Technology,
Bournemouth, United Kingdom
abouchachia@bournemouth.ac.uk

Abstract. The present paper proposes the application of decision trees to model activities of daily living in a multi-resident context. An extension of ID5R, called *E-ID5R*, is proposed. It augments the leaf nodes and allows such nodes to be multi-labeled. E-ID5R induces a decision tree incrementally to accommodate new instances and new activities as they become available over time. To evaluate the proposed algorithm, the ARAS dataset which is a real-world multi-resident dataset stemming from two houses is used. E-ID5R performs differently on activities of both houses.

1 Introduction

Advances in ambient intelligence technology have become more prominent in the last decade yielding innovative and revolutionary applications related to smart environments such as smart homes, smart meeting rooms and classrooms, health monitoring and assistance systems, and smart factories. Usually smart environments aim at ensuring comfort, security, safety for the occupants and efficiency in the management of resources like energy. The technology of smart environments targets the design and development of smart adaptive systems capable of intelligently behaving by taking actions on behalf of the environments occupants for their satisfaction. In this setting, activity recognition plays an important role to achieve this capability, since perceiving and understanding the occupants behavior in the smart environment are crucial issues for the system to make a decision and to perform reasonable actions to the benefit of the occupant. Activity recognition is currently a challenging but exciting research topic because human activities are complex and are performed differently across individuals and become even more complex when the environment is inhabited by multiple occupants, which is the case in most real-world environments. The system needs to track each occupant when performing individual or group activities (e.g., move, seat, watch, garden, etc.) based on sensor readings with the overall goal to recognize what activity is being performed and to assist the occupant by taking actions on his/her behalf. For instance, in a smart home, the system should be

A. Bouchachia (Ed.): ICAIS 2014, LNAI 8779, pp. 182–191, 2014.

able to predict upcoming activities of each resident and send instructions to different smart devices to perform appropriate actions (such as starting a coffee machine once the occupant wakes up in the morning).

So far there has been a lot of effort for modeling human activities of daily living (ADL) in the context of pervasive computing and vision. In the former context, the smart homes are equipped with sensors and actuators, while in the later one, the living environment is equipped with cameras to capture data. Very often the use of cameras in criticized for privacy reasons. Using pervasive sensors allows to overcome the privacy issues and can be either installed in the environment or wearable by the resident.

Most of the published work related to ADL modeling has focused on environment occupied by one resident, called *single occupancy* environment. Many computational models have been used such as neural networks [2, 14, 15, 17], fuzzy rule-based systems [3–5, 9], decision trees [11, 20], hidden Markov models and similar graphical models [10, 12, 18, 19, 22].

So far, most smart home research has focused on monitoring and assisting single individuals in a single space. Since homes often have more than a single occupant, developing solutions for handling multiple individuals is vital. Dealing with multiple inhabitants has rarely been the central focus of research so far, as there have been numerous other challenges to overcome before the technology can effectively handle multiple residents in a single space. However, researchers are now beginning to recognize the importance of applying human activity recognition in smart homes with multiple inhabitants to design and develop real-world application needs.

Existing work on sensor-based activity recognition mainly focuses on recognizing activities of a single user [10, 12, 18, 19, 23]. Considering only single resident occupation is far from real life especially in smart homes. However modeling multiple-resident ADL is more complex because activities can take different forms: (1) Sequential activities, where each activity is performed after another, (2) Interleaving activities, where a single occupant switches back and forth between two or more activities, (3) Concurrent activities, where a single occupant performs two or more activities simultaneously, (4) Parallel activities, where occupants perform different activities , and (5) Collaborative activities, where the occupants work together in a cooperative manner where each occupant performs certain steps/actions of the activity, either together. Thus recognizing the individual occupants, known as the problem of data association and understanding their interaction with each other are key problems [24]. There has been some work on modeling and recognizing multi-resident activities based on pervasive sensors, but most of the work is based on computer vision [8]. The attempts made to model multi-resident activities have heavily relied on graphical models: the HMM [7], variants of HMM like Coupled Hidden Markov Model (CHMM) [6], Parallel Hidden Markov Model (PHMM) [6], Bayesian Networks (BN) [16], dynamic BN or variants of BN like DBN [13], Conditional Randoms Fields (CRF) or variants of CRF like Factorial Conditional Random Fields (FCRF) [25].

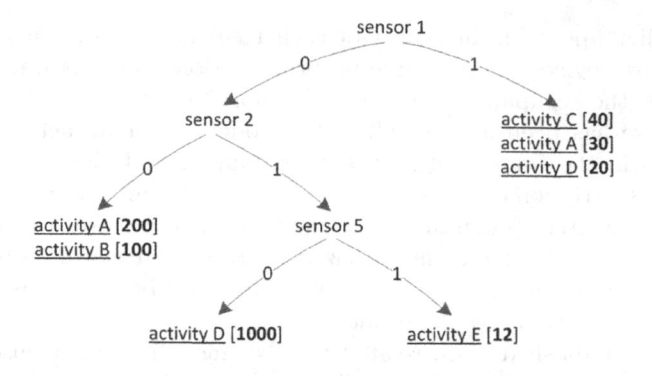

Fig. 1. Example of a decision tree. Each leaf node is multi-labeled (*underlined*) and each class is tagged with the number of occurrences (*bold*).

In this paper we will focus on multi-resident activity classification in the context pervasive computing. Instead of popular graphical models, we will use incremental decision trees (IDT). We propose an extension of ID5R [21], called *E-ID5R*. E-ID5R induces DTs with leaf nodes (class nodes) augmented by contextual information in the form of activity frequency.

The paper is organized as follows. Section 2 explains the process of decision tree induction using E-ID5R. Section 3 provides the experimental evaluation of the approach using ARAS data, Section 4 concludes the paper.

2   Details of E-ID5R

Decision trees are used in the context of this study to classify activities. Each activity is seen as a class and is described by a set of sensor readings. Unlike in conventional decision tree algorithms, in E-ID5R, the leaf nodes can represent single or multiple classes. Next to the class identifier, the number of the instances assigned to the class (class occurrence or class count) is encoded as a class attribute as shown in Fig. 1.

In order to construct a decision tree incrementally as new instances and activities become available, the following three stages are carried out: (1) Construction of an initial tree, (2) classification of new instances, and (3) evolution of the tree.

2.1   Construction of the Initial Tree

Based on a set of instances representing daily activities, where the input attributes are sensor measurements, an initial decision tree is generated using the steps described in Alg. 1. Because many activities can be conducted in the same space and are captured using the same set of sensors, ambiguity characterizes activities. Hence, the decision tree is adapted to accommodate multiple activities in a single leaf node. Figure 1 shows a simplified tree of input data representing

---

Algorithm 1. Decision tree generation

Require: training instances $i \in I$ with unique classification $c(i)$
1. **for all** $i \in I$ **do**
2.   **if** decision tree is empty $|N| == 0$ **then**
3.   Add single node n with all attribute-value pairs as unexpanded set.
4.   Add class $c(i)$ to classes C of node n.
5.   Set occurrence of class $c(i) = 1$.
6.   **else**
7.   Update the decision tree running Alg. 2.
8.   **end if**
9. **end for**

---

sensor measurements and the corresponding activities. Here the sensor measurements are given as binary values (1: emits data, 0: sensor is stale). To decide the activity corresponding to the input, the number of occurrences to the classes (class count) is added as class attribute.

Once the initial tree is constructed it can be used to classify new arriving unlabeled instances. In case the new instances are labeled, we can use them to evolve the initial tree.

2.2 Classification of New Instances

The tree can be used in a subsequent classification of new instances running Alg. 4. In the naive scenario, the number of occurrence encoded as class attribute is used as discriminator in case of a leaf node holding multiple classes.

As an example we examine the classification of a new instance giving a single measurement of *sensor 1 = 1* using the decision tree shown in Fig. 1: The leaf node holds the three candidate classes *activity C*, *activity A*, and *activity D* with the counts *40*, *30*, and *20*. Hence the candidate representing the highest count (*40*) is selected as the class of the new instance (*activity C*).

But if the instances are *time-stamped*, which represents the conventional scenario, the information can be used as discriminative attribute to further extend the approach. Next to the class count, the averaged time stamp (of all learned instances) is encoded as class attribute as shown in Fig.2. The weighted count Q^w of a class candidate $c \in C$ is calculated as follows:

$$Q^w(c) = \frac{Q(c)}{\sum_{i=1}^{C} Q(c_i)} + (1 - \frac{D(c)}{\sum_{i=1}^{C} D(c_i)})f \qquad (1)$$

where C is the set of classes grouped in a single leaf and D is the distance between the time stamp of the instance to be tested $i \in I$, and the averaged time stamp of class c. The weighting of the distance can be tuned by the multiplicative factor f.

If the new instance is labeled with a unique time stamp of *50*, the weighted count of the classes change in the following way. Using Equation 1 and assuming $f = 1$, the count of class *activity C* changes from value 40 to round 0.80. The

---

Algorithm 2. Tree update

Require: instance i
1. **repeat**
2.   Find decision or leaf node n (with classes C) in tree, satisfying the tested attribute-value pairs of instance i.
3.   Update the classes counts at the tested attributes.
4.   Update the classes counts at the non-tested attributes.
5.   **if** n is a leaf node AND $c(i) \in C$ **then**
6.   Add non-tested attribute-value pairs of i as unexpanded set to n.
7.   Increase quantity of class $c(i)$.
8.   **else if** n is a leaf node AND $c(i) \notin C$ AND n does not contain non-tested attributes **then**
9.   Add class $c(i)$ to the classes C in leaf node n.
10.   Set quantity of class $c(i) = 1$.
11.   **else if** n is a leaf node AND $c(i) \notin C$ AND n contains non-tested attributes **then**
12.   Expand the non-tested attribute of n showing the highest information gain, creating one or more subtrees depending on the number of corresponding values.
         {Instance i will not be added in the current iteration}
13.   **else**
14.   Select one arbitrary non-tested attribute of decision node n and create a leaf node n_s.
15.   Assign $c(i)$ as class to leaf node n_s.
16.   Set quantity of class $c(i) = 1$.
17.   Add non-tested attribute-value pairs of i as unexpanded set to n_s.
18.   **end if**
19. **until** instance i was added
20. Transpose the tree following the predecessors of n respectively n_s running Alg. 3.
21. **return**   update succeeded

---

count of *activity A* changes from 30 to 1.13 respectively from 20 to 1.08 in case of *activity D*. Considering the weighted count the new instance is labeled as class *activity A*.

2.3   Evolution of the Tree

Since our approach is based on an incremental decision tree induction algorithm, it can be evolved at any time using classified instances. This allows our approach to adapt to changes in the behavior of the residents over time. The instances can be more fine-grained and eventually new activities can be learned systematically. New arriving instances can be used to evolve the tree by running Alg. 2. The quality of the classification using the proposed approach is shown in the experimental section.

Algorithm 3. Transpose tree

Require: leaf node n
    {Traverse the tree bottom-up starting with n}
1. **while** there is a predecessor n_p of n **do**
2.   **if** $information\_gain(n) > information\_gain(n_p)$ **then**
3.   Swap the places of n_p and n.
4.   Reorder all other subtrees of n_p if there are any.
5.   **end if**
6.   Select n_p as n during the next iteration.
      {Do one step bottom-up}
7. **end while**

Algorithm 4. Classification

Require: new unlabeled instance i
1. Find leaf node n (with classes C) in the tree, satisfying the tested attribute-value pairs of instance i.
2. **if** $|C| == 1$ **then**
3.   **return** i is an instance of class C.
4. **else if** $|C| > 1$ **then**
5.   Select class $c \in C$ having the highest value $Q(c)$.
6.   **return** i is an instance of class c.
7. **else**
8.   **return** i is an instance of an unknown class.
9. **end if**

---

3 Evaluation

To evaluate E-ID5R we use the dataset ARAS (Activity Recognition with ambient sensing) which is known to present a multi-user setting. It contains information about the association (activity, resident), that is which resident performs which activity. Many activities are either parallel or cooperative ones. The dataset covers a full month of labelled activities for multiple residents in two real houses. A total number of 27 different activities is described by the binary measurement force sensitive resistors, pressure mats, contact sensors, proximity sensors, sonar distance sensors, photocells, temperature sensors, and infra-red receivers. Each instance from *House A* or *House B* represents a unique activity (i.e., combination of the residents' activities) combined with the sensor measurements at a given time stamp. The instances from day 1 to day 21 were used to generate and evolve the decision tree. The instances from day 22 to day 28 were used to measure the classification accuracy using the generated tree. Each of the data sets *House A* and *House B* contains $1,814,400$ (day 1..21) learning instances used to construct the decision tree and $604,800$ (day 22..28) test instances to evaluate the classification. The description of the training nad testing data used are shown in Table 1 and Table 2 respectively.

    An example of an ambiguous combination is interpreted the following: The sensors' readings (in *House A*) for the activity *Resident 1 is talking on the phone*

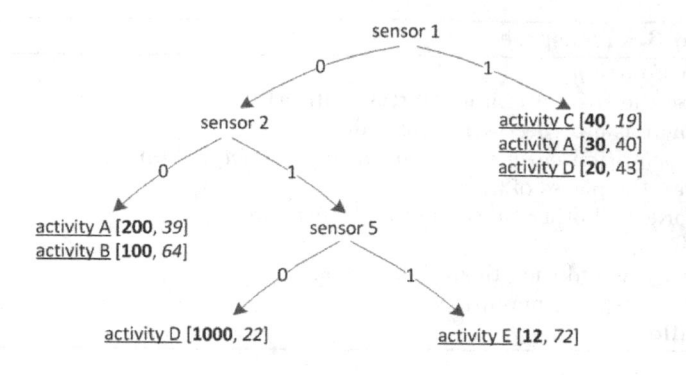

Fig. 2. Example of an enhanced decision tree. Each class is extended with a count (*bold*) and an averaged time stamp (*italic*) of occurrence.

Table 1. Description of the learning data

ID	different classes	Number of ambiguous combinations	ambiguous measurements
House A	243	24,236	3,200 (of total 3,732)
House B	147	6,352	700 (of total 879)

& resident 2 is using the Internet and the activity *Resident 1 is watching TV & resident 2 is using the Internet* are the same. An ambiguous measurement indicates two (or more) activities have the same sensor reading.

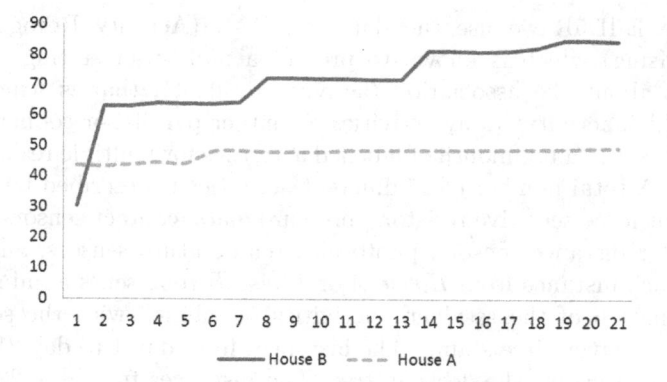

Fig. 3. Percentage of correct classification with respect to the number of days provided as learning data

In Table 3 the result of a number of selected evaluation experiments is shown. Figure 3 shows the number of correct classified instances with respect to the amount of learning data. Although the percentage of correct classified instances

Table 2. Dimension of the test data

ID	Number of		
	different classes	ambiguous combinations	ambiguous measurements
House A	177	11,129	1,660 (of total 2,065)
House B	108	3,768	355 (of total 464)

Table 3. Selected results

ID	Learning instances [day]	Test instances [day]	Correct [%]	Incorrect due to	
				count [%]	no/wrong leaf [%]
House A	1..1	22..28	43.56	15.06	41.38
	1..7	22..28	48.36	30.91	20.73
	1..14	22..28	48.53	38.30	13.17
	1..21	22..28	49.28	40.31	10.41
House B	1..1	22..28	30.47	1.06	68.47
	1..7	22..28	64.19	6.00	29.81
	1..14	22..28	81.08	9.26	9.66
	1..21	22..28	84.45	10.35	5.2

seems to be low, it increases steadily with the number of instances to be learned. The extended approach considering the weighted count as described in Equation 1 improves the percentage of correctly classified instances by an average of 1% only. The performance is very prone to the selected value of factor f and could be improved if an heuristics can be found to predetermine it efficiently.

4   Conclusion

In this paper, an algorithm, called E-ID5R, to induce incremental decision trees is proposed to deal with the classification of multi-resident activities. Initial experiments show that the prediction of activities for House A presents a quite challenging task. The classification rate is insignificantly as much low as 40%. Clearly the parallel and cooperative activities need a better modeling than straight and naive application of decision trees. In the case of House B, the results are much better approaching 82% when the first half duration is used for training and the second is used for testing.

Considering the outcome of the set of experiments, the efficiency of multi-labeling and the use of counts must be further analysed, especially the effect of value of factor f in Equation 1.

References

1. Alemdar, H., Ertan, H., Incel, O.D., Ersoy, C.: ARAS Human Activity Datasets in Multiple Homes with Multiple Residents. In: 2013 7th International Conference on Proceedings Pervasive Computing Technologies for Healthcare (PervasiveHealth), pp. 232–235 (2013)

2. Begg, R., Hassan, R.: Artificial Neural Networks in Smart Homes. In: 〈
   J.C., Nugent, C.D. (eds.) Designing Smart Homes. LNCS (LNAI), vol. 4C
   146–164. Springer, Heidelberg (2006)
3. Bouchachia, A., Vanaret, C.: GT2FC: An Online Growing Interval Type-2
   Learning Fuzzy Classifier. IEEE Transactions on Fuzzy Systems (in Press, 2C
   doi:10.1109/TFUZZ.2013.2279554
4. Bouchachia, A.: Fuzzy classification in Dynamic Environments. Soft Compt
   ing 15(5), 1009–1022 (2011)
5. Bouchachia, A.: An Evolving Classification Cascade with Self-Learning. Evolving
   Systems 1(3), 143–160 (2010)
6. Chiang, Y., Hsu, K., Lu, C., Fu, L., Hsu, J.Y.: Interaction Models for Multiple-
   Resident Activity Recognition in a Smart Home. In: IEEE/RSJ International Conference on Intelligent Robots and Systems, pp. 3753–3758 (2010)
7. Cook, D., Crandall, A., Singla, G., Thomas, B.: Detection of Social Interaction in
   Smart Spaces. Journal of Cybernetics and Systems 41, 90–104 (2010)
8. Du, Y., Chen, F., Xu, W., Li, Y.: Recognizing Interaction Activities using Dynamic
   Bayesian Network. In: Proceedings of the 18th International Conference on Pattern
   Recognition, pp. 618–621 (2006)
9. Hagras, H., Doctor, F., Callaghan, V., Lopez, A.: An Incremental Adaptive Life
   Long Learning Approach for Type-2 Fuzzy Embedded Agents in Ambient Intelligent Environments. IEEE Transactions on Fuzzy Systems 15(1), 41–55 (2007)
10. Hu, D., Zhang, X., Yin, J., Zheng, V., Yang, Q.: Abnormal Activity Recognition
    based on HDP-HMM Models. In: Proceedings of IJCAI 2009, pp. 1715–1720 (2009)
11. Isoda, Y., Kurakake, S., Nakano, H.: Ubiquitous Sensors based Human Behavior
    Modeling and Recognition using a Spatio-Temporal Representation of User States.
    In: Proceedings of the 18th International Conference on Advanced Information
    Networking and Applications, pp. 512–517 (2004)
12. Khan, S., Karg, M., Hoey, J., Kuli, D.: Towards the Detection of Unusual Temporal
    Events during Activities Using HMMs. In: Proceedings of UbiComp 2012 (2012)
13. McCowan, I., Gatica-Perez, D., Bengio, S., Lathoud, G., Barnard, M., Zhang, D.:
    Automatic Analysis of Multimodal Group Actions in Meetings. IEEE Transactions
    on Pattern Analysis and Machine Intelligence 27(3), 305–317 (2005)
14. Mozer, M.: The Neural Network House: An Environment that Adapts to its In-
    habitants. In: Proceedings of the American Association for Artificial Intelligence
    Spring Symposium on Intelligent Environments, pp. 110–114 (1998)
15. Li, H., Zhang, Q., Duan, P.: A Novel One-pass Neural Network Approach for Ac-
    tivities Recognition in Intelligent Environments. In: Proceedings of the 7th World
    Congress on Intelligent Control and Automation, pp. 50–54 (2008)
16. Lin, Z., Fu, L.: Multi-user Preference Model and Service Provision in a Smart Home
    Environment. In: Proceedings of IEEE International Conference on Automation
    Science and Engineering, pp. 759–764 (2007)
17. Lotfi, A., Langensiepen, C., Mahmoud, S., Akhlaghinia, M.: Smart Homes for the
    Elderly Dementia Sufferers: Identification and Prediction of Abnormal Behaviour.
    Journal of Ambient Intelligence and Humanized Computing 3(3), 205–218 (2012)
18. Pérez, Ó., Piccardi, M., García, J., Patricio, M.A., Molina, J.M.: Comparison Be-
    tween Genetic Algorithms and the Baum-Welch Algorithm in Learning HMMs for
    Human Activity Classification. In: Giacobini, M. (ed.) EvoWorkshops 2007. LNCS,
    vol. 4448, pp. 399–406. Springer, Heidelberg (2007)

19. Sarkar, J., Lee, Y., Lee, S.: ARHMAM: an Activity Recognition System based on Hidden Markov mined Activity Model. In: Proceedings of the 4th International Conference on Ubiquitous Information Management and Communication (ICUIMC 2010), pp. 484-492 (2010)
20. Stankovski, V., Trnkoczy, J.: Application of Decision Trees to Smart Homes. In: Augusto, J.C., Nugent, C.D. (eds.) Designing Smart Homes. LNCS (LNAI), vol. 4008, pp. 132–145. Springer, Heidelberg (2006)
21. Utgoff, P.: Incremental Induction of Decision Trees. Machine Learning 4, 161–186 (1989)
22. van Kasteren, T., Noulas, A., Englebienne, G., Kroese, B.: Accurate Activity Recognition in a Home Setting. In: Proceedings of UbiComp 2008, pp. 1–9. ACM (2008)
23. van Kasteren, T.L.M., Englebienne, G., Kröse, B.J.A.: Hierarchical Activity Recognition Using Automatically Clustered Actions. In: Keyson, D.V., et al. (eds.) AmI 2011. LNCS, vol. 7040, pp. 82–91. Springer, Heidelberg (2011)
24. Wang, L., Gu, T., Tao, X., Lu, J.: Sensor-Based Human Activity Recognition in a Multi-user Scenario. In: Tscheligi, M., de Ruyter, B., Markopoulus, P., Wichert, R., Mirlacher, T., Meschterjakov, A., Reitberger, W. (eds.) AmI 2009. LNCS, vol. 5859, pp. 78–87. Springer, Heidelberg (2009)
25. Wang, L., Gu, T., Tao, X., Chen, H., Lu, J.: Recognizing Multi-user Activities using Wearable Sensors in a Smart Home. Pervasive and Mobile Computing 7(3), 287–298 (2011)

Author Index